THE
SHACK
REVISITED

There Is More Going on Here
Than You Ever Dared to Dream

C. BAXTER KRUGER, PH.D.

Foreword by Wm. Paul Young
#1 *NY TIMES* BESTSELLING AUTHOR OF
THE SHACK

New York   Boston   Nashville

The author is represented by Ambassador Literary Agency, Nashville, TN.

FaithWords
Hachette Book Group
1290 Avenue of the Americas
New York, NY 10104

www.faithwords.com

Printed in the United States of America

RRD-C

First Edition: October 2012
10 9 8 7 6 5

FaithWords is a division of Hachette Book Group, Inc.
The FaithWords name and logo are trademarks of Hachette Book Group, Inc.

The Hachette Speakers Bureau provides a wide range of authors for speaking events. To find out more, go to www.hachettespeakersbureau.com or call (866) 376-6591.

The publisher is not responsible for websites (or their content) that are not owned by the publisher.

Library of Congress Cataloging-in-Publication Data

Kruger, C. Baxter.
The shack revisited : there is more going on here than you ever dared to dream / C. Baxter Kruger ; foreword by Wm. Paul Young. — 1st ed.
p. cm.
ISBN 978-1-4555-1680-3 (trade pbk.) — ISBN 978-1-4555-2263-7 (large print trade pbk.) — ISBN 978-1-4555-1679-7 (hardcover)
I. Title.
PS3611.R845S53 2012
813'.6—dc23
2012021192

Praise For

THE SHACK REVISITED

"THE SHACK REVISITED is Baxter's masterpiece. On the canvas of *The Shack* he has distilled the heart of the Trinity. This book is a Bible School for all of us, expounding the heart of the God who is love. A must read."
>
> —Malcolm Smith, International Bible Teacher and author of *The Power of the Blood Covenant*

"The completion of the book *(The Shack)* that fascinated us all by the only hand and mind that could."
>
> —Rev. John Jennings, Vancouver

ALSO BY C. BAXTER KRUGER

Parable of the Dancing God

God Is For Us

The Great Dance

Jesus and the Undoing of Adam

Across All Worlds

For Laura
O beautiful daughter of mine,
You have made me smile every day of your life.

CONTENTS

FOREWORD

To all those who took the time to read and study *The Shack*, to those who bought several copies or a case or more and gave them away and e-mailed me your wonderful stories, I want to say, "Thank you, and please read *The Shack Revisited*." If you want to understand better the perspectives and theology that frame *The Shack*, this book is for you. Baxter has taken on the incredible task of exploring the nature and character of the God who met me in my own shack. A Mississippi theologian who cut his intellectual teeth in Aberdeen, Scotland, with the Torrance brothers, Baxter is a unique cross of intellectual brilliance and creative genius. He fashions lures that are so beautiful people hang them on their walls rather than actually fish with them, which to Baxter is a "crying shame." According to him, everything in creation should be put to its intended use, whether bass, beer, or Barth. He is a master of making difficult things understandable for the rest of us. If you found hope and encouragement through *The Shack*, this book will help you take more steps in knowing the love of Papa, Sarayu, and Jesus.

It has now been a few years since I penned a story for my six mostly grown children, trying to get it done by Christmas in the busyness of working three jobs and "life." I thought I was building them a rowboat, you know the kind, with a couple of oars and just enough room to take them out on the lake two at a time. Surprising everyone, especially me, it came out a supertanker that has since plowed its way through the ocean of humanity, leaving behind a cosmic wake. If you chance a glance at the name of this ship, you will see it is christened *God's Sense of Humor.*

My spiritual upbringing was eclectic and mostly solitary. Even though I attended Bible school and seminary, it was for me a lonely journey accompanied by the one-dimensional voices of dusty pages and cassette speeches and sermons. One wouldn't call Sören Kierkegaard exactly "fun" company, but along with him and others such as Jacques Ellul, George MacDonald, Malcolm Smith, Jean Vanier, C. S. Lewis, and a host of dead and living writers and theologians—and a lot of rock 'n' roll—I made my way through the wastelands and into...what? I wasn't sure. I had discovered that the island on which I was a castaway was also inhabited by a plethora of musicians and poets, writers, thinkers, and comedians, each with something to share: sometimes an insight, sometimes an encouragement. *The Shack* has also been a raft on which I have journeyed out into the vastness of the sea to discover a family of faith that I had not known; I had heard the names, but never met them in person. I discovered my roots, and found that my family tree extended to names like Athanasius and Torrance, Barth, Polycarp, Irenaeus, and so many more, crossing boundaries set by religious divisions and faith cultures.

There has been a tumult of response to *The Shack,* the vast majority of it positive. In e-mails alone I have well over a hundred thousand stories sharing how the book has intersected the lives of precious people on wildly divergent journeys. From the "helping" community, those who actually work in the arenas of healing with real people by way of psychology, spiritual formation, step programs, psychiatry, pastoral care, and so on, I have yet to receive one negative comment or review. What matters to these healers is that something actually works and is of value and aid to those they care for and treasure.

Criticisms have come almost exclusively from religious folk, and I am not intending the term in a pejorative sense. Of course there are those who have taken a position without having read the book for themselves, thereby discounting their right even to pretend an opinion, but there are others who truly feel the weight of responsibility to protect the "flock of the faithful" and to defend God against the intrusion of heresy or "seductive doctrines." We are grateful for these brothers and sisters who are part of the family conversation, and we have carefully considered their responses.

The Shack was never intended to be a systematic theology or another book of pragmatic proof texts useful for badgering unwitting unbelievers into religious submission. It is fiction and it is story. It is an utterly human tale, rife with the mystery of journey and failure, of loss and uncertainty, of deep and precious desires and questions. It is a scratching at the surface of formulaic religion and performance-driven culture to see if behind their murky exteriors we might excavate a rumor of glory, or sense a breath of life that might gently fan the embers of hope and the will to authenticity.

Please don't misunderstand me; *The Shack* is theology. But it is theology wrapped in story, the Word becoming flesh and living inside the blood and bones of common human experience. If you believe, as I do, that everything finds its source, meaning, value, identity, worth, security, and significance inside relationship, and foremost in one's relationship with God, then all of life falls within the purview of theology, the living word of God's reality and presence.

What you have in your hands, or what you are listening

to, is the beginning of what Baxter and I hope will be more to come. This book sets the framework and boundaries; it is an attempt to paint a "bigger picture," elucidating a pre-Enlightenment, pre-Reformation, indeed an early Church vision of the beautiful life of the Father, Son, and Holy Spirit and their dream for the human race. Here Plato and dualism have no voice. This perspective and vision, visible through the window that *The Shack* has provided, is now enlarged and articulated here in accessible and comprehensible language; and I hope the emerging picture that Baxter is painting on this word-canvas stuns you into wonder, worship, and possibility.

Eventually Baxter and I would like to deal, among other things, with history to help us understand how we got so far off-course, with theology that asks the hardest and best questions, and with the implications that must necessarily arise out of such conversations. If what we are trying to unveil and communicate is true, how does this affect our thinking about heaven, hell, evangelism, homosexuality, work, the role of women, politics, religion, science, the sacred-secular divide, commerce, education, the nature of the Church, the process of transformation, healing, and everything else?

We would then like to see this reality worked out in the flesh of everyday experience. We hope to gather together people who can communicate with us what this vision looks like in their own spheres of interest and passion: astrophysics, mothering, arts, media, music, plumbing, farming, fathering, business leadership, pastoring, caring for the planet, medicine, day laboring, teaching, dance, you name it.

Many of us grew up on the ship of Western Enlightenment rationalism and dualism—a vessel that, without a course correction, will find itself grounded on the beach of increasing irrelevance. This ship's intelligentsia can be found in the galley, lost in the bowels of deep and mysterious conversation while the world goes sailing by and the rest of us slumber in our Great Sadness. I don't believe we need a new theology; rather, we must revisit the early and initial, and better understand these roots; we must cultivate the vision of the original "evangels," who saw all of existence and reality only in the light of the person of Jesus, and his relationship with his Father and the Spirit.

So with open arms, my friend Baxter and I, along with myriad others, invite you to revisit the world of *The Shack*, a world where Papa's affection is unending, Jesus' faith in you is as "strong as cabbage," as Baxter would say, and the Spirit's hope is wider than the cosmos; a world where *you* matter and Papa is especially fond of *you*!

—Wm. Paul Young
Author of *The Shack*

Prologue

THE CADILLAC STAND

In mid-October of 2007, Wendy Marchant of Sault Ste. Marie, Canada, rang me on the phone. Her first words were, "Baxter, I am not getting off the phone until you promise me that you will read a book called *The Shack*." My first thought was *Wendy, come on, not you.* From time to time people send me manuscripts of "the best book that has ever been written." And then two or three days later an e-mail follows wanting to know what I thought of the book. But Wendy is no stranger; in fact, she is a dear friend, a sister who loves me and prays for me and my family all the time. So with my mind shuffling between *not again…but this is Wendy*, I asked her what the book was about.

"Baxter, I am not going to tell you; it would ruin it. Just trust me on this one."

"Okay, Wendy, here's what I will do. Deer season is just around the corner, so I will get this book and put it on the top of my deer-stand reading pile." And I did.

A month later, on the opening day of gun season, I headed for my deer stand, *The Shack* dutifully placed in my backpack. Now understand, I am not much of a deer hunter. I have only killed three deer in my entire life. But I love being in the woods. So some years ago my friend Jeff and I built what we affectionately call "the Cadillac stand," complete with tin roof, carpet, and two seriously comfortable chairs. For me it's more an outdoor study and a private sanctuary with fantastic views. In the Cadillac I read, write, pray, and sometimes hunt. So I walked up the stairs, got everything situated, sat down, and opened *The Shack*.

The opening words from Willie's introduction got my attention: "Who wouldn't be skeptical when a man claims to have spent an entire weekend with God, in a shack no less?" *So*, I thought to myself, *this is a book about a man meeting God in the woods, in a shack. That's good. I wonder if this shack is an old hunting camp? But* which *God? That's the question, and please tell me this is not going to be the same old, same old.* But then came the story of Mack's "dad" tying him to a tree and beating him for two days, and then the phrase "the Great Sadness," and then the Multnomah princess story—*then Missy*—and then I found myself crying my eyes out in the Cadillac.

With my soul ripped open, I wailed. When they found Missy's dress in the shack, I stood up, blew my nose, dried my tears, and shook *The Shack* in my right hand. "William P. Young! I don't know who you are, but I promise you this: if you deliver the same old distant, untouchable, legalistic god who scans the universe with his disapproving heart as the answer to this gut-wrenching trauma, I will take your book and walk two hundred yards, lean it against a tree, and personally eliminate this copy from the cosmos."

But the brother delivered. Paul Young knows Jesus' *Abba*. *The Shack* is not about the disapproving god of our fallen imaginations; it is about the shocking fondness of the triune God for *sinners*. It is about the freedom of the Father, Son, and

Spirit to love and to embrace us in our terrible brokenness. It's about the determined passion of the blessed Trinity[1] to deliver us from ourselves, so that we can live loved—because we are. We belong to the Father, Son, and Spirit. We always have, and always will. We just can't see it. And because we can't see it, we live with the poisoning weight of Mack's burden, which we unwittingly share with all around us, including creation.

There is no more beautiful picture of the truth of the triune God than the scene of Papa lifting Mackenzie Allen Phillips off his feet in the greatest hug in the universe. I was stunned, and thrilled, and thrilled again. Somewhere inside we all know it to be so, that this is what Jesus' *Abba* is like, that this is the truth that sets us free, that this divine love is real. It just does not square with our heads, with our entrenched ideas, laden as they are with our proof texts and wounded hearts—with what Athanasius called "mythology."

I read all afternoon, determined to finish before dark. But I didn't make it. So I sat riveted in the Cadillac with a flashlight in my mouth until my son texted me that he was waiting at our base camp.

---

1. "God in three persons, blessed Trinity" is the last line in the great hymn "Holy, Holy, Holy," written by Reginald Heber, an Anglican minister, for Trinity Sunday. The tune is called Nicaea, named after the Council of Nicaea in AD 325. (On the history of this hymn, see Kenneth W. Osbeck, *101 Hymn Stories* [Grand Rapids: Kregel, 1982], pp. 94–95.) The phrase "blessed Trinity" from this hymn haunted me—in a good way— from my early days. I discovered that it was widely used in the ancient Church before its divisions, and has continued to be ever since, across the diverse theologies of the Church worldwide. It is ancient and modern and ecumenical. "The blessed Trinity" speaks of the goodness, the rich and abounding fullness, and the overflowing *life* of the Father, Son, and Spirit; and I think it speaks of the hope that this "blessed" life holds the secret of ours.

The Story Behind *the Story*

Never intended for publication, *The Shack* was written by William P. Young (known to his friends as Paul) as a story for his children. He had two aims: first, to give a gift that would express his love for his kids; and second, "to help them understand what had been going on in his inside world" (14),[2] as his friend Willie put it. Paul's goal was to get the story to Office Depot before Christmas to make fifteen copies for his children, his wife, and a few others. But even working three jobs, there wasn't enough money. Eventually copies were made, and the story circulated through his family and friends. He was encouraged to have it published as a proper book, but found that it was rejected by every publisher he contacted as being "too out of the box" or "having too much Jesus." For Paul, its actual publication as a real book, now one of the bestselling books in history, is *lagniappe*, as the Cajuns say—a little something extra. His dream was fulfilled when the first copies were made and his children had a story that would explain something of their father's journey into the real world.

I heard Paul say that he reached the point in his life when he cried out, "Papa, I am never again going to ask you to bless something that I do, but if you have something that you are blessing that I could share in, I would love that. And I don't care if it's cleaning toilets or holding the door open or shining shoes." And Papa replied, "Paul, I'll tell you what, how about I bless this little story you are writing for your kids? You give

---

2. Throughout this book, the numbers in parentheses are the page numbers of material quoted from *The Shack*. There are two editions of *The Shack* with different paginations. I am using the pagination from the second edition, which generally is two numbers higher than the first edition.

it to yours, and I will give it to mine." The rest, as they say, is history.

But is it? There is far more going on in an average person's life than anyone would dare to dream. And that is certainly true of Paul Young. *The Shack* is not a novel written by an academic who finally learned to communicate with regular people. There is a story behind the story—several stories, in fact, but I will stick to Willie's explanation: "to help them understand what had been going on in his inside world" (14). The inside world, the world of the invisibles, of pain and turmoil, of shame, broken hearts, and broken dreams, is the world that drives us all, and especially the larger-than-life tale in *The Shack*. The story behind the story is the gut-wrenching hell that Paul Young suffered in his own life. I have seen a picture of Paul when he was six years old. He looked like an old man—weary, miserable, spent, and terribly sad. His eyes screamed despair. The picture made me cry. But that is the beginning of this story we have all—or at least most of us—come to love.

By the time Paul was six years old, he had been emotionally abandoned, physically and verbally beaten, and sexually abused—repeatedly. To say the least, he was crippled inside from his early days in life. No child—no person—can withstand such trauma. It creates a lethal roux[3] of shame, fear, insecurity, anxiety, and guilt. These invisibles coalesce into a damning, debilitating, and unshakable whisper: "I am not all right. I am not good, not worthy, not important, not lovable,

---

3. *Roux* is a French cooking term taken up by the Cajuns. In a heavy pot, butter or oil is heated and flour is added, while stirring constantly. When the flour is golden or brown, bell pepper, onion, and celery, the "Holy Trinity" of Cajun cooking, are added. When the vegetables wilt, stock is added. The flavors of the roux permeate whatever is then added to the pot.

not human,"[4] which haunts every single moment of life. How does a child, or anyone, cope with an inner world of such anguish? No one can.

As a fish was not made to live on the moon, we were never designed to live in shame. But what do you do? Where do you go? Most of us bury it all in a garbage can in the back room of our souls, and move on. Or try to. *But what we bury rules us.* What we don't know that we don't know will destroy us. "I am not" becomes "I will be," and we dream a dream of becoming. "If I can just get married and have children..." "If I can just get that job or promotion, that money, that car, that house, that power, that position, that new relationship..." And off we go. But such "things" are incompetent to address spiritual pain. They never work, though we will defend them till they kill us. So we medicate, go on autopilot, check out; or we stay busy, we get involved in a great cause, manage other people's inner worlds, live through our children, or just stay drunk in one way or another. It's too much to cope with head-on.

Paul Young turned to religion, partly because it was the environment he grew up in and therefore readily available, and partly because it presented a possible way to perform his way into becoming valuable. He was born in Alberta, Canada, but before his first birthday found himself on the mission field in the highlands of Netherlands New Guinea (West Papua). Around the age of six, as was required by the particular mission board, he was shipped off to boarding school. Before he turned ten, the family unexpectedly returned to Canada, and by the time he graduated from high school, Paul had attended

---

4. For more of my thoughts on "I am not," see my lecture series "Inside the Soul: An Anatomy of Darkness." This series is available on our website, perichoresis.org.

thirteen different schools. His dad had made the change from missionary to pastor.

> These facts don't tell you about the pain of trying to adjust to different cultures, of life losses that were almost too staggering to bear, of walking down railroad tracks at night in the middle of winter screaming into the windstorm, of living with an underlying volume of shame so deep and loud that it constantly threatened any sense of sanity, of dreams not only destroyed but obliterated by personal failure, of hope so tenuous that only the trigger seemed to offer a solution.[5]

Religion was the only world Paul knew, the cards he had been dealt. So he played them. He believed in the "religious" version of Christianity. He had to. With "I am not good" whispering in every breeze, he set out to prove that he was. He graduated at the top of his class in college, became a shining star; a people-pleasing, religious performer on his way to the top. But every moment involved the exhausting task of hypervigilance, constantly scanning each group, each discussion, each meeting and moment to manage people's impressions of himself. For how could Paul, how can any of us, let people know of the dying inside?

With one hand pushing down on the lid of his garbage can, he smiled, taught the Bible, and became the "nice guy," the counselor, while keeping everyone at a safe distance. But he found no relief from the raging turmoil in his inner world. He cried out to God for healing, rededicating himself and his life a hundred times, until his "rededicator" finally burned out. His life became a form of hiding, while he desperately

---

5. From Paul's personal journal. See theshackbook.com/willie.

searched for relief and help anywhere he could find it. But there is no healing in religion. Healing happens when you meet Jesus in your garbage can—or your shack—a place Paul, like most of us, tried hard to deny even existed.

He performed himself into ministry, into business, into marriage, into fatherhood, trying to the point of exhaustion to become an authentic human being while hiding the underlying shame and personal failures.

A single phone call rocked his world forever—two words, in fact: "I know." Kim, Paul's wife, had found out about the affair he was having with one of her friends. An affair is one way that shame works its poison in our lives. There are millions of others, of course, but one is that we turn to another person, a "magical other"[6] who will be our all, our life, our salvation. I suspect Paul found out what the poet meant when he said, "Hell hath no fury like a woman scorned."[7] But that's not the whole truth. Heaven has no ally like a woman who knows how to love. The dedication in Paul's book reads, "To Kim, my Beloved, thank you for saving my life."

While Mackenzie's weekend at the shack represents eleven years of Paul's actual life—eleven years of pain and emotional torture, depression, and mere flashes of hope—it was Kim's heroic love wrapped in fury that held it all together. From a human perspective, without Kim and her heart, Paul Young would probably be dead, tucked away in some cold asylum, or an empty man still performing. There would have been

---

6. See James Hollis, *The Eden Project: In Search of the Magical Other* (Toronto: Inner City Books, 1998); and Hollis, *The Middle Passage: From Misery to Meaning in Midlife* (Toronto: Inner City Books, 1993). See also C. Baxter Kruger, *Across All Worlds: Jesus Inside Our Darkness* (Jackson, MS: Perichoresis Press, 2007; Vancouver: Regent College Publishing, 2007), pp. 7ff.

7. Adapted from William Congreve's poem "The Mourning Bride," 1697.

no story to tell—at least, not one about meeting the blessed Trinity in the garbage can.

On the other side of hell, as real freedom and life began to dawn, it was Kim who insisted that Paul write something for the children to explain his journey and newfound liberation. She didn't mean a book, and neither did Paul, but most folks are thrilled that it all turned out this way. On more than one occasion, I have heard him speak of Kim and their children with tears streaming down his face. The book was born in the crucible of life, of trauma and abuse; of empty religion, misery and betrayal; of mercy, love, and reconciliation. Luther said somewhere that God makes theologians by sending them to hell. In hell, of course, no one is interested in mere theology. In the emptiness of grief, in the pain, the trauma of suffering, we are not interested in pseudo-promises, intellectual masturbation, or "Skippy, the wonder-Christ," as my friend Ken Blue puts it. What we learn in hell is that we want out. We learn desperation for life, for healing, for real salvation, for a Savior who saves here and now, who reconciles, who heals our brokenness and delivers us from our shame. We need something that works.

This is the story *behind* the story. *The Shack* could have easily been titled *From Hell to Heaven*, or *From Overwhelming Shame to Being Loved into Life*, or *How Jesus Healed a Screwed-Up Man*, or even *With Gods Like Ours, No Wonder We Are So Sad and Broken*. For the story is about hell and heaven, trauma, shame, and finding love—the real Jesus accepting a broken man; and it is about the Father, Son, and Spirit finding us in the far country of our terrible and powerless mythology—to share their life with us. For the truth behind the universe is that God is Father, Son, and Spirit; and the one unflinching purpose of the blessed Trinity is that we would come to taste and feel, to know and experience, the very trinitarian life itself.

What Paul and Kim have lived through and have discovered in the love of Papa, Jesus, and Sarayu is the "joy inexpressible and full of glory" that Peter talked about,[8] and the abounding life that Jesus promised.[9] They cannot go back to the same old do-more-try-harder religion with its properly attested Bible verses. Like C. S. Lewis, in the midst of misery they were "surprised by joy."[10]

Some have taken offense at the theology of *The Shack*. Paul's response is not one of theological argument or biblical prooftexting, though he is very adept at both. His response is his own life and relationships. He would say, "I have a T-shirt from hell—several of them, in fact. Religion doesn't work anywhere, and especially there, but the Father, Son, and Spirit came to find me in my hell. They accepted me, loved me, embraced me, and are healing me with their love." I think Paul would also ask a simple question: "How's *your theology* working for you?" And, knowing Paul, he would follow that with, "How does your wife or husband and your friends think your theology is working for you?" So, while *The Shack* is a story for his children, it is a bit more complicated than that. This story is a matter of life or death. Paul Young is serious. He wants his own children to see the disastrous incompetence of religion to heal our broken souls, and he wants them to know the astonishing liberation of Papa's embrace.

The Father, Son, and Spirit, whom he calls Papa, Jesus, and Sarayu, are not myths like Santa Claus, the white, blue-eyed Jesus, and the tooth fairy. They are real. They meet us in our pain; in our anger, bitterness, and resentment; in our

---

8. 1 Peter 1:8.

9. See John 10:10.

10. *Surprised by Joy: The Shape of My Early Life* is the title of Lewis's autobiography (London and New York: Harcourt, Brace, 1956).

shame and guilt and powerlessness; in our miserable, broken relationships—and in our deadly religion—and there they love us into life and freedom. Hence the second dedication: to "all us stumblers who believe Love rules. Stand up and let it shine."[11]

The Story Within *the Story*

Like Paul Young, though for different reasons, Mackenzie Allen Phillips is a shattered man. A few years ago he began living a parent's worst nightmare: his youngest daughter, Missy, was kidnapped, murdered, and thrown away. "It all happened during Labor Day weekend, the summer's last hurrah before another year of school and autumn routines" (27). Mack took three of his kids on a camping trip; it was then that Missy was taken. Since then Mack has been trapped in "*The Great Sadness*,"[12] as he calls it, a gross and unholy cesspool of his own helplessness, Missy's absence, and the silence of God. He is surrounded by four great kids and his wife, Nan, who knows how to love, but Mack's inner world is as gnarled as a box of loose coat hangers. He is trying, trying to live in his grief, but hell itself would be a relief for those who suffer the loss of a child. It is just wrong. Overwhelming.

You will never again hear your daughter's laughter, see her smile, or hear her speak your name—except in nightmares. There will be no sleepovers, no first dates, no boyfriends, no proms, no field trips, no shared pain, no surprises. It's all over, gone, like the last ray of light before dark. And then there is silence. The grief of it all, the despair and anger and guilt and

---

11. From Bruce Cockburn's song "Mystery," on the album *Life Short Call Now* (True North Records, 2006).

12. On "The Great Sadness," see pp. 14, 18, 26, 27, 66, 76, 81, 94, 98, 103, 116, 117, 118, 163, 171, 198.

powerlessness swirl together to cast a spell of numbness on your being. Your mind is dazed. Your capacity to notice, to connect, to feel—to feel alive, to feel others, to feel anything—slows like molasses in winter as the hurt dissolves the color of a rose, and the world becomes essentially joyless. And then the horrible quiet of absence begins eating away the memories (168).

The Great Sadness drains the life of your already-broken soul, stealing your very "sense of being alive" (76). Then there are the horrible dreams of powerlessness. Mack dreams of being stuck in mud, frantically trying to scream a warning to Missy, but no sound ever emerges from his screams (27, 118). He wakes in a sweat, emotionally tortured, full of guilt, stewing in regret, helpless and despairing. Then there is the question of God. Why did this happen? Where was God? Why did he allow Missy to be taken? Didn't he care? Mack's mind races, trying to find some way to make sense out of such appalling injustice. But anger, blame, resentment fester in the scars of his wound:

> "You don't believe that Father loves his children very well, do you? You don't truly believe that God is *good*, do you?" [Sophia asked.]
> "Is Missy his child?" Mack snapped.
> "Of course!" she answered.
> "Then, no!" he blurted, rising to his feet. "I don't believe that God loves all of his children very well." (158, my italics)
> "Isn't that your *just* complaint, Mackenzie? That God has failed you, that he failed Missy? That before the Creation, God knew that one day your Missy would be brutalized, and still he created? And then he *allowed* that twisted soul to snatch her from your

loving arms when he had the power to stop him. Isn't God to blame, Mackenzie?"...

"Yes! God is to blame!" (163, my italics)

Lost in the cosmos of his pain, Mack is left holding the bag of God's incompetence. In such a place, "reality, looked at steadily, is unbearable."[13] Bewildered and angry, he has quietly become a broken, tired ghost of a man. The days, months, and years pass by, mired in his Great Sadness. Then, on an icy winter day, he slips and slides his way to his mailbox to discover a single note—*from God*:

Mackenzie,
It's been a while. I've missed you.
I'll be at the shack next weekend if you want to get together.

—Papa (18)

And so begins the tale of the healing of Mackenzie Allen Phillips. His liberation involves the thrilling love of the Father, Son, and Spirit in patient, tender care and astonishing respect for Mack. They meet him in his nightmare and nurture him through a *revolution* in his notions of God, the purpose of human existence, who he is and who others are, the meaning of Jesus' death, and what it means to live life.

While Paul Young may never have intended the story for publication, that is not to say that the Holy Spirit didn't have plans of his own. The wild popularity of *The Shack* tells us that something in this story strikes a very deep and common chord. And while Mack is a fictitious character, he is

---

13. C. S. Lewis, *A Grief Observed* (New York: Bantam, 1976), p. 32.

no foreigner to any of us. This is the story *within* the story. We are Mackenzie; he is us. We may not have lost a child so brutally as Mack, but not one of us left our own childhood without wounds, and I dare guess that most of us have had a bellyful of pain and bitter disappointment. Mack's hurt is intense, and his pain raises questions that are deep, and they are *our* questions, too. He is caught between the proverbial rock of a terrible tragedy and the hard place of a God who is silent, if not cruel. And that hard place haunts us. Mack has nowhere to go in his pain. His religion is inept at best. He is alone, on his own, bearing the horror of Missy's death as a man with no answers. So the story within the story is that *The Shack* is our story, too, the story of our pain and blindness, of the God who seems so absent, so uncaring and impotent when it really matters, and of our lives paused in shame. But it is also the story of our liberation—if we want it.

In that moment when Papa opened the door of the shack and embraced a broken, saddened Mackenzie Allen Phillips in utter love, was it not the case with you that an ancient hope sprang to life in your soul? Did you not cry? It's a love story that we desperately want to believe, but we can't. We know it's true. But how could it be? One scene raises a universe of questions. Could God be this good? Could I be so wrong? Could it be this simple? Yes! Yes! Yes!

Mack found no real help in the very "religion" with which many of us have grown up. To be sure, he eventually found serious healing, but the price was the deconstruction of almost everything he had ever been told about God, about himself and others, about life—though not of what he had heard whispered to him in the Spirit. And here is the fascinating part for me as a theologian. What Mackenzie discovered was the sheer goodness and love of the Father, Son, and Spirit, the ancient truth that once changed the world. *The Shack* is the voice of the early Church calling us back from our craziness to our true home in the Father, Son, and Spirit.

The story within the story is that Paul Young—through the tragic life and healing of Mackenzie Allen Phillips—has found a way to steal behind the watchful dragons[14] of our deism, legalism, and rationalism, and introduce us to the truth that sets us free. And the truth is a person (97), who shares life and all things in other-centered love with his Papa, in the wonderful freedom of the Holy Spirit. *And* a person who has crossed all worlds to find us in our pain. *And* a person who brought his Papa and the Holy Spirit with him. Somewhere inside we know it's true. But we're afraid. For when you pull on this thread, a lot of rug begins to unravel. Nevertheless, just when you fear that your world is vanishing, you discover that Someone is weaving a new carpet of unimaginable simplicity, freedom, and life.

In the midst of the story, when Mack is being loved through a fifteen-or-so-step process of healing, Sophia exhorts him with words that all lovers of life must heed: "Maybe your understanding of God is wrong" (166); and then Sarayu, "Be willing to reexamine what you believe" (199).

The Phone Call

A little over a week after I read *The Shack* in the Cadillac stand, my son and I were watching Eli Manning and the New York Giants on TV, when my cell phone rang. It was Sunday

---

14. The imagery of "watchful dragons" comes from C. S. Lewis's essay "Sometimes Fairy Stories Say Best What's to Be Said," in *On Stories, and Other Essays on Literature*, ed. Walter Hooper (New York: Harcourt, Brace, 1982), p. 47. I am grateful to Cary Stockett for sharing the image with me.

afternoon. As I looked at the number, my son asked who it was. "I don't know this number. Where is the 503 area code?"

"Got no idea," he said. "It's not from around here."

"I don't either," I muttered, and moved my finger to mute the call, when something told me to answer.

"Hello, this is Baxter."

"Baxter, this is Paul Young."

The name didn't register, at all. *I don't know a Paul Young*, I thought to myself as my mind reeled through people I have met in my travels.

"You may know me as William."

"William Paul Young," I whispered to myself, the name still not registering. Then it hit me, and I blurted out, *"William P. Young?"*

"I am," he said in a way that I could tell he was enjoying himself.

"The William P. Young?"

"Well, I don't know about the 'the' part, but I am William P. Young. My friends call me *Paul*."

"Are you the dude who wrote like the best book that has been written in the last five hundred years?"

"I don't know about that, but I wrote *The Shack*."

"Dude! Why in the world are you calling *me*? The whole world wants to talk with you."

"Well, I got an e-mail from your friend Tim Brassell. He said that I needed to get in touch with you because you have written the theology that goes with *The Shack*. So I called."

It took me a full five minutes before I could believe what was happening. And then I told him about the Cadillac stand, and he laughed, and then I asked a thousand questions, and he answered most of them.

An hour and a half later we said good-bye, and I immediately phoned Tim and told him what had happened. I was already scheduled to do a conference for Tim and Bill Winn at Bill's church in Virginia in April, so I was eager to get Tim and Bill to invite Paul, which they did.

Since that phone call and the April conference,[15] Paul and I have become close friends, and I have had the privilege of teaching with him on *The Shack* in three countries. It is always amazing to hear his story, and equally amazing that so many millions of people relate so readily both to Mackenzie's struggle and to Paul's life.

Let me relate a story that gives some perspective on Paul, and a hint on the appeal of *The Shack*. Paul and I were touring across Australia in November 2008. We were with singer-songwriter Vanessa Kersting and just settling in for a flight from Melbourne to Brisbane. Vanessa and I were sitting together, and Paul was somewhere behind us, when over the intercom came the captain's voice: "Ladies and gentlemen, this is the captain speaking. Today we have a very special guest on board." Smiling, I turned to Vanessa and said, "Someone found out that Paul is on the plane." She smiled, too, and then the captain said, "Today is Baxter Kruger's fiftieth birthday." With that the passengers erupted in cheers and applause. I was shocked, and a little embarrassed, and as I turned around, waving and thanking the people, I caught the gleaming eye of Paul Young, grinning from ear to ear like a little boy who had surprised his parents with a special gift. Such a gesture meant the world to me on my birthday, especially as I was halfway around the planet from my own family. But what struck me was that in spite of all the trauma that Paul had endured, he was getting to play.

What Willie said about Mack is true of Paul:

---

15. This conference, "Rediscovering Jesus," is available on our website, perichoresis.org, and through thegreatdance.org.

But I have to tell you that I've never been around another adult who lives life with such simplicity and joy. Somehow he has become a child again. Or maybe more accurately, he's become the child he never was allowed to be; abiding in simple trust and wonder. (249–50)

I think this freedom sings throughout the story. And it's the haunting tune we all long to hear—and to live to. For it is our song, too.

PART ONE

SOME FIRST
THOUGHTS ON
PAPA

1

THE SHOCKER

*Well, Mackenzie, don't just stand there gawkin' with your
mouth open like your pants are full.... Come and talk to me
while I get supper on.*

—Papa

In an old abandoned shack in the outback of the Oregon
mountains, Mackenzie Allen Phillips is shocked by three
unusual characters. It is supposed to be a showdown with
God in "the place of his nightmares" (71), the very place where
his Missy was murdered. But the three people he meets, a
large African American woman with beaming eyes, a strong
carpenter of Middle Eastern descent, and an Asian-looking
woman who appears and disappears at will, are nothing like
the God Mack *imagined* he would meet. In fact, the God he
imagined is a no-show.

In all, Mack makes four trips to the shack. The first is the
terrible night when the authorities find fragments of Missy's

red dress, and blood on the wooden floors. The second, several years later, is when Mack answers an invitation from Papa, his wife's favorite name for God. Mack has mixed emotions, to be sure. He is a little intrigued, a little scared, and a lot angry. He borrows his friend's Jeep and heads out, knowing that he is driving "into the center of his pain" (76).

After several hours of driving, Mack parks the Jeep a mile or so from the shack, but he can only take five steps before the knot in his gut makes him panic. "Please help me!" (77) he cries out, but there is no answer. At length he manages to follow the treacherous trail until he sees the shack. "The shack itself looked dead and empty, but as he stared it seemed for a moment to transform into an evil face, twisted in some demonic grimace, looking straight back at him and daring him to approach" (79). The fact that Mackenzie takes another step toward the shack is a lesson in courage, or anger. He has a lot to talk to God about.

Standing at the door, his mind flashes back to that terrible night, his emotions in turmoil. He calls out to God, but as before, there is no answer. Then again he calls and again there is no answer. Courageously facing his fear of what may be inside, Mack opens the door. And that's just it: there is nothing inside. No God, no life; just emptiness, shadows, the barren nothingness of the god of our fears, and the bloodstains of his Missy. Mack's god, our god, the god of our fallen imaginations, is not real—never has been, and never will be. But the trauma this god inflicts is real to us.

This is a brilliant move on Young's part. Without a single theological word, he has ripped open the tragedy of Western theology—and made us feel it. At this moment in the book, and hopefully at this point in history, the sterility of that imaginary god is exposed for all to see. To be sure, Mack's Great Sadness is rooted in the horrible loss of Missy, but it's also rooted in the terrible absence of God. That is a lonely place.

Inside, alone and helpless, Mack explodes with pain. "Why? Why did you let this happen? Why did you bring me here? Of all the places to meet you—why *here*? Wasn't it enough to kill my baby? Do you have to toy with me too?" (80). In a fit of rage he all but destroys the room, exhausting himself as he throws a chair and beats the floor with one of its broken legs. And then his pain, his anger, his wrath at God are funneled into three screaming words: "*I hate you!*" (80). It is the scream of honesty, the only real response when our pain and the cold, heartless impotence of this god collide in real-life tragedy. *I hate you!*

He slumps down in tears, engulfed in his Great Sadness. Once again, taking "aim at the indifferent God he imagined" (80), he shouts sarcastically:

So where are you? I thought you wanted to meet me here. Well, I'm here, God. And you? You're nowhere to be found! You've never been around when I've needed you—not when I was a little boy, not when I lost Missy. Not now! Some "Papa" you are! (80–81)

I'm done, God…I can't do this anymore. I'm tired of trying to find you in all of this. (82)

I hate you! The last word of the human race, trapped in the great darkness. But such awful desolation is not the end of the story. For the lover of our souls meets us in our pain. This, too, is a brilliant move, to my mind, and one of the great themes running throughout *The Shack*. Unlike the indifferent god of our imaginations, the Father, Son, and Spirit do in fact meet us in our pain, in our tragedy, and especially in our darkness and sin. It is not so much—as we will see—that the blessed Trinity is absent to the rest of our lives; it is that, in the trauma created by the collision of life and the false god of our imaginations, we begin to get new eyes.

Having screamed his final word, rejecting god, Mackenzie leaves the shack and heads back to the Jeep. It is then, after he has spoken his "peace" with god, that the world changes—his world and, hopefully, ours. Thirty or so yards toward the Jeep, the woods come alive with light. A bizarre life shines in the stillness of Mack's disgust. A month of spring's thaw unfolds in a few short moments. New hope emerges as the snow melts around him, and the flowers unveil their glory. Intrigued yet cautious, he makes the decision to go back to the shack. But it, too, has changed. No longer a dilapidated shack, it is now a finely built log cabin with a white picket fence, and smoke wending from the chimney. He thinks he can hear *laughter* (83). Mack has no idea what lies before him, but it is not to be missed that his first hint was laughter.

But how is a man supposed to believe such a miracle? Half convinced that he has lost his mind, Mackenzie doesn't know what to think, or what to do. But it's too late. Standing on the porch trying to decide if he should knock, Mack, like the prodigal son, never gets a chance to say a word. The door flies open. A large African American woman, whose face beams with life and love itself, runs to embrace him, lifting Mackenzie off the ground in joy while shouting his name as if she has known and loved him all his life.

Mack is stunned silent, clueless as to who this woman is, but finding his soul drinking in every ounce of the moment. Who doesn't want to be embraced? Who doesn't want to be called by name by someone smiling with delight? His defenses are up, to be sure, but his heart is helplessly melting. Shocked but delighted, bewildered yet moved to tears, he loves the way she shouts his name. " 'Mack, look at you!' she fairly exploded.

'Here you are, and so grown up. I have really been looking forward to seeing you face to face.... My, my, my, how I do love you!' And with that she wrapped herself around him again" (85). You can see the wheels turning in Mack's mind: *Who is this woman? And why is she here? How does she know me, and why does she care? What on earth is going on?*

But he hardly has time to process what is happening before an Asian-looking woman, whom he can barely see, invades his space, brushing his cheek. As best he can tell, she is dressed something like a gardener, but she is almost invisible, shimmering in light. "'I collect tears,' she said" (86). Then Mack notices a Middle Eastern man leaning against the doorjamb. He is rather ordinary-looking, but strong, and his smile somehow speaks volumes. "Mack knew instantly that he liked him" (87). Covered in sawdust, with a tool belt around his waist, he looks like he might be a carpenter.

Overwhelmed, Mack tries to steady himself, asking somewhat humorously, "Are there more of you?" (87).

"'No, Mackenzie,' chuckled the black woman. 'We is all that you get, and believe me, we're more than enough'" (87).

Less than thirty minutes ago Mack was fuming at god, screaming out, *"I'm done! I hate you!"* as his final verdict. Now he finds himself in the astonishing embrace of a black woman who obviously knows him and loves him. Mackenzie has no clue what to do or say. Even though he is still hurting, still stewing in anger at the god of his imagination, Mack stands surrounded by two beautiful women and a carpenter, the three of whom somehow know him and accept him—even *like* him—just as he is. He feels strangely at home. He feels noticed and known, cared for, even wanted and certainly welcomed. Then he catches the unmistakable whiff of his own mother's perfume coming from the black woman. Still guarded—and who wouldn't be—he feels tears welling up in his eyes.

And so Mackenzie Allen Phillips unexpectedly finds himself included in a fellowship of love. In a few short hours he will marvel at their relationship, at their other-centeredness, mutual respect and delight, and the way they accept him as he is. Little does he know that this gentle acceptance will transform him from the inside out.

In many ways the whole story of *The Shack* is crammed into this scene, as are some rather large theological issues. It's a picture that stirs longed-for hope within us, and begs a thousand questions—from the character of God to the fact that Mack was included before he repented and believed, from the purpose of the Incarnation to the meaning of Jesus' death, from what it means to be human to the real meaning of heaven and hell. And we will get to these in due course. But first, a simple question: What if this moment—this scene of Papa's embrace—is what happens to us when we die? What if we wake up on the other side hearing Papa shout our name, surrounded by Sarayu collecting our tears, and Jesus, covered in sawdust from the coffin for our Great Sadness?

Let me go a little further. What if it's already true *now*? What if we are already so known and loved and welcomed *now*?

Lesson One of the story is that we are Mackenzie. The astonishing embrace enfolding him is the truth about us. We are known, loved, and delighted in by the Father, Son, and Spirit, just as we are, whether we believe in God or not. The truth is we have already been embraced by Jesus' Papa and by the Spirit. That is what the coming of Jesus was all about. The blessed Trinity has already met us in our shacks. In Jesus they have pitched their tents inside our garbage cans. We belong to the Father, Son, and Spirit. We always have, and always will; Jesus has seen to that personally. But like Mackenzie, we have wrong eyes; there is so much hurt, we cannot possibly know the truth or believe it—yet. But so it is.

2

THE DANCING GOD

I'm not who you think I am, Mackenzie.
—Papa

One reviewer of *The Shack* wrote of meeting critics who were "deeply disturbed" by Young's daring portrayal of the Trinity "as eccentric personalities with offbeat ways of communicating their message." These critics accused him of "blasphemy," labeling Young "a post-modernist for whom 'truth' meant nothing." Then the reviewer wrote:

> I can admit to a sense of shock when I realized in the course of reading that Young had chosen to portray God our Father as an absolutely enchanting, powerfully-mothering, African-American woman. But I will also admit that it wasn't too long in my reading before I found myself wanting to sit at her kitchen table and to enjoy her cooking, her conversation, and

her maternal affection. The beauty of the fellowship generated by her presence was what many of us have sought for a lifetime and so rarely experienced.[1]

This is beautifully stated, and it gets to the heart of the question that Young's Papa raises for all of us. Who doesn't want to be so loved, so known, so accepted? Who doesn't want to sit at Papa's table and enjoy her cooking and delight? But on what basis could we be so bold as even to dream of such a thing? We are talking about God here, remember, the Ultimate One. Yet, as my friend Ken Courtney asks, "that's what we want, isn't it?" We will come back to our desire to be known and accepted in a moment. But first we must deal with another question.

Does this "absolutely enchanting, powerfully-mothering, African-American woman" say anything to us about the real God? Can we dare believe that Jesus' Father is as good as this Papa? My answer is simply, "Of course." The picture of the Father's heart painted by Young is straight from Jesus himself. This heart, overflowing with love and delight, is not a fantasy of Paul Young. This is the ancient love that fired the universe. This is the untarnished truth. If anything, the enchanting love and sheer goodness of Papa's heart, beautiful as they are, nevertheless pale in comparison to Jesus' portrayal of his Father in his most famous parable.[2]

The background of this parable is the critique of Jesus by the religious leaders called the Pharisees. They don't like Jesus. His freedom to be with broken people is disturbing, if not

---

1. King David, review of *The Shack*, Leadershipjournal.net.

2. See Luke 15. On the father and his prodigal and religious sons, see my book *Parable of the Dancing God*, available as a free download on our website, perichoresis.org. It is also available through InterVarsity Press.

embarrassing. He doesn't play by their rules, and the broken people are "listening intently" to what he has to say.[3] And, get this, the "broken people" are the dreaded tax-gatherers who were themselves Jewish but collected taxes for the Romans, often lining their own pockets through overtaxation. They were despised by the rest of the Jews. Of course, Jesus made one of them his disciple, and later went out of his way to find Zaccheus, a *chief* tax collector. When Jesus found him up in a tree, he said, "Zaccheus, hurry and come down, for today I must stay at your house."[4]

And then there were the "sinners," the lawbreaking drunkards, the harlots, the conniving swindlers, those so shamed and beaten down they wouldn't dare even look up at heaven. You have to appreciate the irony here. The ones who are lost are not the sinners who are listening to Jesus, but the religious people who have no problems, at least in their own minds.

So the Pharisees and the scribes are fuming at Jesus for allowing the likes of such folks to hang around. You can see their minds working: *After all, he's making a pitch at being at least a great prophet, if not the Son of God himself. If anything, he should be holier than us, yet there he is fraternizing with blasphemers and winebibbers. Go figure.* So they level what they believe will be an exposing accusation at Jesus. You can almost see it on *Saturday Night Live,* the robed religious elite having their secret whispering sessions, finally coming up with just the right damning allegation to throw the light on this charlatan. And then they practice their grimace of insolence, so their critique will drip off their noses with poignant contempt.

What is their great criticism? "Both the Pharisees and

---

3. Luke 15:1 *The Message.*

4. Luke 19:5.

the scribes began to grumble, saying, 'This man receives sinners and eats with them.'"[5] That's it: he receives sinners, and eats with them! There is obvious disdain in their accusation; they don't even have the courtesy to speak his name, calling Jesus "this man" or "this fellow." The problem is that to receive someone and share a meal with them in this culture is a sign of real solidarity. This is how you treat family. So Jesus is acting like he is family with the tax collectors and sinners. The Pharisees are dumbfounded. "How can he do this? He is supposed to represent God. Jesus has lost his mind."

Jesus must have been a little stunned, if not angry, at the extraordinary blindness of this religious lot. Their accusation is loaded with a question: "How do you, Jesus, a self-respecting rabbi with disciples, explain your bizarre relationships? These people deserve nothing but to be outcast, forever shunned by God and his people. And here you are eating with them, declaring to the world that they are family."

They did not have baseball in those days, of course, but if they did, Jesus would have been a pitcher. For he loved throwing theological curveballs to the self-crowned religious elite. And he wasn't shy about firing a blazing inside fastball to back them off the plate and get their attention.

He responds with three stories—and if you think Paul Young's Papa is shocking, just wait till you hear what Jesus tells the Pharisees about *his* Father. The sinners, sitting at Jesus' feet, could hardly wait for what was about to happen. But you've got to admire the Pharisees' self-confidence. They have picked a fight with Jesus. It is carefully calculated, and in their minds there is no way that Jesus can escape without embarrassment.

---

5. Luke 15:2.

So Jesus faces them with his own questions. Here is my loose paraphrase of Luke 15:

> Which of *you* would not go after one of your own sheep, if you discovered that it was lost? And when you found it, which of you would not invite your friends and neighbors to celebrate its safe return? I didn't think so. So hear me. I tell you, *that's* the way it is in heaven. In fact, there will be more joy over one sinner who gets the truth about my Father, than over ninety-nine "righteous" persons who think they don't need help.
>
> Or what woman here, if she loses one of her ten coins, would not light a lamp and search carefully until she finds it? (Note the "search carefully" part.) And when she finds it, who among you would not call your friends and neighbors to rejoice with you? I didn't think so. So hear me. I tell you, there is joy in the presence of the angels of God over one sinner who gets the truth about my Father.
>
> Here's another story. A father had two sons; he loved them both. One got it into his head that he wanted to see the world. The other kept his list of dos and don'ts. The father divided his wealth between them. The younger son blazed a trail to the far country, squandering his money on wine, loose women, and riotous living. He humiliated his father and embarrassed his family with his feral ways. The whole town knew; the whispers were everywhere.
>
> When the money ran out, the boy began to starve. Reduced to pilfering food that he was feeding to pigs (an utter horror for a Jewish person), he remembered that the servants of his father ate quite well. So he

decided to go home, and knowing that he had proved himself unworthy of his father's love, he would pitch a plea for a job and some food as a servant.

So he headed home. But his father saw him when he was but a speck on the horizon. His heart filled with joy, the father ran out, embraced his son, and kissed him again and again—foul stench and all. Then he shouted to his servants, "Quick! Get my best robe and put it on him, and get the family ring and put it on his finger, and new sandals for his feet. And bring out the prized calf, and let's have a party! For my son was lost and has come home."

Then, I suspect, there was a long pause as Jesus let the shocking, almost unbelievable story sink in. Then he looked to the broken people with an assuring smile and a nod, and then he stared at the Pharisees.

This is what *my* Abba, my Papa, is like. *This* is why I am here, and this is why I receive sinners and share meals with them. They belong to my Father. He loves them forever. They are family. Just like the sheep belonged to the shepherd, and the coin belonged to the woman, and the two boys belonged to their father, you belong to my Father.

But the story is not over. You see, the older son, list in hand, was in the fields carrying out his duties. He heard the music and dancing, and called one of the servants for an explanation. "Your brother has come home. Your father's commanded a feast!" When the older son heard of the father and his party, he stalked off fuming, fit to be tied. The father himself came out looking for him, doing his best to convince him to join the party.

Then the son shouted, "*Look here!* I have never once disobeyed you, and you have never once given me a prized goat for a party for my friends. But when this whoremongering son of yours straggles in from the wine country, you embarrass yourself running down the streets, and receive him back! I even heard you kissed the swine-smelling derelict. *That is not fair!*"

Grieved and bewildered, the father looked his son in the eyes. "My child, you have always been here *with me*, and I have *already* given you everything that I have. How could we not rejoice over your brother? For he was dead and now has begun to live. He was lost to life in my house, but now has been found."

We are not told what happened when Jesus finished telling these stories. But surely the broken people cheered, and then cried in their shocked hope. They had never heard of a father like this. They identified with the lost sheep, the lost coin, and the younger son. And Jesus was telling them that *they* were accepted and loved by his Father just like this Jewish patriarch loved his broken son. Like the shepherd, Jesus' *Abba* has come after his lost sheep. Like the woman, Jesus' Papa has scoured the house of his universe to find his lost coin. And like this Jewish father, Jesus' *Abba* has embraced and kissed us in our shame, and commanded a feast in his joy. So what's the real difference between an African American woman embracing a broken, angry white man, and a Jewish father embracing his wayward son? Both are stunning pictures of the truth.

Paul Young is not saying that God *is* a black woman, any more than Jesus is saying that God *is* a Jewish patriarch. But both are using a shocking story to help us know the real truth about Jesus' Father, and the truth about who we are.

And what of the older brothers of the world, the Pharisees who create their own religious way to God, make lists, and keep them perfectly? I suspect that Jesus told these stories primarily for the Pharisees. That is why the older brother's story comes last. Jesus knows his Papa is "especially fond" of them, too. They belong, just as the tax-gatherers and sinners do. In fact, the father in the story embraced this older son in his religious pride, entreating him in the power of the Spirit to join the party.

I wonder if the Pharisees got it. I wonder if they saw themselves in the older brother. Jesus is the Father's arms embracing all of us, including them. He is the Father's heart entreating the religious among us to put the ledger down and to learn from him about his Father's heart. He is the "wealth" divided between them. Like Mackenzie, who has more in common with the Pharisees than he does with the wayward son, the Pharisees, too, are already loved and included.

3

LIGHT FROM LEWIS

Sarayu began humming the same evocative tune he'd heard earlier.... The melody stirred Mack deep inside, knocking again at the door.
—The Shack

As you have probably gathered by now, I suspect that the fingerprints of C. S. Lewis are all over *The Shack*. And nowhere more so than in the riveting scene when Papa runs across the porch and lifts Mackenzie off the ground with a hug as wide as the universe. Such a scene is born from a long and brutal journey, winding through great hurt into the discovery of the love of the Father, Son, and Spirit and the freedom *to be*.[1] Both Young and Lewis write as grown men who have learned

---

1. For a great song on this, see Dave Ligenfelter, "Free to Be Me," available at songsfromtheshack.com.

to play again; they write, as someone said to Lewis about his writing, "as though you enjoyed it."[2]

I have listened to Paul share his story for hours and hours in three different countries. He is always the same. His voice sounds like a blend of the voices of Kevin Costner and Tom Hanks, and he grins like Donald Sutherland, as if he knows something that you don't, but are about to, and he will enjoy every minute of your awakening. What Paul knows is that Papa is good, and that you are accepted as you are, and he knows that you believe that you are not. For me, Paul's voice, his grin, his eyes anticipating your surprise, all come together when Papa shouts, "Mackenzie Allen Phillips!" on the front porch.

Within us all there lies a broken dream, "our inconsolable secret,"[3] as Lewis calls it, that is so precious to us we protect it with a thousand defenses. "The secret which hurts so much," Lewis says, "that you take your revenge on it by calling it names like Nostalgia and Romanticism and Adolescence."[4] We know that we are made for glory, but we've only known hints of its joy. In the midst of life we long for more. Something is missing; creation is aflame with a glory we cannot touch, but we know it's ours. We are moved by ancient music, but cannot find the great dance. So "we pine," as Lewis says.[5] But such pining is too much to bear. So we bury our longing, and protect our dream's sleep.

Back in my college days at Ole Miss, I once bumped into

---

2. C. S. Lewis, *The Grand Miracle and Other Selected Essays on Theology and Ethics from "God in the Dock,"* ed. Walter Hooper (New York: Ballantine Books, 1970), p. 156.

3. C. S. Lewis, *The Weight of Glory: And Other Addresses* (Grand Rapids: Eerdmans, 1965), p. 4.

4. Ibid.

5. Ibid., p. 11.

Miss Mississippi. I had met her several times, so we greeted one another. It was around Homecoming, so as we talked I asked her who she had a date with for the big weekend. She paused for a moment, and then said, "Baxter, I don't have a date. In fact, no one ever asks me out."

I was shocked. "How in the world do *you* not have a date? I would have thought your phone never stops ringing."

"I don't know," she said. "No one calls me."

Every now and then I think about how odd it was that the reigning Miss Mississippi hardly ever had a date. One day it dawned on me. There is a huge risk in picking up the phone and asking someone like her for an evening out. Rarely does a "No" feel good, even a polite one; but somehow it seems to hurt more if the "No" comes from someone of standing. Perhaps it's better not to run the risk, and just settle for something else.

What if the grand promises of the New Testament, of abounding life, of the river of living water, of love, of a kingdom of righteousness, joy, and peace in the Holy Spirit, turn out to be a sham, a terrible trick of the gods? What if we find a closed door at the end of our longing? What if we hear that dreaded and shattering "No"? What if at last we miss the great dance altogether? Better not to listen for the music. Better to put the phone down. Better to bury the dream.

In this world it is best to keep such romanticism at bay. "Grow up," we say to ourselves, "put such silliness aside, and just get on with it." Perhaps it's better to compromise with our hearts and live a half-life than to risk the prospect of such a bitter disappointment. But then we hear a rumor in the wind, a line from a song; we see a smile, or a sunset; or we read the scene of Papa shouting Mackenzie's name, or hear the "haunting tune" of Sarayu (132, 234), and our insides tremble with hope. Our dream is awakened.

Such is the burden of being alive. How could we dare run

the risk? There is no pain more bitter than the death of a deep dream, and no dread as terrible as its awakening without hope. But what if Papa is real? What if Jesus is passionate that we know his Father with him? What if the Holy Spirit is determined that we live in the freedom of Papa's embrace?

Lewis was a rare academic who harnessed his great mind in the service of his heart's pain, until he was at last "surprised by joy."[6] As such, his writings sing the song of the longing heart.[7] He knows about our dream, and he knows the truth. He was aware of "almost committing an indecency"[8] in bringing up our inconsolable secret. But how can a man who has met Jesus' Papa be silent?

As a boy in Ireland, Lewis was smitten by an encounter too beautiful for words. It was only a fleeting moment, but it was real, and "in a certain sense," he says, "everything else that had ever happened to me was insignificant in comparison."[9] Thankfully, he could never let it go, and his whole life became a long quest to discover what that encounter, and others like it in his youth, were all about. He came to call them "stabs of joy." A "stab" because it hurt, and "joy" because even the pain of the stab was better than anything else in life. But what was it that Lewis encountered? What were the "stabs of joy"? What is our inconsolable secret? What exactly is our dream

---

6. *Surprised by Joy: The Shape of My Early Life* is the title of Lewis's autobiography (London: Harcourt, Brace, 1956).

7. Much of this chapter is a reworking of my essay "From Ghosts to Persons: C. S. Lewis' Vision of the Christian Life." This essay is available as a free download on our website, perichoresis.org.

8. Lewis, *The Weight of Glory*, p. 4.

9. Lewis, *Surprised by Joy*, p. 16.

all about? It has to do with Papa's smile, and Lewis has written beautifully about it.

In his famous sermon, now an essay published separately as *The Weight of Glory*, one of the finest sermons ever penned, you can find three profound insights into our inconsolable dream. The first we might call the desire to be baptized. I don't mean baptism in the sense of water or the church sacrament; I mean baptism in the sense of being immersed in something to the point of being utterly filled with it. Lewis is writing about beauty, the simple pleasure of seeing something beautiful, and about how in seeing it we want more. And this *wanting more* is surely part of what awakens in our hearts as we read about Papa's embrace.

> We do not want merely to *see* beauty, though, God knows, even that is bounty enough. We want something else which can hardly be put into words—to be united with the beauty we see, to pass into it, to receive it into ourselves, to bathe in it, to become part of it. That is why we have peopled air and earth and water with gods and goddesses and nymphs and elves—that, though we cannot, yet these projections can enjoy in themselves that beauty, grace, and power of which Nature is the image. That is why the poets tell us such lovely falsehoods. They talk as if the west wind could really sweep into a human soul; but it can't. They tell us that "beauty born of murmuring sound" will pass into a human face; but it won't.[10]

I think I have read this paragraph a hundred times over the years. It never ceases to amaze me. There is so much here.

---

10. Lewis, *The Weight of Glory*, pp. 12–13.

Notice the words "to be united with the beauty we see, to pass into it, to receive it into ourselves, to bathe in it, to become part of it." And I wonder if Lewis is right when he suggests that our fairy tales are really about this deep dream, that they are the projections of our longing hearts. The longing is not so much about beauty as it is about being filled, baptized. But filled with what?

In *Mere Christianity*, Lewis notes the biblical distinction between *bios* and *zoe*.[11] Although both words are translated as "life" in our English Bibles, they mean two different things. Lewis says that human beings in their natural condition, from their mother's womb, have *bios*—biological life—but not *zoe*, or spiritual life. The difference between the two, Lewis says, is like the difference between a photograph and a real place, a statue and a real man.[12] We could say it is the difference between broken, sad, and angry Mackenzie, and Mackenzie embraced and delighted in by Papa, Jesus, and Sarayu.

"This world is a great sculptor's shop," writes Lewis. "We are the statues and there is a rumor going round the shop that some of us are some day going to come to life."[13] The filling we long for is a filling with real spiritual life, not *bios* but *zoe*. But what is this spiritual life? What is *zoe*?

The second aspect of longing Lewis writes about in *The Weight of Glory* has to do with reunion. It is a longing "to be reunited with something in the universe from which we now feel cut off,"[14] and "to be acknowledged, to meet with some

---

11. C. S. Lewis, *Mere Christianity* (New York: Macmillan, 1952), pp. 139–40.

12. Ibid., p. 140.

13. Ibid.

14. Lewis, *The Weight of Glory*, p. 12.

response."[15] Here Lewis shifts from the abstract to the personal and relational, from discussions of filling and fullness and life to being noticed, heard, and known—to fellowship.

But there is yet a third dimension. For it is not merely fellowship for which we long, but fellowship of a certain kind. In the essay Lewis talks about glory in terms of fame. Not the fame of Hollywood—"not fame," Lewis says, "conferred by our fellow creatures"—but fame of a much more profound nature: "fame with God, approval or (I might say) 'appreciation' by God."[16] He elaborates:

> Nothing is so obvious in a child—not in a conceited child, but in a good child—as its great and undisguised pleasure in being praised.[17]
>
> To please God...to be a real ingredient in the divine happiness...to be loved by God, not merely pitied, but delighted in as an artist delights in his work or a father in a son—it seems impossible, a weight or burden of glory which our thoughts can hardly sustain. But so it is.[18]

Lewis moves from longing as the desire to be filled (baptized) to the desire to be reunited, reconnected, and known (fellowship), and now to the desire to be a thrill to the heart of God. It is when you combine these three that you come very close not only to the soul of the universe, but also to naming our own inconsolable secret. When Papa embraces Mackenzie, our inner world leaps with hope that it could be

---

15. Ibid., p. 11.

16. Ibid., p. 8.

17. Ibid., p. 9.

18. Ibid., p. 10.

so for us. What we want is to see Papa smile at us. We want to be a delight to the Father's heart, and to be so filled with his pleasure that our whole being dances in it. And *that* brings us within a hairsbreadth of the blessed Trinity and the great dance of the triune God, not to mention the stunning dream of the blessed Trinity for the human race.

Lewis was shocked at this. He said it never crossed his mind that what he longed for was God. "No slightest hint was vouchsafed me that there ever had been or ever would be any connection between God and Joy."[19] But gradually it began to dawn on him that behind the whole universe was Something vast and deep and ancient and beautiful, and very alive.

> And that, by the way, is perhaps the most important difference between Christianity and all other religions: that in Christianity God is not a static thing—not even a person—but a dynamic, pulsating activity, a life, almost a kind of drama. Almost, if you will not think me irreverent, a kind of dance.[20]

Behind Lewis's longing and ours is "the first dance," the original dance, the fellowship of the Father, Son, and Spirit. This fellowship is not boring, joyless, sad, or empty, and certainly not religious. This is a living fellowship of passion and delight and love, of creativity and music and joy, of glory and oneness and life—*zoe.*

The secret longing of our souls is to be taken into *this* circle and given a place in it, to pass into it, to bathe in it and be filled with *this* life, to be noticed and known and embraced, to share in the very delight and pleasure that the Father has

---

19. Lewis, *Surprised by Joy*, p. 230.

20. Lewis, *Mere Christianity*, p. 153.

for his beloved Son, to share in their joy together in the Spirit, and to live in its freedom. As Lewis says, "The whole dance, or drama, or pattern of this three-Personal life is to be played out in each one of us."[21]

Such a thought is almost unbelievable, but I think it is tucked away within us, and wrapped up in a box labeled "Too Risky." Such a longing is too much to bear. What could be more painful than to hope for such a dream and then miss it? And who among us actually believes that we could possibly be "a real ingredient in the divine happiness"? Why would God smile at us? So we bury our dream, and move on with life. Then we read of Papa's shout, full of such passion and love and delight, and the dream is awakened.

It hurts to hope that it could be so. But what if it is already true?

---

21. Ibid.

4

WHAT'S IN A NAME?

Nobody knows what horrors I have saved the world from
'cuz people can't see what never happened.

—Papa

Only the Lord knows how a boy from south Mississippi could be a die-hard Minnesota Vikings fan, but I was.[1] And my mom and dad gave me the unheard-of present of going to New Orleans to see my beloved Vikings play in person against the Saints, known in those days as the "aints" (blessedly, times have changed).

The three hours it took to drive to New Orleans seemed to me an eternal day. But we finally got there, and my dad parked the car. We took a trolley to the old Tulane Stadium. It

---

1. This story was originally published in my book *The Great Dance: The Christian Vision Revisited* (Jackson, MS: Perichoresis Press, 2000; Vancouver: Regent College Publishing, 2005), pp. 81ff.

was a magnificent afternoon, and the game was everything I had dreamed it would be, including a decisive Viking victory.

After the game we were walking down the exit ramp when I looked over the rail and saw three buses lined up, and I recognized the huge men boarding the buses as the Viking players themselves. Without thinking, I ran down the ramp and somehow made my way to the players. I actually shook hands with Carl Eller and was inches away from Alan Page and Wally Hilgenberg. And Coach Bud Grant himself stood not five feet from me. As he leaned over to sign an autograph his hat fell off, and I got to pick it up and give it back to him. Needless to say, I was in heaven.

Then, one by one, the buses began to drive away. I remember watching them go beside the stadium and turn left, out of sight. When the last bus was gone, the greatest of all fears seized my little heart. I suddenly realized that I had no idea where my parents were, and worse, that they had no idea where I was. I looked around and there was not another person in sight, not one. To this day, it is a mystery how the crowd around those buses disappeared so quickly, but they did. There was not one single human being to be found. Sheer panic gripped me. Within seconds I was scared out of my mind. I did not have a clue what to do. My heart was racing so fast I could not even think.

Twelve years old, New Orleans, Tulane Stadium, and it was getting dark. I was a long way from being street-smart, but I knew to the roots of my soul that I was in trouble. At some point it dawned on me to find a policeman, but there were none. I could not find another person, let alone a policeman, and I walked around that entire stadium at least three times.

By this time I was frantic and crying my eyes out. There were plenty of houses around, but I was not about to go to one for help. The only thing I knew to do was to try to find my way back to the car. I thought of the trolley that we had taken to the stadium, but which one? North and south were meaningless to me on the streets of New Orleans, and I had no idea which direction to go anyway. I did not even remember any street names. But I had some money in my pocket, so I found a trolley car and got on and told the driver that I was lost. He told me to get in the back of the trolley and keep my eyes peeled, and if I saw anything, to pull the cable and he would stop.

As the trolley made its way around New Orleans, I jumped from one side to the other, pressing my face against the cold windows, hoping, just hoping, that I would see something that I recognized—a tree, a building, a street, a parked car, who knows—maybe even my parents. But it did not happen. I rode that trolley all the way back to the stadium.

"Son," the driver said, "we have made the circuit. What do you want to do?" Not knowing what else to do, I got off and walked around the stadium all the way back to where the buses had been. Alone and scared to death, I sat down under an oak tree in a pile of leaves. I remember fiddling with a stick and crying, but there were no more tears. It was pitiful.

But things got worse. As I sat there, my twelve years of life flashing before my eyes, the stadium lights suddenly went off. I have never experienced darkness like that. Nearly forty years later I can still see the darting, haunting shadows of that place and still smell the concrete and hear the leaves rustling in the cold wind. I don't know how long I sat there, but it seemed like hours, certainly longer than the eternal ride to the stadium. It was so dark. I was so alone and cold.

And then suddenly, the stadium lights came on, and before I knew what was happening, I was on my feet running around the stadium. Someone had to have turned the lights on, and

I was determined with the fire of the universe to find them. And then it happened. Over the noise of my footsteps and the pounding of my fears, I heard the most blessed sound in all of New Orleans. It was the most blessed sound I had ever heard in my life: one word, "Baxter!"—shouted by my father.

No one had to tell me what to do. No one had to tell me what that word meant. No one had to tell me how to apply the word to my life. My name, shouted by my father, spoke the hope of a thousand volumes. The overwhelming fear, the frantic searching, the anxiety, all took a left turn like the buses and were gone. And in their place arose the simplest and most wonderful of all things: security, assurance, rest.

I had no way of knowing it at the time, but I was being given a world-class education on how to live life. It would be years before I could begin to understand the significance of what happened. The story is a living parable with two simple points.

First, it's not just about a young boy lost in New Orleans, desperately searching for his family. It's about *us*, the human race. *We* are on the trolley car. It is a streetcar named Scared to Death, but who can admit it? We don't know who we are or why we are here, or what's going to happen next. It's a fearful world. And we are trapped on the streetcar going in circles. Again and again we hear, "Son, we have made the circuit. What do you want to do?" Some of us have given up and gone to entertaining ourselves, others sleep in one way or another, some stay busy, some pretend that all is well or that they have it figured out; but when there is an odd sound, we all betray ourselves as we glance out the window, hoping to see something that will give us a hint of home, of hope, of peace.

Second, my trauma in New Orleans is a dramatic picture of the truth that *life* is all about hearing Papa shout our name. It is truly no more complicated than that. When we hear Jesus' *Abba* shout our name, it baptizes our inner worlds with unearthly assurance. In the New Testament this unearthly assurance is called *parrhesia* (par-ray-see-uh): confidence, freedom, boldness, assurance. We are so made as to live our lives baptized in such assurance. That is how we are wired. We have been designed, so to speak, to hear Jesus' Papa. And when we do, peace happens, assurance settles our souls, unexpected joy fills the room of our broken lives. We see with new eyes, and we see glory everywhere.

I have heard a year's worth of sermons on "the will of God," and some shame-filled ones on "settling for God's second best." I believe the will of the Father, Son, and Spirit for us is that we would know what Jesus knows, that we would see what Jesus sees, and that we would experience what Jesus experiences when he looks his Father in the face. Think of what Jesus feels when he looks into his Father's eyes and hears, "You are my beloved Son, in whom my soul delights." I dare say it's not sadness or fear; not anxiety, dread, or hopelessness. I think Jesus' soul is baptized with unearthly assurance, with a freedom and confidence and hope that are born in his Father's heart. Jesus gets to live life in the joy of that baptism, in the freedom of the Spirit. The dream of the blessed Trinity is that *we* will, too. We will get to be mothers and fathers, friends and neighbors, golfers and poets and gardeners, ditchdiggers and teachers in the assurance of Papa's voice. *Heaven. Zoe.*

I love the scene in *The Shack* when Papa says to Mackenzie, "Just follow my voice" (91). It is no more complicated than that. But oh, Lord, there are so many voices. Jesus' Papa loves us forever, and shouts our name with a smiling face, but we have weird ears. There are childhood wounds, the voices of our disappointed parents, the sermons on the angry god, the constant whisper: "I am not worthy, I am not important, not lovable, not good enough, not okay." There are divorces and financial crises, abuses and the betrayal of friends, overwhelming losses, all conspiring together to drown out Jesus' Father's voice.

As you read this, I want you to find a mirror and stand in front of it. I want you to stare yourself in the face, look yourself in the eyes, and as you do I want you to say these words out loud: "I am good." Then say them again: "I am good." And then a third time: "I am good." Why is it so hard to say "I am good"? Is it because we have reached another conclusion about ourselves, a conclusion based on real-life experiences? Is it because of what we have been taught in church? Perhaps we have a definition of goodness that clearly excludes us. Perhaps we have crowned ourselves as the ultimate judge of goodness.

The truth is that Jesus has crossed all worlds to find us. He became what we are, entered into our world of confusion, and boarded the trolley car. He found his way into our darkness, into the scary places inside our souls. And there he pitched his tent forever—and he brought his Papa and the Holy Spirit with him. We can't say "I am good" because we don't know who we are and what glory lives within us. For inside of us all, because of Jesus, is nothing short of the very trinitarian life of God, with all of its goodness and beauty, its righteousness and holiness, its joy unspeakable, its love and laughter. "I am good" because Jesus and his Father and the Holy Spirit have found me and live in me.

What will happen when the great dance of trinitarian life and love and freedom, when that beauty and goodness and righteousness of the Father, Son, and Spirit—already within us—gets loose, so to speak, to run rampant in our lives and relationships, in our work and play?

What is keeping it from happening? What is in the way? What do we bring into the equation of the trinitarian life that is being shared with us every moment? What keeps us from believing Papa's shout? It is simple, but not easy. Like Mackenzie, we are not neutral. We bring a load of rubbish to the kitchen conversation.

5

THE TWO GODS

Good souls many will one day be horrified at the things
they now believe of God.
—George MacDonald

What if instead of Papa, it was Mack's real dad who flung the door open and ran toward him, drunk again, stick in hand and eyes full of rage, ready for another round of beatings? Huckleberry Finn's dad was a drunk, too, and mean as a snake. When Huck heard his dad calling his name, he ran for his life. For the one thing Mack and Huck knew was that their fathers were not *for* them. There was no baptism of unearthly assurance. Theirs was a baptism of outright fear.

I once asked Paul about his favorite line in his book. He responded quickly, "That's easy: 'Freedom is an incremental process'" (97). We want a quick fix, but that's not how it works. The freedom of living loved is not the sort of thing that happens overnight. Hearing Papa takes time. We are all so wounded and blind; we bring a lot of baggage into our hearing. Life, history, wars and beatings, abusive parents, evil systems, and our own invisible world of assumptions and prejudices all work against us, shouting that God is like Mack's real dad, and Huck's. He could not possibly be *for* us. And if God is not *for* us, we certainly don't want to hear him shouting our name.

It would take an entire weekend of love, acceptance, and conversation before Mack could begin to hear the truth. And for Paul himself, Mack's weekend at the shack represents more than a decade of his own life. Lewis's journey was much the same. He says that his imagination was baptized when he was reading one of George MacDonald's books, but that it took years before that baptism reached the rest of him.[1] There is something deep within us that tells us it can't be so, that God cannot be *for* us. Even Missy, who called God "Papa" like her mother, nevertheless thought that God was "mean" (33) and wondered if she would have to die. Perhaps all this talk of the love of Papa is just romanticism.

Yet we know that God is good, else we would not care a whit about problems in life. They wouldn't be *problems* really, they would just be life: the way it is. But we know that it is not supposed to be this way. This is why tragedy is so *tragic* to us and hurts so brutally; we know that life is supposed to be good.[2] We have heard the music. We have tasted of something beautiful, and somehow we know we belong to it. It is

---

1. See C. S. Lewis, *Surprised by Joy: The Shape of My Early Life* (New York: Harcourt, Brace, 1956), p. 181; and Lewis's introduction to George MacDonald's *Lilith* (Grand Rapids: Eerdmans, 2000), p. xi.

2. For more here, see my book *The Great Dance: The Christian Vision Revisited* (Jackson, MS: Perichoresis Press, 2000; Vancouver: Regent College Publishing, 2005), pp. 88ff.

our own despair, our own frustration and pain that tell us we are made for peace. For how can you be homesick if you have no home? How can you despair if you don't know that you are meant for abounding life?

We are in two minds. Even Papa made Mackenzie "nervous" (119), and her offer to be the Papa he had never had "was at once inviting and at the same time repulsive" (94). It all translates into a question of serious importance. Is God really *for* us? Note this depiction of Jesus' Father:

> The bow of God's wrath is bent, and the arrow made ready on the string, and justice bends the arrow at your heart, and strains the bow, and it is nothing but the mere pleasure of God, and that of an angry God, without any promise or obligation at all, that keeps the arrow one moment from being made drunk with your blood.[3]

This image of Jesus' Father is from Jonathan Edwards's famous sermon, "Sinners in the Hands of an Angry God." Thankfully, this is not the full picture of Edwards's vision, but it is unfortunately the most famous sermon in American history.[4] It makes sense to our broken, wounded minds. Needless to say, it stands in dramatic contrast to Young's Papa and

---

3. Jonathan Edwards, "Sinners in the Hands of an Angry God," in *The Works of Jonathan Edwards*, vol. 2 (Edinburgh: Banner of Truth Trust), p. 9.

4. Jerry Falwell ranks Edwards's sermon first in his book *25 of the Greatest Sermons Ever Preached* (Grand Rapids: Baker, 1983). Note George MacDonald's lament: "From all copies of Jonathan Edwards' portrait of God, however faded by time, however softened by the use of less glaring pigments, I turn with loathing." In his *Unspoken Sermons: Series I, II, III* (Whitethorn, CA: Johannesen, 1999), p. 540.

her determined love. Edwards's God is full of wrath, bound by a law of abstract justice. We have failed; we deserve to suffer. God is angry. You wouldn't expect this God to say, "I have really been looking forward to seeing you face to face. It is so wonderful to have you here with us. My, my, my, how I do love you!" (85).

The anger of Edwards's God, terrible as it is, may not be as bad as his arbitrariness. He is aloof. He has no obligation to his own creation. Love is not an essential part of his being; it's merely an option. He is not *for* us. And it is this divine *ambivalence* toward us that causes our real hearing problems. Why should he not let the arrows fly? Who wants to hear this God call our names? Who really wants to go to this God's heaven?

But in Young's Papa there is no ambivalence at all. There is not a shred of indifference or neutrality. There is no Maybe, or Perhaps, or If-Then. Young's Papa is *for* us, always has been, and always will be. She doesn't even *have* a quiver of arrows. Love is the core truth of her very being: "I *am* love" (103); "The God who is—the I am who I am—*cannot* act apart from love!" (104).

Most of us, like Mackenzie, while wanting to believe, have too many shadows and a thousand questions. What about wrath? What about holiness and judgment, faith and repentance, heaven and hell? God cannot simply love us because that's the way he is. Don't we have to do something?

> Mack knew that what he was hearing, as hard as it was to understand, was something amazing and incredible. It was as if her words were wrapping themselves around him, embracing him and speaking to him in ways beyond just what he could hear. Not that he actually believed any of it. If only it were true. His experience told him otherwise. (104)

As I read through *The Shack*, especially the conversations about goodness and love, I thought again and again of Athanasius, one of the early Church heroes. Note what he says about Jesus' Father:

> The God of all is good and supremely noble by nature. Therefore he is the lover of humanity.[5]
>
> As, then, the creatures whom He had created... were in fact perishing, and such noble works were on the road to ruin, what then was God, being Good, to do? Was He to let corruption and death have their way with them? In that case, what was the use of having made them in the beginning?...It was impossible, therefore, that God should leave man to be carried off by corruption, because it would be unfitting and unworthy of Himself.[6]

I first read Athanasius when I was a senior at Ole Miss, having followed up a footnote in C. S. Lewis's *God in the Dock*. As a son of the Bible Belt, I was shocked when I read the two statements quoted above, and the many more I found like them. *This Athanasius fellow*, I thought to myself, *writes as if the Father loves us passionately, as if he is for us, not against us*. The God of Athanasius is all heart, intent on the single-minded purpose of blessing us beyond our wildest dreams. It's as though we are the reason for the whole creation—the apple of his eye. He has stunning dreams for us, and he won't let them go. This Father doesn't have to have his arm twisted

---

5. In Khaled Anatolios, *Athanasius: The Coherence of His Thought* (London: Routledge, 1998), p. 40.

6. Athanasius, *On the Incarnation of the Word of God* (London: A. R. Mowbray, 1963), §6.

by Jesus to love us, or to forgive us. He is not distant, aloof, uncaring. He is thrilled with his creation, and loves us all. For Athanasius, Jesus is the proof.

This was a different world and a different God from that of the Calvinism of my youth. The sheer love of Athanasius's God captured my imagination. Far from being a stern Judge ever watching with his disapproving heart, or the faceless, nameless omni-being, Jesus' Father is good, and "therefore he is the lover of humanity." What, then, is *this* Father to do when his creation, when Mackenzie Allen Phillips, when you and I are trapped in such dastardly confusion and on the road to ruin? Throw up his hands and scream at Jesus, "I *knew* this would happen! I never should have let you talk me into such a stupid thing as creating human beings! You can go and fix it if you want, but know this: I don't care; let them squirm and die in the miserable mess they have made. They have offended me. They make me sick. Where is my quiver?"

In Athanasius's view, it never crossed the Father's mind to go back on his lavish dreams for the human race. He is not fickle; he did not grudgingly grant us life, only to watch for an excuse to abandon us. He is good, and therefore loves us forever. Inconceivable as it may be to us, before the creation of the world the Father, Son, and Spirit set their love upon us, and dreamed of the day when we could be included in nothing less than the very life and goodness, the fellowship and joy, the unbridled delight that they share together from all eternity. As Papa says to Mackenzie, "We created you to share in that" (101).

> It was unworthy of the goodness of God that crea-
> tures made by Him should be brought to nothing
> through the deceit wrought upon man by the devil;
> and it was supremely unfitting that the work of God

in mankind should disappear, either through their own negligence or through the deceit of evil spirits. As, then, the creatures whom He had created...were in fact perishing, and such noble works were on the road to ruin, what then was God, being Good, to do?[7]

When Adam fell, when he introduced independence and thus chaos, dying, misery, and death into the world of God's dreams for us, the response of the Father, Son, and Spirit was as simple as it was passionate: "No! No! No! Not on our watch! We did not create *you* to perish, to die, to live in such appalling pain and blindness and brokenness. We created you to share in our life, to taste and feel and know and experience what we have known from all eternity."

Adam chose to go it on his own, as we knew he would, and everything got messed up. But instead of scrapping the whole Creation we rolled up our sleeves and entered into the middle of the mess—that's what we have done in Jesus. (101)

Papa's unflinching heart reflects the passionate love of Athanasius's God, and putting the two in vivid contrast with Edwards's God helps us see a confusion at work in our own hearts, or at least a duality. Like an overturned tackle box, the two pictures of God have left our beliefs in a tangled mess. How can we hear Jesus' Papa call our names, and believe it when we do, when there are two very different Gods knocking around in our minds? It is, I fear, even more complicated than this, for our notions of God shape our understanding of why God created us, of who we are, of what happened in

---

7. Ibid., §6.

Adam and then in Jesus, and of the very nature of life, just to name a few.

And there is another question lurking here. How have we developed our ideas about God? Who told us? Was it our parents, our church, a religious leader, the Bible, or are our ideas of God a compilation of various notions that just seem right to us? Or do they arise from our wounds? Perhaps, like Mack's, our view of God is influenced by iconic figures such as Gandalf (75) or Santa Claus. Or could our God be our own image writ large and projected into heaven, as Papa said to Mack?

> The problem is that many folks try to grasp some sense of who I am by taking the best version of themselves, projecting that to the nth degree, factoring in all the goodness they can perceive, which often isn't much, and then call *that* God. And while it may seem like a noble effort, the truth is that it falls pitifully short of who I really am. I'm not merely the best version of you that you can think of. I am far more than that, above and beyond all that you can ask or think. (100)

For Mackenzie, hearing Papa was largely about the removal of his alien ideas. As Papa said in a simple but loaded statement, "I am not who you think I am, Mackenzie" (98).

PART TWO

Jesus, His Father, and the Holy Spirit

6

Summary of the
Trinitarian Vision

The heart of the New Testament is the relationship between
the Father and the Son in the Holy Spirit.

—James B. Torrance

Mackenzie's meeting with Papa, Sarayu, and Jesus is a weekend within a much, much larger story. As we have seen, the weekend represents eleven years in Paul's own life. But both Paul's life and Mackenzie's weekend fall within the larger narrative of the purposes of the triune God for the human race. The beautiful portrayal of the relationship between Jesus, Sarayu, and Papa (107, 122ff.)—its nonhierarchical nature (121ff.), their amazing freedom to embrace Mackenzie in his anger and pain and unbelief (84ff.), the shocking nail scars on Papa's wrists (97, 104, 109, 166, 224), and Jesus' profound comment that he did not come to be an example for us to follow but to share his own life with us (151, 114f.)—all point back to this larger story. We must take time to think about it. If we don't, we are apt to miss some of the healing the story offers us. This is important, and very relevant to our own lives, hurts, and freedom.

Paul's larger vision is rooted in "the evangelical theology of the ancient Catholic Church,"[1] to borrow a phrase from theologian Thomas F. Torrance. This vision involves you, me, and everyone else on the planet in a breathtaking relationship with Jesus' Father—the Papa we always wanted. It is trinitarian, incarnational, relational, thoroughly biblical, Christ-centered, and cosmic. It is the truth being told in every line of Paul's book. I want to explore this trinitarian vision as a way of opening our eyes to the larger context of the book so that we will have a framework for understanding the various topics and issues raised in *The Shack*. But first I will attempt a brief summary of the trinitarian vision.

From all eternity, God is not alone and solitary, but lives as Father, Son, and Spirit in a rich and glorious fellowship of utter oneness. There is no emptiness in this circle, no depression or fear or insecurity. The trinitarian life is a great dance of unchained communion and intimacy, fired by passionate, self-giving, other-centered love and mutual delight. This life is unique, and it is good and right. It is full of music and joy, blessedness and peace. And this love, giving rise to such togetherness and fellowship and oneness, is the womb of the universe and of humanity within it.

The stunning truth is that this triune God, in amazing

---

1. This is the subtitle of Thomas F. Torrance's book *The Trinitarian Faith: The Evangelical Theology of the Ancient Catholic Church* (Edinburgh: T&T Clark, 1988).

and lavish love, determined to open the circle and share the trinitarian life with others. As Papa said to Mack, "We want to share with you the love and joy and freedom and light that we already know within ourself" (126). This is the one, eternal, and abiding reason for the creation of the world and of human life. There is no other God, no other will of God, no second plan, no hidden agenda for human beings. Before the creation of the world, the Father, Son, and Spirit set their love upon us and planned for us to share and know and experience the trinitarian life itself. To this end the cosmos was called into being, the human race was fashioned, and Adam and Eve were given a place in the coming of Jesus Christ, the Father's Son, in and through whom the dream of our adoption would be accomplished.

Before Creation, it was decided that the Son would cross every chasm between the triune God and humanity and establish a real and abiding union with us. Jesus was predestined to be the mediator, the One in and through whom the very life of the triune God would enter human existence, and human existence would be lifted up to share in the trinitarian life.

When Adam and Eve rebelled, ushering chaos and misery into God's creation, the Father, Son, and Spirit did not abandon their dream, but wonderfully incorporated our darkness and sin into the tapestry of the coming Incarnation. As the Father's Son became human, as he submitted himself to bear our anger and bizarre blindness, and as he gave himself to suffer a murderous death at our hands, he established a real and abiding relationship with fallen humanity at our very worst—and he brought his Father and the Holy Spirit with him. It was in Jesus himself, and in his death at our bitter hands, that the trinitarian life of God pitched its tent in our hell on earth, thereby uniting all that the Father, Son, and

Spirit share with all that we are in our brokenness, shame, and sin, thus adopting us into their circle of fellowship.

In the life and death of Jesus, the Holy Spirit made his way into human pain and blindness. Inside our broken inner worlds, the Spirit works to reveal Jesus *in* us so that we can meet Jesus himself in our own sin and shame, begin to see what Jesus sees, and know his Father with him. The Holy Spirit discloses Jesus to us so that we can know and experience Jesus' own relationship with his Father, and be free to live in the Father's embrace with Jesus. As the Spirit works, we are summoned to take sides with Jesus against our own darkness and prejudice, and take the "incremental" (97) steps of trust and change. As we do so, Jesus' own anointing with the Spirit—his own fellowship with his Father, his own unearthly assurance, his own freedom and joy and power in the Spirit—begins to express itself in us, not diminishing our own uniqueness as persons but augmenting and freeing it to be expressed in our relationship with the Father, in our relationships with one another, and indeed with all creation, until the whole cosmos is a living sacrament of the great dance of the triune God.

It is this trinitarian vision that forms Young's core beliefs, and they inform every page of *The Shack*. While it would take twenty volumes to set out the details and nuances of these ideas, it is important that we take some time to explore the leading thoughts here more carefully.

In most great stories there is a twist that no one sees coming; something happens that catches both the characters and the readers by surprise. And once it happens, everyone's understanding of the story changes. In *The Shack*, the twist—at least the main one—is Papa. In the biblical story, it's the incarnation of the Son of God. Not a single character in the long drama of Israel anticipated that God would come in person. While not at all inconsistent with the love of Israel's Lord, such personal presence wasn't even a blip on Israel's radar of possibility. After all, there had been four hundred years of prophetic silence; who would ever have dreamed that the Lord himself would suddenly appear? But according to John the Baptist, Matthew, Mark, Luke, and John, even doubting Thomas and Saul of Tarsus, this is exactly what happened.

Jesus Christ stepped into Israel's history not merely as a great prophet, a revolutionary priest, or even the best of Israel's kings. He stepped into Israel's history as the One Israel called "the Lord." The shocker of the New Testament is that Israel's Lord became human. The Creator, the One in and through and by and for whom all things were created and are constantly sustained, entered into his own creation and became one of us—*Immanuel*, "God with us."

In itself, the identification of Jesus with Israel's Lord, the Creator of the heavens and the earth, was not necessarily at odds with Israel's nonnegotiable commitment to monotheism. It was surely a shock and perhaps unbelievable, but it simply meant that the Lord himself had come in person. *But Jesus was not alone.* And this was the rub, or perhaps I should say, *the revelation*, for the Lord identified himself as "the Son" and lived his life in relationship to One he called "my Father." And in the midst of this remarkable relationship moved One called "the Holy Spirit."

The New Testament fits into Israel's history like a new-found scroll that recasts the whole story in a new light. It is loaded with revolutionary ideas that call for a serious rethinking of everything we thought we knew about God, about creation, and about human life and history. It does not read like a collection of letters from pipe-smoking old men. There is urgency; there is passion; there is scrambling. Every writer stands on his tiptoes, stretching his imagination to see and to say. Jesus rocked the world! His presence was too big, too stunning, too beautiful to be understood, yet it had to be told. His life involved the whole cosmos and every single human being within it. And most important of all, his presence involved God.

For the disciples, Jesus is not a mere prophet heralding the latest divine message. *Jesus is a revolution.* Note the very first verse of John's Gospel: "In the beginning was the Word, and the Word was with God, and the Word was God." These three simple statements carry hitherto unknown and inconceivable ideas about God that are destined to change the world. As a good Jew, John certainly knows the first verse in the Hebrew Bible: "In the beginning God created the heavens and the earth."[2] But John has met Jesus, and "saw His glory, glory as of the only begotten from the Father."[3] While John certainly agrees that God created all things, he cannot leave it at that, for he has seen something that has changed his understanding of everything. Note the parallel and the difference between Genesis 1:1 and John 1:1:

> In the beginning God created the heavens and the earth.
> In the beginning was the Word, and the Word was with God, and the Word was God.

Having met Jesus and beheld his glory, John makes the staggering move of placing Jesus with God in the beginning. In this unprecedented move John is filling out the notion of

---

2. Genesis 1:1.

3. John 1:14.

God with the idea of relationship: the God who created is not alone and solitary, but relational.

While the ancient world was replete with gods and goddesses, John is not simply adding another to the list. The Word or Son who was in the beginning "was with God." The preposition *with* here carries the Hebrew idea of being face-to-face. It is an idea of personal relationship, of intimacy. At the end of his introduction, John adds another image to solidify this point: "No one has seen God at any time; the only begotten God who is *in the bosom of the Father*, He has explained Him."[4] This imagery is not cold or sterile; it suggests profound familiarity, a deep, personal relationship of mutual affection, delight, and love. And John is saying that this beautiful fellowship exists within the very being of God, and thus frames the story of Creation itself. The twist in the tale turns out to be a double twist: first, God has come in person; second, this God is the Son of his Father. In Jesus, the kaleidoscope of human thought turns and all things appear new—*including God*. The incarnation of the Father's eternal Son, anointed in the Holy Spirit, is a flash of eternal light enlightening all human knowledge of God.[5]

4. John 1:18, my italics.

5. Here, see Thomas F. Torrance, *Space, Time and Resurrection* (Edinburgh: Handsel Press, 1976), pp. 42ff.

7

JESUS AND HIS FATHER

Truly, truly, I say to you, the Son can do nothing of Himself,
unless it is something He sees the Father doing....For the Father
loves the Son, and shows Him all things that He Himself is doing.

—Jesus

From the very beginning, the Hebrew Bible proclaims God as the Creator of the heavens and the earth. And at no point does it give the impression that the Lord is only marginally interested in his creation. God is not an abstract divinity, a deistic creator who makes the universe, sets it in motion, and then steps back to let it fend for itself or go its own way. Neither is God a legalist who appears long enough to dispense a set of sacred rules and then leaves with the threat of a future, final reckoning. The God of the Bible is an involved God. He is the God *of* Abraham, Isaac, and Jacob; the covenant God; the Lord, who stoops in grace to call Abraham to himself and binds himself in relationship to Abraham and Israel.

However, even given the Lord's personal involvement, and given the wonderful care for and relationship he has with his people, there is nonetheless always a profound distance between the Lord and Israel. Even Moses, the archetypal servant of the Lord, was permitted only to see the "back" of God.[1] And the high priest, whom the Lord chose to minister in his presence, was permitted to enter the holy of holies, the place of the Lord's dwelling, only once a year—and then only after going through an elaborate system of cleansing.[2]

It is in this context of involvement and personal relationship, yet reservation and distance between God and Israel, that Jesus Christ appears in Israel's history. And he does so with what can only be described as shocking familiarity with God. To begin with, Jesus speaks about God from a position of assurance: "For God *so* loved the world, that He gave His only begotten Son....For God did not send the Son into the world to judge the world, but that the world might be saved through Him."[3] Instead of summarizing others, in the style that was typical of the rabbis of his day, Jesus spoke simply out of direct knowledge of God, and did so "as one having authority."[4] "Never has a man spoken the way this man speaks."[5]

Traditionally, the word *amen* ("truly") was "used to affirm, endorse or appropriate the words of another person," but in the speech of Jesus, *amen* was "used *without exception* to introduce and endorse" his own words.[6] "Truly, truly (*amen*,

---

1. See Exodus 33:18–23.

2. See Hebrews 9:1ff.

3. John 3:16–17, my italics.

4. Matthew 7:29.

5. John 7:46.

6. Joachim Jeremias, *The Prayers of Jesus* (Naperville, IL: Alec R. Allenson, 1967), p. 112.

amen), I say to you, unless one is born from above, he cannot see the kingdom of God."[7] Jesus operates with unquestionable authority, not only assuming a position of equality with the Scriptures, but having "the unparalleled and revolutionary boldness to set himself up in opposition to the *Torah*."[8] But his authority is not the kind that arises out of certainty as to the abstract will of God. What we see in Jesus is more deeply grounded. It is authority and confidence arising out of inside knowledge, out of deep and personal familiarity with the very heart of God. This is the primer, as it were, which alerts us to something far more profound than a prophetic presence.

In the entire Old Testament there are only fifteen[9] places where God is actually called "Father," and even then it is in general terms—God is the Father of Israel[10] or of the King,[11] who represents Israel. The fatherhood of God is certainly present in the Old Testament, but it is nothing like the central point of Israel's thinking about God. But in Jesus we encounter One standing within Israel who speaks of God as *Father* more than one hundred times in John's Gospel alone (179 in all four Gospels). At times it seems as if every other statement begins with "The Father"; for example, in John 5:21–22 Jesus says, "For just as the Father raises the dead and gives them life, even so the Son also gives life to whom He wishes. For

---

7. John 3:3, my translation. See also 1:51; 3:5, 11; 5:19, 24, 25; Matthew 5:18, 26; 8:10; Mark 3:28; 8:12; 9:1, 41; Luke 4:24; 12:37.

8. Joachim Jeremias, *New Testament Theology* (New York: Scribner's, 1975), p. 253. See, for example, Matthew 5:22, 28, 32, 34, 39, 44.

9. See Jeremias, *The Prayers of Jesus*, pp. 11ff. It is to be noted that there are more than 250 references to God as Father in the New Testament.

10. See Isaiah 63:16; 64:8.

11. See 2 Samuel 7:14.

not even the Father judges anyone, but He has given all judgment to the Son."

The phrase "the Father" is virtually a refrain in Jesus' famous Sermon on the Mount. And, as we have seen, the Father himself is the theme of Jesus' most famous parable.[12] There is not a single instance in the entire Old Testament, including the Psalms, of an individual addressing God in prayer as "Father"; yet Jesus, in stunning contrast, prays to God as Father in all his prayers—with the exception of the cry from the cross,[13] which is a quotation from Psalm 22:1.

In Jesus, the conception of God as Father moves from the periphery to center stage. No longer is it simply there lurking in the background; in Jesus it becomes the focus. And this betrays a personal consciousness of God on Jesus' part that is well beyond receiving a prophetic word to proclaim. It betrays a profound intimacy with God—a unique relationship with him.

The intimacy and the uniqueness of his relationship with God is conveyed all the more powerfully by the Aramaic word *Abba*, the word Jesus would have used, rendered in Greek by the Gospel writers as *Pater* (Father).[14] *Abba* is the word of a child addressing his or her father. This is not the language of distance or formality, not the language of Jewish reservation or reticence, nor of religion or servile fawning. *Abba* is the language of thoroughgoing naturalness and assurance, of awareness of real belonging. It is respectful and honoring, but

---

12. See Luke 15:11–32.

13. See Matthew 27:46; Mark 15:34.

14. See Jeremias, *The Prayers of Jesus*, pp. 55–57; and *Theological Dictionary of the New Testament*, ed. Gerhard Kittel, vol. 1 (Grand Rapids: Eerdmans, 1966), pp. 5–6.

its main nuance is endearment and intimacy. As James D. G. Dunn says:

> It is difficult therefore to escape the conclusion that Jesus said "Abba" to God for precisely the same reason that (most of) his contemporaries refrained from its use in prayer—viz., because it expressed his attitude to God as Father, his experience of God as one of unusual intimacy.[15]

Abba suggests an image of unceremonious closeness and warmth, of undaunted familiarity and at-homeness *with God*.

What are we to make of the fact that Jesus addresses God not only as *Father*, but as *Abba*, Papa? According to Jeremias, this venture in language "was something new and unheard of,"[16] perhaps revolutionary. This, of course, is a matter of scholarly debate.[17] What is not debatable is the striking fact that more than sixty times in the Gospels (nearly forty times in John) Jesus uses the phrase "my Father," which has no parallel in the Hebrew Bible. And according to Jeremias, it has

---

15. James D. G. Dunn, *Jesus and the Spirit: A Study of the Religious and Charismatic Experience of Jesus and the First Christians as Reflected in the New Testament* (Philadelphia: Westminster Press, 1975), p. 23.

16. Joachim Jeremias, *The Prayers of Jesus*, p. 62. "We can say quite definitely that there is *no analogy at all* in the whole literature of Jewish prayer for God being addressed as Abba," p. 57. In another work, *The Central Message of the New Testament*, Jeremias comments, "To a Jewish mind it would have been irreverent and therefore unthinkable to call God by this familiar word" (New York: Scribner's, 1965), p. 21.

17. Note Dunn, *Jesus and the Spirit*, pp. 26ff; William C. Placher, *Narratives of a Vulnerable God: Christ, Theology, and Scripture* (Louisville: Westminster John Knox Press, 1994), pp. 58ff.; and James Barr, "'Abba' Isn't 'Daddy,'" *Journal of Theological Studies* 39 (1988): 47.

no parallel in all the literature of Judaism.[18] No biblical Jew would have dared conceive of such a standing with God. It would have been blasphemously familiar, which is the very accusation the Jewish leadership leveled at Jesus.[19]

The plain and astonishing fact is that this language was commonplace for Jesus. At the age of twelve, for example, he queries his parents, who have been searching for him at least two days: "Why is it that you were looking for Me? Did you not know that I had to be in *My Father's* house?"[20] And straightaway in his public ministry, Jesus, in John's Gospel, cleanses the temple with the words: "Take these things away; stop making *My Father's* house a place of business."[21] Again and again Jesus refers to God not only as "Father," but as "my Father." And as a correlate he refers to himself not only as *a* Son but as *the* Son. In terms of the Bible, Jesus' relationship with God, whom he called "Father," "my Father," and *Abba,* is in a class by itself.

The uniqueness of this relationship is confirmed from God's side in the divine declaration about Jesus: "Thou art my beloved Son, in whom my soul delights,"[22] which is proclaimed from heaven in dramatic fashion on at least two

---

18. See Jeremias, *New Testament Theology,* pp. 61ff.; Jeremias, *The Prayers of Jesus,* pp. 18–29; and Jeremias, *The Central Message of the New Testament,* p. 17.

19. See John 5:17ff. and 10:33.

20. Luke 2:49, my italics.

21. John 2:16, my italics.

22. Matthew 3:17, my translation. This declaration is a conflation of three Old Testament statements: Genesis 22:2; Psalm 2:7; and Isaiah 42:1. For more on this declaration, see Thomas A. Smail, *The Forgotten Father* (London: Hodder and Stoughton, 1980), p. 77.

occasions—at Jesus' baptism and after his transfiguration.[23] This statement declares the presence of the unique and only Son of God. At the Transfiguration, this declaration was spoken to the three disciples with a nuance of rebuke, for in his excitement Peter wanted to build three tabernacles—one for Jesus, one for Moses, and one for Elijah. Evidently he conceived of the three on equal terms. And the scriptural writer makes sure we understand that it was *while* Peter was suggesting building the three tabernacles that the word of declaration was spoken—as if to say, "*Peter*, what are you doing? This is not another Moses. This is not another Elijah. This is not merely the long-awaited Messiah. This is *my* Son, *my* beloved and only *Son*."

What we encounter in Jesus' assumption of such authority, in his whole approach to God, in his extraordinary language and confident familiarity with God, and in God's own declaration from heaven to and about him, is a divine-human relationship that is unparalleled in biblical Israel. Throughout Israel's history we see mutual personal involvement between God and humanity, but there is always distance. God is always transcendent in his presence; he is always other. We see Moses spending days with God on the mountain, so much so that his face glowed. We read of Abraham as the friend of God, and we hear David called the man after God's own heart. But of no one do we ever read the divine declaration: "Thou art my beloved Son, in whom my soul delights." And we never read, "*Abba*, Father," in response to God.

The relationship between Jesus the Son and the God he called "my Father" was an exclusive and intimate relationship so unthinkable to the Jews that they took up stones to kill him for blasphemy. For in "calling God His own Father,"

---

23. Mark 1:11 and 9:7; Luke 2:22 and 9:35; Matthew 3:17 and 17:5.

he was "making Himself equal with God."[24] They could only take his familiarity as undiluted arrogance. This relationship collapsed the distance between God and man, placing Jesus where no human being in the Bible had ever been placed—in the closest proximity to God, in the bosom of the Father[25] as *the* Beloved, in shocking intimacy with God.

The language of Father and Son, the address "my Father," and the declaration "my Son," the access, the confidence and at-homeness of Jesus with God, all place him in a singular relationship with God. As P. T. Forsyth said, "In Jesus Christ we have one who was conscious of standing in an entirely unique relation to the living God."[26] But this relationship is not static, nor is it a matter of mere status or words. It is a living relationship, taking shape in action. The declaration "Thou art my beloved Son, in whom my soul delights," is both a revelation about Jesus' identity and a revelation of the Father's heart toward him. "*Abba*, Father," likewise, is not only the verbal response of Jesus; it is the description of his life.

Jesus was not a deist. For him, God was not an infinite, unmoved omnipotence or a nebulous force who created the universe and then moved on to higher things. Neither was God a bookkeeping legalist. For Jesus, God was the passionate, present, and embracing Father who was utterly *for him*, and this fact filled Jesus' heart. Jesus was loved and lavishly embraced, and he knew it. "My Father," not religion, is Jesus' response, and it is the response of his whole being and life. As we see so graphically in the cleansing of the temple,[27] zeal

---

24. John 5:18.

25. See John 1:18.

26. P. T. Forsyth, *The Person and Place of Jesus Christ* (London: Hodder and Stoughton, 1909), p. 285.

27. See John 2:13ff.

for his Father and for his Father's honor is Jesus' answer. "My food is to do the will of Him who sent me and to accomplish His work."[28]

Jesus lives by relating to God as his Father, by seeking him and knowing him as Father and loving him with all of his heart, soul, mind, and strength. His life is not really *his* at all; it is *sonship*. He never lives on his own, doing his own thing, following his own agenda. He has no self-interest. "Not what I will, but what you will be done,"[29] is not just the prayer in Gethsemane; it is the prayer of his whole life. It is a travesty, therefore, to speak of Jesus merely as Jesus, as a man, who did this or accomplished that. Every breath he drew, every act and decision he took, every moment he lived, every word he uttered, was not merely as Jesus, but as the Father's Son in direct relationship with him: "I do nothing on My own initiative, but I speak these things as the Father taught Me."[30] "I can do nothing on My own initiative. As I hear, I judge."[31] "The words that I say to you I do not speak on My own initiative, but the Father abiding in Me does His works."[32]

The declaration "Thou art my beloved Son, in whom my soul delights," and Jesus' response, *"Abba*, Father," reveal a passionate *fellowship*. There is nothing cold or distant or hesitant, and certainly nothing legal about it. It is heart-to-heart, overflowing with mutual delight, devotion, and communication. Recall here, in *The Shack*, Jesus' pride in Papa and his adoration for the way she treated Mackenzie: "Papa, I loved watching you today, as you made yourself fully available to

28. John 4:34.

29. Mark 14:36, my translation.

30. John 8:28. See also 8:26, 38, 40.

31. John 5:30.

32. John 14:10.

take Mack's pain into yourself, and then give him space to choose his own timing" (109). And hear also Papa's pride and joy in Jesus:

> "Yup, I love that boy." Papa looked away and shook her head. "Everything's about him, you know. One day you folk will understand what he gave up. There are just no words." (193)

Young here captures the warmth and mutual affection in the relationship between Jesus and his Father. This mutual affection and pride translate "Thou art my beloved Son" into "The Father loves the Son, and shows Him all things that He Himself is doing."[33] And the affection and pride translate "*Abba*, Father," into "The Son can do nothing of Himself, unless it is something He sees the Father doing; for whatever the Father does, these things the Son also does in like manner."[34] The Father is utterly riveted to his Son's every move; he is the *beloved* Son. And the Son is in tune with his Father's heart and filled with joyous passion for its pleasure. "I always do the things that are pleasing to Him."[35]

This is a relationship of the deepest affections of the soul. There is no dead ritual, no facade or shame or hiding or reticence. The Jesus of the New Testament is so aware of God's presence, so aware of the present God as his Father, and so confident in his relationship with him; and in turn his Father has such earnest joy in him and affection for him, that they share everything and live in utmost fellowship. The formula "Thou art my beloved Son" and "*Abba*, Father," signals a living,

---

33. John 5:20.

34. John 5:19.

35. John 8:29.

personal, and active relationship of profound love and togetherness, a rich and blessed communion in which all things are
shared.

The uniqueness and intimacy of this relationship are
given verbal expression in the amazing statement of Jesus in
Matthew 11:27:

> All things have been handed over to Me by My
> Father; and no one knows the Son except the Father;
> nor does anyone know the Father except the Son, and
> anyone to whom the Son wills to reveal Him.

Jesus boldly claims here to be the recipient of "all things"
from the Father—not a few things, not even the main ones,
but *all things*.[36] As he says elsewhere, all authority in heaven
and on earth,[37] all judgment and the very power of life,[38] have
been given to him. Indeed, he says, "all things that the Father
has are Mine."[39] But here, in Matthew 11:27, the phrase "all
things" is qualified and made all the more remarkable by the
next part: "and no one knows the Son except the Father; nor
does anyone know the Father except the Son." This statement
shifts the meaning of "all things" from abstractions to the
concrete realm of persons, encounter, and communion.

Jeremias interprets the verse in this way:

> Like a father who personally devotes himself to
> explaining the letters of the Torah to his son, like a

---

36. See also John 3:35.

37. See Matthew 28:18.

38. See John 5:22, 26.

39. John 16:15.

father who initiates a son into the well-preserved secrets of his craft, so God has transmitted to me the revelation of himself, and therefore I alone can pass on to others the real knowledge of God.[40]

This interpretation is helpful on two fronts. First, it highlights the fact that the phrase "all things" refers fundamentally not to *things* at all but to the revelation of God. Second, it highlights the fact that Jesus is the unique recipient of this revelation. The Father has personally devoted himself to transmitting the revelation to Jesus alone.

But this interpretation is misleading in that it does not capture the deep and rich *communion* that is involved in this revelation. Revelation is not a thing or a doctrine, mere information that can be transmitted from mind to mind. Revelation involves the unveiling or uncovering of God's *Self* in personal disclosure. What one encounters in revelation is not simply facts about God, or even accurate information, but God in person. Revelation involves an encounter with the person beyond the words, and gives rise to communion. This is exactly why Jesus does not say, "No one knows the truth about God." He says, "No one knows *the Father*." For what is unique about Jesus is not only that he has received the revelation of God, but that this revelation is the unveiling to him of *the Father himself.*

In Matthew 11:27 Jesus is claiming that he stands alone within a closed circle of personal encounter with the Father himself. What he has and knows that no one else has or knows is *the Father*, and what the Father has and knows that no one else has or knows is *the Son.* The accent is upon the mutual knowing of persons—and upon the fact that this mutual

---

40. Jeremias, *The Prayers of Jesus*, p. 51.

knowing is deep and rich. Thus, *knowing* here is not data processing, but communion. It is the interchange of souls, involving self-exposure and mutual sharing of the innermost being. So much so that, comparatively speaking, no one else qualifies as really *knowing* the Father or the Son at all.

Here we are approaching the heart of the relationship of the Father and Son. It is a fellowship involving an incomparable level of personal encounter in love. As we have seen, John introduces his entire Gospel stressing the sheer closeness, the face-to-face intimacy of Jesus and the Father. This is the deep truth we hear in the declaration "Thou art my beloved Son, in whom my soul delights," and Jesus' response, "*Abba*, Father." The declaration and the response point us to a relationship of warmth and love, which gives rise to an abounding fellowship. For the gift of the Father to Jesus is not a thing, not a word, not information or abstract authority or power, but *himself* in passionate love. And likewise, the response of Jesus to his Father is not merely one of outward obedience. He responds by loving the Father with all of his heart, soul, mind, and strength.

Our thinking is being led from a consideration of unique standing and position to that of personal encounter and communion of the most intimate and profound kind. The relationship of the Father and the Son is a communion of *self*-giving love so real and true and personal that Jesus says not only that he *knows* the Father, but that he is *in* the Father and the Father is *in* him.[41] Such language, straightforward and simple as it is, stretches the frontiers of our imaginations. What could it possibly mean? Here is a relationship so beautiful and deep and personal that Jesus and his Father *dwell in* one another.

---

41. See John 14:10–11, 20.

And they do so to such a degree, so to speak, that Jesus says: "He who believes in Me, does not believe in Me but in Him who sent Me. He who sees Me sees the One who sent Me."[42] "He who has seen Me has seen the Father."[43] "I and the Father are *one*."[44]

42. John 12:44–45.

43. John 14:9.

44. John 10:30.

8

THE HOLY SPIRIT

*The grace of the Lord Jesus Christ, and the love of God,
and the fellowship of the Holy Spirit, be with you all.*

—Saint Paul

You can spend your life studying something, only to find again and again that it outclasses your best ideas. When it comes to the Holy Spirit, I confess that I love the Spirit's passion and joy, respect for us and love for the broken, and affirmation of everything that lives and hints of beauty. I even love the Spirit's out-of-the-box ways. But to *explain* the Holy Spirit is another matter altogether, and no theologian worth his or her salt would claim otherwise. Let me pause here for a moment and clarify a simple biblical fact about the Holy Spirit. Sometimes Jesus speaks of the Holy Spirit using the pronoun *he*, while the Greek word for spirit (*pneuma*) is neuter and the Hebrew word *ruach* (wind, spirit) is feminine. As a way of stealing behind our prejudices, Paul Young portrays the Holy Spirit as an Asian woman called Sarayu. Personally, I find it somewhat offensive to use the pronoun *it* for the Holy Spirit. Most of us are at ease with "he," yet the masculine does not tell the whole biblical truth, and neither does the feminine. While "she" may appear a touch daring or perhaps sacrilegious to some, the feminine has the deep and ancient biblical support of the Hebrew word.[1] Like *pneuma* and *ruach*, *sarayu* is a word for refreshing wind (in an Indian language), and it sounds better than Pneuma or Ruach as a name.

I have read many books, ancient and modern, on the Holy Spirit, but I know of no book that speaks as beautifully and biblically about this person of the Trinity as *The Shack*. As a gesture of gratitude to Paul, and in the hope of helping us all understand the Holy Spirit more personally, I have chosen to use the feminine pronouns *she* and *her*.

Now back to my main point. We all know, scholarly and academic arguments aside, that the Holy Spirit is God of God. While I could probably string together something of a biblical argument, with a few historical footnotes, as to why we should rethink the ancient Church's conclusions about the Holy Spirit, I would never dream of raising them with the Spirit in person. Somehow I know better. And that may be the point. When we finally face the Holy Spirit ourselves, I suspect not a one of us will say, "But you didn't say whether...," or "You weren't that clear on..."

Since the Enlightenment, the West has been locked in an overly rationalistic view of knowledge. Compared to the

---

1. Of the generally recognized 89 times *ruach* refers to the Holy Spirit in the Old Testament, only 9 are masculine, and not without some ambiguity. The other 80 are feminine, 44 of which (including Genesis 1:2 and throughout Judges) are accompanied by feminine verbs, et cetera. For more here, see R. P. Nettlehorst, "Appendix 3: The Holy Spirit in the Old Testament," http://www.theology.edu/journal/volume3/spirit.htm.

"hard facts" of science or the logic of "pure reason," any talk of intuitive knowledge, of personal encounter with Jesus, or of knowing *in the Spirit* has largely been dismissed as subjective romanticism. But as Pascal said, "The heart has its reasons, which reason does not know."[2] Faith in Jesus Christ is rooted in personal encounter, not in abstract logic or in the wisdom of the age, or in "scientific fact"—and thank the Lord, for whatever "scientific fact" is, it seems to change as often as a politician's opinions. This does not mean that faith in Jesus is illogical or unscientific, but simply that its basis is a real encounter with Jesus through the Spirit.

On his mission of persecution, Saul of Tarsus was struck blind by a light from heaven as he traveled the Damascus road. He heard a voice addressing him, "Saul, Saul, why are you persecuting Me?" Saul answered with a question: "Who are You, Lord?" And he got his answer: "I am Jesus whom you are persecuting."[3] Saul was shocked, to say the least, but he did not argue, and that is what fascinates me. Something indisputable had happened. Saul was a bright and highly educated man, and he had an awful lot to lose, but this revelation of Jesus simply and quickly outweighed his trained judgment and intense prejudice. The appearance of Jesus rocked Saul's world and led him into a massive change in his way of thinking. Saul of Tarsus became Paul the great apostle and bondslave of Jesus Christ:

> And when I came to you, brethren, I did not come
> with superiority of speech or of wisdom, proclaiming

---

2. Blaise Pascal, *Pensees: Thoughts on Religion and Other Subjects* (New York: Washington Square Press, 1965), 277.

3. Acts 9:3ff.

to you the testimony of God. For I determined to know nothing among you except Jesus Christ, and Him crucified. And I was with you in weakness and in fear and in much trembling, and my message and my preaching were not in persuasive words of wisdom, but in demonstration of the Spirit and of power, so that your faith would not rest on the wisdom of men, but on the power of God.[4]

It is this inner world of Pascal's "reasons of the heart" and Paul's "demonstration of the Spirit and of power" that the Spirit loves. To speak of such a world may make a rationalist suspect that we have "a few 'roos loose in the top paddock," as the Aussies say, but it was a reality to Saul of Tarsus and to millions of others throughout history.

In one of Paul Young's extra-*Shack* essays he talks about the beauty of ambiguity, and indeed of its necessity.[5] *Ironclad rules negate the need for real relationship.* We don't have the original letters from John, Paul, or Matthew, or any from Moses, David, or Isaiah, and that is probably for a reason. If we did, we would likely obsess on the documents themselves, rather than pursue knowing the Lord of whom they speak. And what I know about the Holy Spirit is that her passion is fellowship with the living Jesus himself, not merely facts about him. Information is important, as are facts, but one can be in possession of all the facts yet miss their meaning.[6]

---

4. 1 Corinthians 2:1–5.

5. See Paul Young's essay "The Beauty of Ambiguity," posted on his official website, windrumors.com.

6. See C. S. Lewis, "Transposition," in *The Weight of Glory: And Other Addresses* (Grand Rapids: Eerdmans, 1965), p. 28.

The Spirit knows that the meaning of the words is Jesus. As Sarayu said, "The Bible doesn't teach you to follow rules. It is a picture of Jesus" (200). "Life and living is *in him* and in no other" (198).

From the beginning, the Bible is about the Lord's desire— not as need, but as love's expression—for real relationship with us, his mere creatures. We matter. As Papa said to Mackenzie, "We carefully respect your choices" (125). What we think, what we misunderstand, what we are utterly clueless about matters to the Lord (121f.). The Holy Spirit walks with us as we are, not as we are supposed to be or as we pretend to be on Sunday, but as we are in our strong-willed blindness, independence, and judgment. And she works in the invisible world of the heart in order that we may encounter Jesus, and experience—against our own prejudices—the life he shares with us in his relationship with his Father.

Throughout Israel's history we see a certain irrepressibility about the Spirit. She is grieved by Israel's disinterest and obstinate rebellion; with the Lord, her heart breaks as the leadership of Israel turns toward idols and the wisdom of the nations around them. *But she never gives up.* Again and again she finds a farmer, or a tender of sheep and sycamore figs, or a donkey, who will listen to her voice. And the Spirit's voice is always odd to us, always foreign to the way everybody thinks. The apostle Paul says that the things of the Spirit are foolish to the natural mind.[7] But this was not new in Paul's day. From the fall of Adam onward, the Spirit—to our way of seeing things—is odd, out of touch, foolish. She is inconceivable.

It's a scary thing to realize that while the Lord made us in his own image, we have been creating him in our own ever

---

7. See 1 Corinthians 2:14.

since.[8] I will have more to say later about Adam's fall and the projections of our fallen minds, but for now the point is that the Holy Spirit is passionate about our coming to know Jesus and his Father as they are. The Spirit knows that we will experience a life beyond our wildest imaginations when we see the Father's face and know his heart, and she knows that we don't. And the Spirit is intently doing something about it. In patience, kindness, and tenderness she walks with us as we are, in our craziness; she never gives up. And the Holy Spirit finally finds, in Jesus, her listening and faithful man; she goes wild with life, with joy, with healing and miracles and deliverance, and nothing in the cosmos will ever be the same.

It is not too difficult to set out the New Testament's vision of Jesus and his Father. That, I suspect, is the Holy Spirit's point: the record she has left is all about revealing Jesus to us so that in Jesus we can know his Father with him, and in knowing Jesus' Father we can experience the shocking and liberating life of his love. It is rather more problematic to set out the New Testament's vision of the Spirit. She is "a *free* Spirit" (123), and "she's *way* out there" (112), as Mackenzie says. From the day of Pentecost on, the Spirit is everywhere and into everything, but never visible and always completely unpredictable (130). She is alive and powerful, and constantly moving. "Mack wondered if she ever completely stopped moving" (122). She inspires witness to Jesus and works within the deepest trenches of the human heart and its wounds. Or, perhaps I should say, she works within the root systems of the gardens of our souls.

---

8. Recall Papa's comment to Mackenzie, "The problem is that many folks try to grasp some sense of who I am by taking the best version of themselves, projecting that to the nth degree, factoring in all the goodness they can perceive, which often isn't much, and then call *that* God" (98).

While she can be lied to, resisted, tested, grieved, insulted, quenched, and blasphemed,[9] she is remarkably comfortable with the sinful mess we have made of ourselves and our lives. For me, as we shall see, the garden scene in *The Shack* is one of the most powerful moments in the book. It wonderfully portrays the freedom of the Spirit to dig around in the garden of our broken souls. "Sarayu loved the mess" (140).

To describe the Spirit is like trying to count the waves of an ocean or photograph the air; it is like "tracking a sunbeam" (130). But I will try. And here I have the utmost respect for Paul Young's amazing treatment of the Spirit as Sarayu, which I suspect is his finest contribution to Christian thought. Whatever I do or fail to do, I want to make one point clear at the outset: the Holy Spirit is *about life*. As Sarayu says, "*I* am about the process that takes you to the *living answer*" (200). She is good, and she won't let you go until you find your real life in Jesus—and that means until you come to know that Jesus' Father loves you forever, no matter what. That is what Adam lost; that is what Jesus—in the Spirit—knows; and that is what Jesus—through the Spirit—is now teaching the human race. As Papa says to Mackenzie, "That's why we're here" (100). "This weekend is about relationship and love" (104).

Catching Israel and the world by surprise, no one less than Israel's Lord himself stepped personally into his own creation, became a human being, and dwelt among us.[10] Who saw this coming? What prophet or seer or wise person ever dreamed

---

9. See Acts 5:3; 7:51; Acts 5:6; Ephesians 4:30; Hebrews 10:29; 1 Thessalonians 5:19; Matthew 12:31; Mark 3:29; Luke 12:10; Mark 3:29, respectively.

10. See John 1:14.

of such grace? It was the shocker of cosmic history. But as shocking as the Incarnation was, it was even more surprising that the *Lord* Jesus lived his life in constant *relationship* to the One he called "my Father." This relationship is so deep, so pure and good and right, it defies imagination. Jesus not only knows the Father; he knows the Father in a way that no other human being has ever known him. And his knowledge, his communion, his fellowship with the Father is so true and intimate, so intensely personal and unclouded, that Jesus says he is *in* the Father and the Father is *in* him. And at no point does the New Testament allow us to think of the Spirit as a mere spectator of the communion between Jesus and his Father. The Holy Spirit lives in the middle of this astonishing relationship.

According to the Scriptures, Jesus was conceived by the Holy Spirit,[11] baptized in the Spirit,[12] led and empowered by the Spirit,[13] given great joy by the Spirit,[14] cast out demons by the Spirit,[15] heard his Father in the Spirit,[16] and offered himself to his Father by the power of the Spirit.[17] From his conception to his death, resurrection, and ascension, Jesus' life was thoroughly filled with the Holy Spirit. Epiphanius, one of the early church theologians, spoke of the Holy Spirit as "in the midst of the Father and the Son" and as "the bond

---

11. See Matthew 1:18, 20; Luke 1:35.

12. See Matthew 3:16; Mark 1:10; Luke 3:22; John 1:32.

13. See Matthew 4:1; Mark 1:12; Luke 4:1, 14.

14. See Luke 10:21.

15. See Matthew 12:28.

16. See Matthew 3:16–17; Mark 1:10–11; Luke 3:22.

17. See Hebrews 9:14.

of the Trinity."[18] The Holy Spirit is always in the middle of Jesus' fellowship with his Father.

The image of the Spirit descending as a dove upon Jesus at his baptism, which harks back to the Spirit hovering over creation[19] and points forward to the outpouring of the Spirit at Pentecost,[20] is a picture of what we might call the Spirit's "betweenness." The Holy Spirit is the "Go-Between God,"[21] to borrow a great phrase from John Taylor. Known in the early church as "the modesty of God," the Spirit does not like to be the center of attention. She hides herself, preferring to work behind the scenes. Her passion is fellowship: she loves to connect people. She is the "Overcomer of the Gap" and the "Space Between," as Richard Rohr puts it so beautifully.[22] Like the lighting of a great cathedral, the Holy Spirit loves to illuminate others so that encounter and fellowship can take shape—for life happens in relationship.

In an almost offhand comment, the apostle Paul says, "For the kingdom of God is not eating and drinking, but righteousness and peace and joy in the Holy Spirit."[23] This comment speaks to the heart of the Holy Spirit's passion. Righteousness means right relationship, relationship that functions out of other-centered love and goodness, mutual respect, and honor. Peace means the cessation of conflict and strife. It is the calm-

---

18. Cited by Thomas F. Torrance in *The Trinitarian Faith: The Evangelical Theology of the Ancient Catholic Church* (Edinburgh: T&T Clark, 1988), p. 328.

19. See Genesis 1:2.

20. See Acts 2:1ff.

21. See John V. Taylor, *The Go-Between God* (London: SCM Press, 1972).

22. Richard Rohr, *The Naked Now: Learning to See as the Mystics See* (New York: Crossroad Publishing, 2009), p. 169.

23. Romans 14:17.

ing of our own inner worlds and the calming of the world at large, *and* peace involves the presence of blessing, well-being, shalom. Righteousness and peace create room for joy. Joy is about gladness and delight, about freedom to be, freedom to be present for others and to be open for fellowship, freedom to share and appreciate life in gratitude.

As life is formed in relationship, in personal encounter, in knowing and being known, the Holy Spirit specializes in the inner, invisible world that makes such communion possible. As the One who gives life, the Spirit is inherently about relationship. She is at once the keeper of the gardens of our souls (89) and the surgeon of our inner eyes (209). She is the Spirit of encounter, of fellowship, of intimacy and sharing.

While it would take several volumes to chart all that the Bible has to say about the Holy Spirit, there are several simple points that need to be highlighted. First, while there are many spirits, there is only one unique or special Spirit *of God*. Very closely related to the presence of the Lord and the Word of the Lord, the Spirit of the Lord comes from outside creation and always commands awe and respect. She is remarkably free to be present and active within creation, yet is never domesticated, manipulated, or controlled. In Israel's history she is called the Spirit of the Lord,[24] the Spirit of God,[25] Holy Spirit,[26] the Spirit of Wisdom,[27] the Good Spirit,[28] and the

---

24. Judges 3:10; 6:34; 11:29; 13:25; 14:6, 19; 15:14; 1 Samuel 10:6, 10; 11:6; 16:13, 14; 1 Kings 18:12; 22:24; 2 Kings 2:16; 2 Chronicles 18:23; 20:14; Isaiah 11:2; 40:13; 61:1; 63:14; Ezekiel 11:5; 37:1; Micah 3:8.

25. Genesis 1:2; Exodus 31:3; 35:31; Numbers 24:2; 1 Samuel 19:20, 23; 2 Samuel 23:2; Job 33:4; Ezekiel 11:24.

26. Psalm 51:11; Isaiah 63:10, 11.

27. Exodus 28:3; Deuteronomy 34:9.

28. Nehemiah 9:20; Psalm 143:10.

Spirit of grace.[29] Sometimes, when God is speaking, he calls the Holy Spirit "my Spirit."[30] In Isaiah 11:2 the Spirit is called "the spirit of wisdom and understanding, the spirit of counsel and strength, the spirit of knowledge and the fear of the LORD."

Second, the Spirit makes her first appearance at Creation itself and is involved with God and the Word of God in the creating and forming of all life:

> In the beginning God created the heavens and the earth. The earth was formless and void, and darkness was over the surface of the deep, and the Spirit of God was moving over the surface of the waters.[31]

While the Spirit is brooding over creation, the Word of God is spoken, "Let there be light," and the command comes to fruition. This pattern is repeated until it comes to the forming of humanity. Then the command "Let there be" is replaced by "Let Us make man in Our image."[32] Later we are told, "Then the LORD God formed man of dust from the ground, and breathed into his nostrils the breath of life; and man became a living being."[33] While technically the Spirit is not mentioned here in the breathing of life, in other places the association is clear: "The Spirit of God has made me, and the breath of the Almighty gives me life."[34] "By the word of

---

29. Zechariah 12:10.

30. Genesis 6:3; Isaiah 30:1; 42:1; 59:21; Ezekiel 36:27; 37:14; 39:29; Joel 2:28, 29; Haggai 2:5; Zechariah 4:6.

31. Genesis 1:1–2.

32. Genesis 1:26.

33. Genesis 2:7.

34. Job 33:4; see also Genesis 6:3.

the LORD the heavens were made, and by the breath [Spirit] of his mouth all their host."[35] As the Nicene Creed affirms, the Spirit is "the Lord and giver of life."[36]

Third, while giving life to all creation, the Spirit of the Lord appears personally within Israel's history, but only rarely. There are fewer than one hundred references to the Spirit in the Hebrew Bible, and through all of that history only two hundred or so people in Israel ever have direct dealings with the Spirit of the Lord. When the Spirit is present and active, she gives power,[37] wisdom and discernment,[38] and creative and artistic gifts.[39] She particularly loves to inspire the prophets with the Word of the Lord,[40] and anoint kings, priests, and leaders.[41] On the surface it appears that the Spirit acts randomly, as she is prone to come and go at will—or, to use Paul Young's word, "evaporate" (90)—and never stays anywhere for long. This is captured well by Young in his portrayal of Sarayu. But the Spirit is concerned with Israel *walking with* and *knowing* the Lord. It is not surprising that for the most part her activity is centered upon the very narrow circle of Israel's leaders—Moses, Aaron, and Joshua, for example; as well as judges, wise men, priests, kings, and prophets. These chosen few were called to participate in the Lord's communication with Israel, and to lead Israel's response to the Lord. It

---

35. Psalm 33:6.

36. See John 6:63; 2 Corinthians 3:6.

37. See Judges 3:10; 6:34; 11:29; 13:25; 14:6, 19; 15:14.

38. See Genesis 41:38f.; Daniel 4:8ff.; Exodus 31:3; 35:31; Numbers 11:17ff.; Deuteronomy 34:9.

39. See Exodus 35:30f.

40. See Numbers 11:17ff.; 2 Chronicles 24:20; Nehemiah 9:30; Ezekiel 2:12, 14, 24; 8:3; 11:1, 5, 25; Micah 3:8.

41. See 1 Samuel 10:6, 10; 16:13; 2 Samuel 2:23; 2 Chronicles 20:14.

is within this group of mediators, not with Israel at large, that the Spirit primarily works.

The book of Genesis was written to help Israel understand who they were and why they had been chosen by the Lord. The writer begins with God creating the heavens and the earth, and ultimately Adam and Eve. After describing what is called "the Fall," the writer places Abraham, and thus Israel, within the context of God's redemptive plan. The assumption in Genesis, and in the Bible as a whole, is that the Creator wants to be in relationship with humanity, and that within this relationship the Lord is determined to bless his creation with fullness and life.

After Adam's fall, the Lord called Abram (Abraham) and through him reestablished relationship with fallen humanity. Abraham's descendants became a nation in covenant with the Lord, chosen to be the people through whom redemption would be worked out for the world. At the heart of this covenant relationship was the Lord's declaration, "I will be your God, and you will be my people."[42] This declaration contains three critical truths, of which two are obvious and one is more implicit, but all are equally important. The first is the rather amazing fact that the Creator of the heavens and the earth is determined to have a relationship with mere creatures. The second is the even more startling fact that the Lord takes responsibility for the human side of the relationship. The second clause, "and you will be my people," is not in the first instance an invitation, but part of God's *declaration* to

---

42. See Exodus 6:7; Leviticus 26:13; Jeremiah 7:23; 11:4; 24:7; 30:22; 31:1, 33; 32:38; Ezekiel 11:20; 14:11; 36:28; 37:27; Hosea 1:10; 2:23; Zechariah 2:11.

Israel. We could interpret it this way: "I will be your God, and I will see to it that you come to know me and live in my fellowship." The third truth is that as Israel *knows* the Lord and as they dwell together in fellowship, inconceivable blessing and life will flower within Israel and spread to the ends of the earth and beyond.

The emphasis in the declaration is not on ownership, but on relationship and fellowship. The blessing of the Lord is not dispensed mechanically, religiously, or legally; it is the fruit of fellowship with the Lord. As Jesus said, "This is eternal life, that they may *know* You, the only true God, and Jesus Christ whom You have sent."[43] It is as Israel knows and walks with the Lord that the great blessing comes into being.

Since it is the Spirit who gives life, and since life comes through *knowing* the Lord, the Spirit is not uninterested in Israel's relationship with the Lord; she is inherently passionate about it. She is the Spirit of relationship, of encounter, of revelation and response. The Spirit sets the table, so to speak, so that the Lord and Israel can meet. She is at work on God's side reaching out to Israel, and she is at work on the creaturely side helping Israel know, respond to, and walk with the Lord so that life and blessing and shalom can flower.

But it is here that disaster struck Israel, as king after king, prophet after prophet, and priest after priest forsook the Lord and his love. The first clause of the covenant, "I will be your God," never failed, as the Lord was ever faithful to Israel. But the second clause, "and you will be my people," hardly got a foothold as the chosen leadership of Israel and Judah grieved the Spirit. Following the nations around them, they worshipped foreign gods and led the people into idolatry.

The covenant fellowship was broken and the blessing of

43. John 17:3, my italics.

the Lord withered on the vine, so to speak. In the Spirit the great prophets bore the Lord's anguish and broken heart as they repeatedly warned Israel and summoned the nation back to the Lord. But the leadership had a mind of its own and, with few exceptions, did what was right in their own eyes. Their resistance to the Spirit eventually led to Israel's exodus from the Promised Land.

In the bitterness and shame of captivity the Spirit of the Lord, ever passionate for relationship and life, began to give a new vision for Israel. The second clause in the divine declaration, "and you will be my people," had miserably failed; but it was prophesied that the day would come when things would be dramatically different. The Lord himself would raise up a faithful servant—a true King, a true Priest, and a faithful Prophet. This vision had been in the making since Moses,[44] but was now projected into the future.

It was not clear whether this faithful servant would be the whole nation of Israel itself, a group of individuals, or perhaps even just one person,[45] although Peter tells us that the Spirit who inspired the prophets was the Spirit of Christ.[46] But it was clear that a new day was coming. It would be a day of deliverance from all captivity, and from the darkness and deadness of the human heart itself. It would be a day of forgiveness and healing, of breathtaking blessing upon Israel, and through Israel upon the whole earth. Under the inspiration of the Spirit, a new age of international and, indeed, cosmic blessing appeared on the horizon. This deliverance and blessing, this *new* covenant relationship, would come about when the Lord raised up his faithful servant and anointed him with

---

44. See Deuteronomy 18:15ff.

45. See Isaiah 49:1–6.

46. See 1 Peter 1:11.

the Spirit. This Messiah (the Anointed One) would *know* the Lord, and in *their fellowship* together, the great blessing of the Lord would be released in Israel and flow to the ends of the earth and beyond.[47]

It is in this hopeful expectation of the coming of the Anointed One that the Hebrew Scriptures close.

After centuries of silence, the wild figure of John the Baptist stepped out of the wilderness. He was full of the Holy Spirit, with a mission to prepare the way for *the Lord*. Clothed with camel's hair and a leather belt, John began baptizing and preaching. His activities created a stir among the people and so caught the attention of the Jewish leadership. They sent a delegation to ask him the question, "Who are you?"[48] After a brief and animated discussion, John declared: "I am a voice of one crying in the wilderness, 'Make straight the way of the LORD,' as Isaiah the prophet said."[49] "After me One is coming who is mightier than I, and I am not fit to stoop down and untie the thong of His sandals. I baptized you with water; but He will baptize you with the Holy Spirit."[50]

The Old Testament closed with hope that the Lord would raise up a faithful servant who would be anointed with the Holy Spirit. This servant would *know* the Lord, and through him the great blessing of salvation and life and kingdom would come to fruition. It was John the Baptist's calling and privilege to identify Jesus as this long-awaited Anointed One. But at first not even John recognized the real identity of Jesus:

---

47. See Ezekiel 11:16–20; 36:22–30; Jeremiah 31:27–34; 32:37–41.

48. John 1:19.

49. John 1:23.

50. Mark 1:7–8.

I have seen the Spirit descending as a dove out of heaven; and He remained upon Him. And I did not recognize Him, but He who sent me to baptize in water said to me, "He upon whom you see the Spirit descending and remaining upon Him, this is the One who baptizes in the Holy Spirit." I myself have seen, and have testified that this is the Son of God.[51]

As we have seen, the Spirit of the Lord was at work within Israel's history, but only rarely, and only within a select group of people. But in Jesus things changed dramatically, in two directions. First, the already very narrow circle of the Spirit's *personal* activity was narrowed even further to *Jesus alone*. Apart from Mary, Zechariah, Elizabeth, John the Baptist, and Simeon, the Spirit was silent except for her profound presence in Jesus' life. What they had in common was the Spirit's inspiration to bear witness to Jesus. Second, in Jesus, through his life, death, resurrection, and ascension, the Spirit's activity was then broadened at Pentecost when the Spirit was poured out upon *all flesh*.[52] Today, in and through Jesus, the Holy Spirit is at work universally in the *world at large*, convicting the world of sin and righteousness and judgment;[53] but before Pentecost, the Holy Spirit was focused exclusively upon Jesus, who alone among biblical characters was miraculously conceived by the Spirit herself,[54] and upon whom the Spirit came and remained as an immeasurable and abiding presence.

The Spirit gives Jesus life, confidence, power, freedom, joy, and wisdom, but above all she works to enable Jesus to *know*

---

51. John 1:32–34.

52. See Acts 2:17 and Joel 2:28–29.

53. See John 16:8–11.

54. See Matthew 1:18, 20; Luke 1:35.

his Father. This, it seems to me, is the key point. When the apostle Paul writes, "God's love has flooded our inmost heart through the Holy Spirit he has given us,"[55] he is also describing what the Holy Spirit first did in the inmost heart of Jesus. The remarkable fellowship between Jesus and his Father is not separated from the Holy Spirit, as if Jesus' relationship with his Father and his relationship with the Spirit were two parallel railroad tracks that never meet.

In the Incarnation, the Spirit crosses over to the human side of the relationship and prepares a womb for the Son in the virgin Mary. The Spirit gives and sustains the human life of Jesus in conception and as it develops in the womb. And once Jesus is born, the Spirit works between the Father and Jesus, facilitating their relationship. She reveals the Father to Jesus and gives him eyes to see and ears to hear, so that at every level of his life he is free to be the beloved and faithful Son, the true *amen* to the Father. It is from his own experience that Jesus assures his disciples that the Spirit will take what is his and disclose it to them.[56] For that is what the Spirit did in Jesus' relationship with his Father.

It is not an accident that at Jesus' baptism, when the Father declared, "Thou art my beloved Son, in whom my soul delights," the Spirit was present as a dove *between* the Father in heaven and the Son on earth. The Spirit was present throughout the whole of the Son's life as the one in and *through* whom the Father gave himself, revealed himself, and communicated himself to his Beloved.[57] And the Spirit was present as the One who enabled the Son to *hear* the Father's stunning affirmation,

55. Romans 5:5 NEB.

56. See John 16:14.

57. See Thomas A. Smail, *The Giving Gift: The Holy Spirit in Person* (London: Hodder and Stoughton, 1988), pp. 89ff.

to relate to and know the Father as *his* Father, and to love him with all of his heart, soul, mind, and strength. The Holy Spirit is, as Jürgen Moltmann notes, "the eternal light in which the Father knows the Son and the Son the Father."[58]

One of the apparently strangest parts of the gospel story is the way the Spirit, immediately upon Jesus' baptism, compelled Jesus into the wilderness to be tempted by the evil one.[59] This is the way the modern headings lead us to read the story, but it could be the other way around, and I think it is: the Spirit was not leading Jesus into temptation so much as she was using the devil's temptation to give Jesus sharper inner eyes, to lead him into a deeper understanding of his identity and relationship with his Father. For the temptations all have the question of Jesus' identity at their core: "If You are the Son of God, command that these stones become bread…."[60] "If You are the Son of God, throw Yourself down…." The third temptation does not follow the "if You are" formula but is even more odious, as it promises Jesus the kingdoms of this world in exchange for denying his Father and worshipping the evil one.

In all three, the question was the identity of Jesus and whether or not he would live his life in fellowship with his Father, or be independent like Adam and live according to his own ideas. Adam's history, the history of Israel, and our own histories were here being repeated; but this time the Spirit's witness found a ready human heart, as Jesus simply and beautifully rejected the evil one's suggestions and gave himself to his Father. He came away empowered and confident, and his anointed ministry of deliverance and life began.

---

58. Jürgen Moltmann, *The Trinity and the Kingdom: The Doctrine of God* (London: SCM Press, 1981), p. 176.

59. See Matthew 4:1ff.; Mark 1:12ff.; Luke 4:1ff.

60. See Matthew 4:3ff.; Luke 4:3ff.

When we look at the life of Christ from a human vantage point, we see a relationship between God, on the one side, and a Jewish man named Jesus, on the other, that is unparalleled in biblical history.[61] Here is a relationship of profound love, of delight and adoration, of mutual passion and faithfulness, which issues forth in true oneness and union, in deep and creative fellowship. The Holy Spirit is right in the middle of it all. The most profound fruit of the Spirit's presence and activity is Jesus' fellowship with his Father, and in this communion the new covenant, the new relationship between God and Israel with all its blessing, is cut into flesh-and-blood existence. Through the Spirit, the ancient declaration, "I will be your God and you will be my people, and I will dwell among you with all blessing and life," comes to staggering fruition in the life of Jesus.

The beautiful intimacy between the Father and Jesus, the face-to-face fellowship, the togetherness, the union without loss of personal distinction, and the outright life and blessing within it, are as much the fruit of the Spirit as they are of the Father's faithfulness and the Son's love. But how do we talk about this? How do we describe the Holy Spirit's place in this most profound relationship and its abounding life?

Fully aware of the difficulty of describing the Spirit's role in this relationship, yet pushed by her obvious centrality, Augustine spoke of the Spirit as the "bond of love" between the Father and the Son, and indeed as "the love itself."[62] It is in and through the Spirit that the Father loves the Son, and

---

61. See Matthew 11:27; John 1:18; 14:20.

62. Augustine, *On the Trinity*, in *Nicene and Post-Nicene Fathers*, vol. 3 (Grand Rapids: Eerdmans, 1980), VI.5.7; V.11; XV.19.37. See also C. S. Lewis, *Mere Christianity* (New York: Macmillan, 1952), p. 152.

that the Son loves the Father. To my mind, Augustine is following the witness of the Scriptures. From Genesis to Revelation, the Spirit works behind the scenes, not whimsically or arbitrarily as if she has her own plans, but in tandem with the larger purpose of the Lord—fellowship with the human race. She is the Spirit of love, of life, of encounter, of fellowship and union, and exceptionally so in the relationship of Jesus with his Father. From a biblical perspective, if we take the Spirit out of the equation, we have no relationship between the Father and the Son. And without their fellowship, no life takes shape on earth. Her place in this communion is deep and essential; she is the bond of their love.

Nevertheless, to speak of the Spirit as "the bond of love" between the Father and the Son, or as their "love itself," runs the risk of making the Spirit something less than her own person. The love between two people is not itself a third person. This has been a problem throughout Christian history; the Holy Spirit has been impersonalized, often reduced to a mere power or force, or even to something akin to the atmosphere in the room. But, *Star Wars* notwithstanding, you cannot grieve[63] a force; you grieve a person. A mere force, however strong, does not speak. A power does not refer to itself as "I" or "me,"[64] search the deep things and thoughts of God,[65] or lead prayer and worship.[66] A power does not love,[67] or bear witness with our spirits that we are children of God.[68]

---

63. See Isaiah 63:10 and Ephesians 4:30.

64. See Acts 13:2.

65. See 1 Corinthians 2:11.

66. See Ephesians 6:18; John 4:24; Philippians 3:3.

67. See Romans 15:30.

68. See Galatians 4:6.

In the New Testament the Spirit has her own mind, will, and ministry.[69] She speaks, informs, leads, guides, and instructs.[70] She evaluates, appoints leaders, makes decisions, and gives gifts—words of wisdom, of knowledge and faith, gifts of healing.[71] She inspires witness to Jesus;[72] convicts the world of sin, righteousness, and judgment; makes known the mystery of Christ; cries *"Abba! Father!"* in our hearts; and bears fruit in human life.[73] She strengthens, helps our weakness, comforts, brings liberty and freedom, gives fellowship, fills with joy, and produces life and peace.[74]

She is referred to variously as the Spirit of God (or of the Lord); the Spirit of truth; the Comforter or Helper; the Spirit of Jesus, of Christ, of your Father, of him who raised Jesus from the dead; his Spirit; the Lord; the eternal Spirit; the Spirit of adoption; the Spirit of his Son; the Spirit of life in Christ Jesus; the Holy Spirit of promise; the Spirit of grace, of holiness, of glory; the firstfruits, pledge, or down payment.

In her activities the Spirit is not simply the alter ego of the Father or the Son, or simply the One through whom they relate to one another and to creation. She loves and shares love, has her own mind and will, has joy and gives joy. She is a free Spirit, as Paul Young so wonderfully portrays, but not an independent or detached Spirit. As her names reveal,

---

69. See 2 Corinthians 3:8 and Romans 8:27; 1 Corinthians 12:11; Hebrews 2:4.

70. See John 16:3; Acts 8:29; 10:19; 11:12, 28; 13:2; Revelation 2:7, 11, 17, 29; 3:6, 13, 22; 14:13.

71. See Acts 15:28; 20:28; 1 Corinthians 12:4–11.

72. See Acts 2:17–18; 4:8, 31; 2 Peter 1:21.

73. See John 16:8; Ephesians 3:5; Galatians 4:6; 5:22–23.

74. See Ephesians 3:16; Romans 8:2; Acts 9:31; 2 Corinthians 3:17; and Galatians 5:18; 2 Corinthians 13:13; Acts 13:52; Romans 8:6.

the Spirit doesn't act alone; she is profoundly involved in the inner life of the Father and the Son, in their relationship, and in all that they do together.

As the Spirit *of* the Father and the Spirit *of* Jesus, the Holy Spirit has an intimate and deep relationship to both. As the Spirit of the Father *and* the Son, she is in the midst of their relationship and togetherness, the bond of their love. She is so close to both, and to their fellowship together, that it is difficult to know where the line is drawn. Yet, as *the* Spirit, and *the* Holy Spirit, she has her own identity and cannot be reduced to the Father, or to Jesus, or to their communion. As the Comforter, and as the Spirit of truth, adoption, life in Christ, grace, holiness, and glory, she has her own peculiar interests. She loves and shares love and creates fellowship. In her presence people come to know that they are loved by Jesus' Father; they are set free, and fellowship and community form.

I suspect that part of the difficulty surrounding the Spirit is the way we in the West think of a person. According to Boethius's famous (or infamous) definition, a person is "an individual substance of a rational nature." But what if instead of trying to fit the Holy Spirit into this definition of a person and finding her wanting, we reversed the order and let the Spirit expand our ideas of personhood? The Spirit is profoundly other-centered, humble, patient, and good. She loves communication, fellowship, and togetherness. Perhaps we need to modify our notion of personhood to include being a facilitator of fellowship. Perhaps a real person is not simply an individual substance of a rational nature, but one who loves bringing others together to share life, an individual who is other-centered, relational, and full of passion for communion.

In the case of the Holy Spirit, she is so adept at facilitating love, communion, and life that it is difficult to distinguish her from her fruit (which may be why Augustine not only called her the "bond of love," but "love itself"). But why should this mean that she is therefore less a person? Just because the Holy Spirit is so good at facilitating love that she seems to disappear in its midst doesn't mean she is not real.

In the Holy Spirit's world, Jesus sees his Father, and the Father sees his Son, and life and love happen. In her world, people encounter Jesus himself within their own innermost beings, and in their brokenness find healing. In the Spirit, empowerment, freedom, confidence, and assurance take form, as do love, joy, peace, patience, kindness, goodness, gentleness, faithfulness, and self-control.[75] Community, relationship, and life flourish in her.

The Holy Spirit knows how to make the cosmos dance. She found her man in Jesus, and now in Jesus she has found us. Her great joy is that she gets to be in the middle of it all and enjoy the love, healing, and abounding life she brings about in others.

The Holy Spirit is the giver, former, and lover of life. She is "in the midst of the Father and Son," "the bond of love" between them. And now, in Jesus, she is in *our* midst; or perhaps I should say, *we are in hers*. And she won't give up until she is the bond of love between us and Jesus and his Father, and the heavens and the earth and all their inhabitants are alive with the unbridled life of Father and Son *in* the Spirit.

---

75. See Galatians 5:22–23.

9

THE ONENESS OF THE SPIRIT, SON, AND FATHER

By virtue of their eternal love they live in one another to such an extent, and dwell in one another to such an extent, that they are one.

—Jürgen Moltmann

In the context of the rampant polytheism of the ancient world, God first established in Israel that there was only one true God: "Hear, O Israel! The LORD is our God, the LORD is one!"[1] Apart from the politically charged and strange confession "We have no king but Caesar," uttered by the Jewish leadership before Pontius Pilate,[2] the abiding truth of Israel's faith was the fact that there was only one true God, and Yahweh (the LORD) was his name. But from the moment Jesus

---

1. Deuteronomy 6:4.

2. John 19:15.

appeared in Israel's history, a new nonnegotiable was forming within Judaism. For all who encountered Jesus in the Spirit, whether fishermen like John and James or Pharisees like Saul of Tarsus, there was no doubt that Jesus was the Lord God in person. Even Doubting Thomas confessed, "My Lord and my God!"[3]

The Jews and the Greeks accused the Christians of polytheism, for they worshipped the Father, the Son, and the Holy Spirit. But the Christians weren't budging. Whatever else they knew, they *knew* that Jesus was the Lord himself. But then, so was his Father, and the Holy Spirit. Such a confession was blasphemy to the Jews, and utter nonsense to the Greeks. The Christians found themselves in a perplexing situation. On the one hand, they shared Jewish belief in one God. On the other, they would rather die than betray the worship of Jesus as Lord—and many did. But how could the Christians worship and glorify the Father, Son, and Spirit, and baptize in their names, and not worship three Gods? How could three be one, and one be three? How do we talk about this relationship without falling into polytheism on the one side, or denying the divinity of Jesus and the personhood of the Spirit on the other? These questions fueled the controversies that eventually led the Christians to perceive and develop the revolutionary vision of the triune God.

Did Jesus just happen to win the divine lottery? Is he merely a highly favored man who achieved an unthinkable relationship with God? Is his relationship with his Father one of random and exceptional grace on God's part toward the man Jesus, and of exceptional obedience on Jesus' part toward God, forming a divine-human relationship in and through the Spirit that is unparalleled in biblical history? Was Jesus Christ

---

3. John 20:28.

simply a man who knew God to a much greater degree than the rest of the human race?

Could it be that this astonishing relationship between the Father and the Son *in* the Spirit is not something new? Could it be that this relationship did not begin in the womb of the virgin Mary, but is a *divine* relationship predating Creation and subsequently entering into our world? Could it be that this remarkable love and fellowship between the Father and the Son in the Spirit is in fact the *eternal life of God* being lived out before our eyes and revealed to us? Are we dealing here with the truth of God's eternal being, with the way God is and always has been and always will be, or is this seeming tri-unity simply one of many forms that the solitary God assumes from time to time?

Somewhere around AD 200, a priest and theologian from Rome named Sabellius put forward the idea that the one, indivisible God revealed himself in different ways in his relationship to humanity. For Sabellius, there is only one divine Person, but he manifested himself first as the Father, then later as the Son, and finally as the Holy Spirit. This view, known as Sabellianism or modalism, was popular in the Church, as it offered a way of affirming the deity of Christ while maintaining the fact that God is one. The one God appeared in different modes at different times. The problem with this view, of course, is that it admits of no relationship, no interaction between the Father, Son, and Spirit, as there is only one Person who appears in three different modes, but never at the same time. By definition there is no "they," no three distinct Persons, and thus never any relationship between them.

In a way this view guards the deity of at least the *roles* of the Father, Son, and Spirit, but it makes a mockery of Jesus living his life in relation to his Father, and of the Holy Spirit in their midst. Why would the one Person, while he donned the temporary mode of the Son, for example, be so confused and misleading as to pray to another that he called his Father? And why would he baptize himself with the Spirit while another voice from heaven was declaring, "Thou art my beloved Son, in whom my soul delights"? Both Sabellius and his view were condemned as heretical around AD 220.

A second possible solution, and one that was far more popular, was put forward by a Presbyter named Arius (AD 256–336). He was a well-known preacher, and very bright. We don't have much of what he actually wrote, as the Church has a tendency to destroy the work of its detractors; but what we know from those such as Athanasius,[4] who argued against him, seems sensible, at least on the surface.

Arius took seriously the fact that the Father and the Son were distinct persons, and that their relationship was real. But he could not shake his Greek notion of the indivisibility of the one God. For Arius, God is single, end of subject. So for Arius, the Father alone is God, and Jesus is the first and greatest of all God's creatures, through whom God created the rest of the cosmos. In this scenario the singleness of God is safeguarded and Jesus is uniquely honored. And there is even room for an incarnation of sorts, for as the first and greatest of God's creatures, Jesus was not originally a human being.

Arius offered what appeared to be an extraordinary place for the Son as the mediator of creation and of salvation. It is through Jesus, said Arius, that the one God relates to all creation, now and forever. This place of honor spoke to what

---

4. See Athanasius, "Against the Arians," in *Athanasius: Select Works and Letters*, vol. 4 of *Nicene and Post-Nicene Fathers of the Christian Church*, 2nd ser., ed. Philip Schaff and Henry Wallace (Grand Rapids: Eerdmans, 1987). For more on the debate between Athanasius and Arius, see Khaled Anatolios, *Athanasius: The Coherence of His Thought* (London: Routledge, 1998).

the Christians *knew* of Jesus in their Spirit-inspired worship, and thus gained considerable popularity. And Arius was quite adept at arguing his case from the Scriptures. But, as Athanasius was quick to point out, the Arian Jesus—exalted as he was—was nevertheless still a *creature* and not *God*, and could not be considered "the Lord" in the same sense that God the Father was "the Lord."

While Arius was trying to be faithful to the notion that God is one, and find real honor for Jesus, he fell short of the mark. His subtle but real denial of the deity of Jesus Christ carried several serious consequences. First, it didn't square with the apostles' teaching, nor with the believers' worship, nor with the Church's practice of baptism in the name of the Father, Son, and Holy Spirit as commanded by Jesus. Second, it raises questions about the integrity of this Jesus. If he is not divine, why does the Arian Jesus insult the one God by allowing himself to be worshipped and glorified? What kind of God-honoring creature would receive the adoration due alone to the one true God? Third, the character of the Father is also in question. If Jesus is a creature and not God, then there was a time when there was no Son and the Father existed alone and solitary, so that even the Father was not always Father; and if he was not always Father, what is his essential character? Fourth, if Jesus is only a creature, then the salvation and the life he gives, while perhaps better than what we could do as mere humans, falls seriously short of *divine* salvation, and the *eternal life* of God.

Arius and his teaching forced the Church to engage in serious reflection about its faith in Christ. The Church responded at the Council of Nicaea in AD 325, and then at the Council of Constantinople in AD 381, with a clear affirmation of the deity of Jesus and his utter *oneness* with the Father:

We believe in one God
the Father Almighty, Maker of heaven and earth,
and of all things visible and invisible.
And in one Lord Jesus Christ, the only-begotten
Son of God, begotten from his Father before all ages,
Light from Light, true God from true God, begotten
not made, of one substance with the Father, through
whom all things were made....

The Nicene confession, with its litany of Christological affirmations culminating in its strong statement that Jesus is "of one *substance* with the Father" and its pronouncement of anathema on anyone denying this, was designed to call a halt to the notion that Jesus was a creature of any sort and not equal to God the Father. It placed Jesus inside the circle of everything it means to be God.

At Nicaea the teaching of Arius was declared heretical and the oneness of Jesus with the Father was affirmed in no uncertain terms. But what did that actually mean? What does it mean to speak of the utter oneness of the Father and the Son? How can we worship the Father, and the Son, and the Holy Spirit and not be polytheists? How can three be one, and one be three? After the Council of Nicaea, through the leadership of Athanasius and others, the Church followed the apostle John's lead in thinking deeply about relationship, and as it did so a brilliant and revolutionary move took place. The Jewish and Greek notion of "one" was baptized into the world of *relationship*, and filled with "togetherness," or "oneness."[5]

---

5. See John Zizioulas, *Being as Communion* (London: Darton, Longman and Todd, 1985), pp. 27ff.; and Thomas F. Torrance, *The Christian Doctrine of God* (Edinburgh: T&T Clark, 1996), pp. 73ff.

To the Jewish mind, "one God" meant a single, individual, or solitary divine Person. For the Greek, "one God" meant indivisible, simple essence, not subject to partition or liable to change. For the Christian mind, "one God" came to mean three Persons *utterly together.* This is the point of capital importance. "One" undergoes a dramatic shift from an individual thing to relational togetherness or union.

It may seem like a trivial matter, but just think of your relationships, or of your marriage, or of your deepest desires in life. Does your heart not cry out for oneness rather than singularity or isolation? No one wants to be alone. And why not? If we were created in the image of a solitary Person, why would we so crave to be known, and to share our lives with another? Why are our deepest joys and pains relational? It makes sense that if we were created by a single-personed God, we might be wired to live in relationship with this God. But why would a single God wire us with a bent for relationships with one another?

The *sharing* between the Father and Son in the Spirit is so deep and genuine, the *intimacy* so real and personal, that our minds are forced to move even beyond the rich notion of face-to-face fellowship into the world of *mutual indwelling* and *union.* The relationship of the Son and the Father in the Spirit is a living and unobstructed fellowship of love of the deepest order. They *know* one another fully. They live a fellowship of unqualified personal interchange and communion in the Spirit, which is so flawless, so rich and thorough and true, that there is literal mutual indwelling. The Persons pass into one another and contain one another without losing themselves. When one weeps, the other tastes salt, yet they never get so entangled or enmeshed that they lose themselves and become one another. The beautiful word *pericho-*

resis (peri-co-*ray*-sis), my favorite theological word, says both things at once.[6] *Perichoresis* means mutual indwelling, or interpenetration, without loss of individuality: "The doctrine of the perichoresis links together in a brilliant way the three-ness and the unity, without reducing the threeness to the unity, or dissolving the unity in the threeness."[7]

When Jesus says that he and the Father are one, or that if you have seen him you have seen the Father, he is not say-ing that he *is* the Father. Jesus remains his own person, as do the Father and the Holy Spirit, yet their fellowship is so unclouded that they dwell *in* one another; and they dwell in one another to such a degree that, for lack of a better way of saying it, they live in utter union—oneness.

Implicit in the preposition *in* as used by Jesus and John is the idea of *perichoresis*, mutual indwelling without loss of personal identity. It would take centuries of debate before this could be articulated, but the idea of mutual indwelling opened the way for relationship and fellowship and love to be included in the discussion of what it means to be "one." In fact, it transformed the idea of "one" from strict individual-ity to profound togetherness—oneness. And oneness does not negate "one," but fills it with new meaning.

In this move from isolation to profound togetherness, the truth that the Father, Son, and Spirit are distinct Persons is held together with the truth that God is one. For this relation-ship is so deep, this fellowship is so true, this love between the Spirit, Son, and Father is so pure and unclouded, they so

---

6. For a detailed discussion of the meaning of *perichoresis*, see Thomas F. Torrance, *The Christian Doctrine of God*, pp. 168ff.

7. Jürgen Moltmann, *The Trinity and the Kingdom: The Doctrine of God* (London: SCM Press, 1981), p. 175.

mutually indwell one another, that any description short of the word "one" betrays their sheer togetherness.[8]

In our lives such relational oneness is something we long to experience, but in the life of the blessed Trinity it is an abiding reality that continually expresses itself in love and in astonishing creativity and freedom. To me this is one of the most brilliant aspects of *The Shack*. Paul Young beautifully captures the equality, the threeness and the oneness, and the creativity of the relationship. At no point do we ever confuse Papa, Jesus, and Sarayu, and at no point do we think that they are separated in any way. As Sarayu says, "You can't share with one and not share with us all" (108).

This togetherness of the Father, Son, and Spirit is free to express itself in an infant "in the lonely house of Adam's fall,"[9] wrapped in swaddling clothes and lying in a manger— and on a cross, suffering rejection and murder at the hands of the human race. Divine oneness is both the *truth* of the being of the triune God, and the *way* of trinitarian being, ever expressing itself in love and fellowship.[10]

In the context of the Jewish tradition, the disciples of Jesus found themselves walking with One they believed to be the Lord himself—yet One who had a Father, and was

---

8. For more of my thoughts on the oneness of the Father, Son, and Spirit, see my book *Jesus and the Undoing of Adam* (Jackson, MS: Perichoresis Press, 2002), pp. 18ff.

9. Pierce Pettis, from the song "Family," on *Chase the Buffalo* (High Street Records, 1993).

10. "We must not think of this, however, as if we have to do with three individual persons who have some independent existence prior to the mutual relatedness and perichoretic interpenetration. The *perichoresis* is eternal. It is given in the very being of God. To be God is to be Father, Son and Holy Spirit in eternal perichoretic *koinonia*." Trevor Hart, *Regarding Karl Barth* (Carlisle, England: Paternoster Press, 1999), p. 113.

anointed with the Holy Spirit. Through their witness, and indeed through the ongoing revelation of Jesus in the Spirit, the Christian community came to perceive that the astonishing relationship of Jesus, the One he called his Father, and the Holy Spirit was not a form that God assumed for a moment, but a revelation to the human race of the way the one God is from all eternity and forever. What we see in Jesus' life is an unveiling to us of the way God is, always has been, and always will be.

When Christianity says *God*, it says Father, Son, and Spirit, existing in a beautiful, intimate relationship of other-centered love expressing itself in boundless fellowship and unutterable oneness. It does not speak of a being that is isolated or unapproachable, detached or indifferent. It does not speak of a legalist, or a self-centered potentate, or an unmoved mover. God, for the Christian Church—at its best, anyway—is a relational being: three Persons, Father, Son, and Spirit, sharing life and all things in other-centered love and incomparable togetherness.

But we dare not stop here. The minute we mention the eternal relationship of the Father, Son, and Spirit, we have spoken volumes about the entire cosmos and the destiny of the human race. For this trinitarian relationship, this abounding and joyous communion, this unspeakable oneness of love, is the very womb of the universe and of humanity within it.

10

THE LOVE OF THE TRIUNE GOD

God, who needs nothing, loves into existence wholly superfluous creatures in order that He may love and perfect them.
—C. S. Lewis

The way Sarayu, Jesus, and Papa relate to one another in *The Shack*—in love, openness, mutual deference, and simple enjoyment of each other—is all either a gross and ungodly misrepresentation, or a hint at the astounding truth. It intrigued Mackenzie (106ff., 202f.), to say the least. He had never seen anything like it. He was drawn to their relationship, and their way of being. But the whole Trinity thing just didn't make any sense to him. And what difference does the Trinity make anyway? (103).

According to Young's Papa, "It makes all the difference in the world!" (103) and nowhere more than when we think of the possibility of love:

"You do understand," she continued, "that unless I had an object to love—or, more accurately, a *someone* to love—if I did not have such a relationship within myself, then I would not be capable of love at all? You would have a god who could not love. Or maybe worse, you would have a god who, when he chose, could only love as a limitation of his nature. That kind of god could possibly act without love, and that would be a disaster. And *that* is surely not *me*." (104)

In a variation on the argument of the medieval theologian Richard of St. Victor, Papa is saying that there can be no love (or charity, as the older writers called it) without relationship.[1]

For Young's Papa, if God were alone and solitary from eternity, then being other-centered would be out of the question, for there would be no *other* to be centered upon. Relationship itself and fellowship, even being open, personal, and approachable, would be quite foreign to the very *nature* of such a solitary God. "Love," C. S. Lewis says, "is something that one person has for another person. If God was a single person, then before the world was made, He was not love."[2] According to Saint Victor, "No one is properly said to have charity on the basis of his own private love of himself. And so it is necessary for love to be directed toward another for it to be charity. Therefore, where a plurality of persons is lacking, charity cannot exist."[3]

---

1. Richard of St. Victor, "Book Three of the Trinity," in *Richard of St. Victor*, trans. Grover A. Zinn (New York: Paulist Press, 1979), chap. 2ff.

2. C. S. Lewis, *Mere Christianity* (New York: Macmillan, 1952), p. 151.

3. Richard of St. Victor, "Book Three of the Trinity," chap. 2.

Young, Lewis, and Saint Victor raise a great issue. If there is no relationship within God's eternal being, then there is no real basis in God's *nature* for caring about something other than himself, no basis for altruistic devotion to others or for loving a thing for its own sake. The love of a single-personed God would be inherently self-centered, narcissistic, and ultimately about God, not others. A solitary God could love others *for their benefit* only by *shutting off*, as it were, the fountain of his deeper and true nature. That would mean Papa would have only been pretending when she embraced Mackenzie on the porch. Hiding her real nature—self-interest, or private love—she put on the mask of acceptance, all the while waiting to see if *her* desires would be fulfilled. Her embrace (in this scenario) would be not for *Mack's* sake, but ultimately for her own, and thus would have been conditional upon a proper response at some point.

This, it seems to me, is a huge point. Are we loved for what we can potentially bring to God's table, or are we loved for our own sake? Does the love of the Father, Son, and Spirit come with strings attached? Is our existence about relationship, or is it about performance? Is the universe the product of divine self-interest, or need, or perhaps boredom? Are we here to do something for God, for God's benefit?

> "What's important is this: If I were simply One God and only One Person, then you would find yourself in this Creation without something wonderful, without something essential even. And I would be utterly other than I am."
>
> "And we would be without...?" Mack didn't even know how to finish the question.
>
> "Love and relationship." (103)

If God is alone and solitary, then in one way or another we were created for God's benefit, not ours.[4] But given that God is Father, Son, and Spirit, and given that relationship and love form the core of the trinitarian being, then we were "created to be loved" (99), and to live loved, and to love others without agenda (181f.). As Lewis says, "God, who needs nothing, loves into existence wholly superfluous creatures in order that He may love and perfect them."[5]

A few years ago I was playing golf with a friend when the play slowed and we found ourselves on the next tee box with the group in front of us. As we approached, an older man walked toward us, tall with silver hair. I knew immediately that he was a religious glad-hander. He even tilted his head slightly as he cupped his hand to shake mine. I literally asked myself, *I wonder how long it will take before he jumps into his religious pitch?* I will admit to growing shy for a moment and backing away to let my partner be the target. Sure enough, we weren't off the tee box before the glad-hander dropped his first question, the setup.

"You boys go to church?"

I pretended not to hear and headed for my golf bag. My friend, let's call him Samuel, answered.

"Not really... sometimes; I mean, I don't find church very helpful, do you?"

With the touch of one who has no clue that everyone sees right through him, the glad-hander ignored Sam's question and dropped his next.

---

4. For more on creation as our benefit, see Karl Barth, *Church Dogmatics III/1*, trans. G. W. Bromiley (Edinburgh: T&T Clark, 1985), pp. 330–44.

5. C. S. Lewis, *The Four Loves* (New York: Harcourt, Brace, 1960), p. 127.

"Are you saved?"

Sam was quick. "Of course. I believe in Jesus, but that is not my question."

With that it was time to tee off. The glad-hander and his partner gave us the tee and changed the subject completely.

There are some who would say that the glad-hander cared for Sam; that was why he wanted to make sure Sam was saved. But I beg to differ. As it turns out, Sam and I were playing golf that day because he was really struggling with the loss of his wife. He was in a lot of pain. We were having a great conversation about how Jesus meets us in our trauma, and Sam was finding some hope when the glad-hander approached us, dampening the moment with a religious spirit and spoiling our "church."

The Father, Son, and Spirit love us *for our benefit*, not for increasing their membership rolls, or for making themselves look good, or for anything they can get from us. There is no need in the blessed Trinity. It is an overflowing fountain of other-centered love. The shared life of the Father, Son, and Spirit is about giving, not taking; sharing, not hoarding; blessing others with life for their sake, not manipulating for divine control. The Father, Son, and Spirit are focused upon giving themselves for our benefit, so that we, too, can experience real life. They need nothing in return.

This was my point to Sam. Jesus accepts him, meets and embraces him—as he does Mackenzie—right where he is, and is gently leading him to experience his own peace and hope. He wants nothing for himself in return. The Father, Son, and Spirit don't give to get. They meet us in our worlds, in our struggles, miseries, and joys, and they never ignore our real questions—although inside our darkness there are times when it certainly seems so.

The doctrine of the Trinity means that God is a relational being—always has been, and always will be. Relationship, fellowship, self-giving, and other-centeredness are not afterthoughts with God, but the deepest realities of the divine Being. For the Father, Son, and Spirit it is always about love, relationship, and sharing life, not about what they can get from us. We were created that we could be, that we could live and share in the life and joy of the triune God. Jesus' Father is not holding his breath to see if we will jump through the right hoops before he decides our fate. There is no list. We are not here to "glorify God" by our religious performance. We are here to live "in the glory" of the blessed Trinity.

Let's step back for a moment and consider two critical questions that come from Papa's comments to Mackenzie. First, what is the foundation for believing in the love of God? Second, what do we really think about the *nature* of God? If we peeled the onion of divine being, so to speak, what would we find at its core? What lies at the heart of God? If God is a single person, alone from all eternity, then blessing others for their own benefit would be alien to his existence and way of being. In this case, God could not naturally love others for their sake. At best, divine altruism could only be a momentary pretense. But for Young, following the apostle John, God *is* love,[6] or as Papa says, "I *am* love" (103). And here let me cite Jonathan Edwards again: "The apostle tells us that 'God is love'; and therefore, seeing he is an infinite being, it follows that he is an infinite fountain of love. Seeing he is an all-sufficient being, it follows that he is a full and overflowing, and inexhaustible fountain of love. And in that he is an unchangeable and eternal being, he is an unchangeable and

6. See 1 John 4:8, 16.

eternal fountain of love."[7] This love is not self-centered, or a private love of God's self, which could only come with a hidden agenda, but other-centered, altruistic, and unconditional. The deepest truth of the divine *being* is the relationship of love of the Father, Son, and Spirit.

Is there a back door opening to another room beyond this relationship, a room in which we might discover a more profound truth about God? Is there an esoteric secret driving all that God thinks and dreams and does? The relationship of the Father, Son, and Spirit is not the foyer, but the inner sanctum, the very life of God and way of God's being, the simmering soup out of which arise all divine thoughts, acts, and responses.

Papa embraces Mackenzie not because she is having a good hair day and her blood sugar happens to be up, but because that is who she is. She is not pretending. She is being herself. She lives and moves and has her being in relationship with Jesus and Sarayu. As she is with them, so she is with Mack, and with all of us. Papa embraces Mackenzie as a simple expression of her true *nature* and way of being:

> "But why me? I mean, why Mackenzie Allen Phillips? Why do you love someone who is such a screw-up? After all the things I've felt in my heart toward you and all the accusations I made, why would you even bother to keep trying to get through to me?"
>
> "Because that is what love does," answered Papa. (188–89)

On a million front porches Papa will embrace a million Mackenzies. Unless, of course, there is something different

---

7. Jonathan Edwards, *Charity and Its Fruits* (Edinburgh: Banner of Truth Trust, 1982), p. 327.

and deeper about her than her relationship of love with Jesus and Sarayu.

Is there a god behind the back of the blessed Trinity, a divine Ogre in the back room, a cosmic Eeyore, perhaps, or a legalist who at any minute might appear and shame the goodness and love of the Father, Son, and Spirit? Is the relationship of the triune God under restraint, and only allowed expression on, say, Monday and Tuesday? Or is this relationship the abiding constant permeating the universe, the one free and stable, reliable and unchanging reality? If this relationship is not the truth of all truths, then something else ultimately calls the shots, and we can only hold our breath until that something else steps forward.

I suspect most of us live in the frayed world between wanting to believe that we are loved for our own sake and the fear that such love is a pipe dream. Here is a critical question: Do you believe that you can change the Trinity? Can you alter the way the Father, Son, and Spirit relate to one another? I had an argument once with a man who sternly objected to my simple declaration that the Father, Son, and Spirit love us all, and that in Jesus we have all been embraced forever.

"No! No!" he shouted. "You cannot just declare that we were all adopted in Jesus. You don't know these people, or their hearts. You don't know if they have repented and believed in Jesus."

"So," I asked, "what is God's relationship to people before they believe in Jesus?"

"He is their Judge," he replied. "He becomes their Father when they repent and believe."

"So you are saying that people's faith has the power to alter the *being* of God?"

"No, of course I am not saying that."

"Well, it seems that way to me. You are saying that if

someone believes, then God *becomes* their Father, but if they don't, he remains their Judge. Apart from the startling fact that you assume God as Judge is more fundamental than God as Father,[8] what happens to God if they cry out, 'I do believe; help my unbelief'?[9] Is Jesus' Father like a windshield wiper, moving back and forth between being a Father and a Judge?"

Needless to say, the argument did not end well, with both of us convinced that the other had lost his mind. I will have more to say later on the importance and necessity of faith and repentance, and on divine judgment, but for now the point is that we are not to confuse the *character of God* with where we are in our journey of faith, or lack of it. The other-centered love of the Father, Son, and Spirit is the eternal truth of the divine nature, and it is blessedly not dependent upon our faith, or upon anything that we may or may not do, including praying the Sinner's Prayer. As Athanasius said, "The Holy Trinity is no created being."[10] There was never a time when the Father was alone without the Son and the Spirit. Long before the foundations of the world, the character of God was in place. Whether we believe or not, whether we are good or not, whether we ever do one thing right or not, the character of the triune God remains what it is, and always has been, and always will be—love. We are not so powerful as to change the Father, Son, and Spirit.

This is one of many reasons that the Trinity is so critical. For if God were alone and solitary from eternity, then there

---

8. For a powerful critique of such a disastrous notion, see George MacDonald's sermon "Justice," in his *Unspoken Sermons: Series I, II, III* (Whitethorn, CA: Johannesen, 1999), pp. 500ff.

9. Mark 9:24.

10. *The Orations of St. Athanasius Against the Arians* (London: Griffith, Farran, Okeden, and Welsh), I.18.

was nothing for God to love until he created. In that case the solitary God could only *become* a lover, for he was not one *by nature*, and this love could only be a love that grew out of his aloneness and self-interest. And it's more than possible that whatever it was that caused the single-personed God to create and to become a lover could change, and the solitary God would then go back to his essential, nonloving nature. The love of this God is *caused* by something outside of his being. And is this not what we all fear? That something outside the being of God causes him to love us, that his love is conditioned by something other than his nature, and thus that we are the ones who must get it right, trip the love wire, make God's love happen, and keep it happening? No wonder we are so exhausted and unhappy.

> "Why do you love us humans? I suppose, I..." As he spoke he realized he hadn't formed his question very well. "I guess what I want to ask, is why do you love *me*, when I have nothing to offer you?"
>
> "If you think about it, Mack," Jesus answered, "it should be very freeing to know that you can offer us nothing, at least not anything that can add or take away from who we are.... That should alleviate any pressure to perform." (202)

The Christian God is a lover from all eternity, because this God exists as Father, Son, and Spirit in a relationship of other-centered love and beautiful togetherness. The Trinity means that, before Creation, God is love: "Love is the deepest depth, the essence of his nature, at the root of all his being."[11] "God is no lonely monad or self-absorbed tyrant, but one

---

11. MacDonald, *Unspoken Sermons*, p. 421.

whose orientation to the other is intrinsic to his eternal being as God."[12] "In God there is no hunger that needs to be filled, only plenteousness that desires to give."[13] The cause of the love of the triune God is not outside the relationship of the Father, Son, and Spirit. There are no trip wires, no conditions, no reasons, and no way that we can cause the blessed Trinity to love us—or to stop loving us.

Papa's point with Mackenzie is that because relationship and love exist within the being of God from all eternity, we have something we can believe in that we don't cause to be so by our faith, or negate by our unbelief. We are accepted as we are, known and loved for our benefit, embraced forever, because love is the *nature* of the blessed Trinity. So, with the apostle Paul, we can say, "For I am convinced that neither death, nor life, nor angels, nor principalities, nor things present, nor things to come, nor powers, nor height, nor depth, nor any other created thing, will be able to separate us from the love of God, which is in Christ Jesus our Lord."[14]

Here is a reality we can cling to in the midst of abuse and fear, of dying and death, of shame and guilt and doubt, and in the midst of *our Great Sadness*. We certainly may feel cut off, or left out, or abandoned, and who among us does not have a bundle of proofs that it must be so, and hasn't left a trail of wreckage behind us in our pain? But unless the Holy Spirit morphs into a narcissist, and the Father rejects his Son, and Jesus decides he would rather have a divorce, we will never be abandoned or forsaken: "Let us comfort ourselves in the thought of the Father and Son. So long as there dwells har-

---

12. Colin E. Gunton, *Father, Son and Holy Spirit: Toward a Fully Trinitarian Theology* (London: T&T Clark, 2003), p. 86.

13. Lewis, *The Four Loves*, p. 126.

14. Romans 8:38–39.

mony, so long as the Son loves the Father with all the love the Father can welcome, all is well with the little ones."[15] For from all eternity the triune God is love, and the Father, Son, and Spirit relate to us out of their own relating to one another. They love us with their love. There is no other way of being for the triune God.

Jesus' Father loves even Missy's murderer, loves him for his liberation, too (224ff.)—as he does all of us who have made a horrible mess of our lives and the lives of others, and all of us who still believe we are just fine, even the religious glad-hander so lost in his self-importance. "We is all you get, and believe me, we're more than enough" (87). "The God who is—the I am who I am—cannot act apart from love" (102). And love loves the beloved into the freedom to live loved, and to share love; and this love, as my friend Bruce Wauchope says, "picks up the costly tab" of our incessant disasters, and ever works to turn them into good for us, for others, and for all creation. "Because that is what love does" (189). Such is the astonishing truth of the blessed Trinity. It is not an accident that "Fear not" is the most frequent command in the Scriptures.

Let me make two additional points here. First, *all* the characteristics of God are expressions of *this* core nature of relationship and love.[16] The holiness of God, for example, is an expression of the utter uniqueness, the singularity of the trinitarian love. There is nothing like it in the universe. It is in a class by itself, set apart, incomparable. Its beauty, its

---

15. MacDonald, *Unspoken Sermons*, p. 431.

16. For more of my thoughts here, see my book *Jesus and the Undoing of Adam* (Jackson, MS: Perichoresis Press, 2002), pp. 17ff.

goodness, its joy is one of a kind. The righteousness of God speaks not of the conformity of the Father, Son, and Spirit to a law of some sort that stands above them, but of the sheer rightness of their relationship.

Likewise, the wrath of God is not the opposite of love, as if the two were vying for control in God's relationship with humanity. The love of the Father, Son, and Spirit does not play second fiddle to divine anger. As Papa said, "There is a lot to be mad about in the mess my kids have made and in the mess they're in. I don't like a lot of choices they make, but that anger—especially for me—is an expression of love all the same" (121). Wrath is the love of the triune God in passionate action, saying "*No!*" It is love's fiery opposition to our destruction. Likewise, the judgment of God is not the divine "dark side" finally having its say. To judge is to discern, to see into a matter and understand what is wrong in order to make it right and whole. Thus, as Pope Benedict said, "The judgment of God is hope, both because it is justice and because it is grace."[17] And as Sophia says in *The Shack*, "Mackenzie, judgment is not about destruction, but about setting things right" (171). The faithfulness of God, the blessedness and fullness, the power and wisdom, the joy and patience are all trinitarian and relational; all are fueled by, and expressions of, the same astonishing, other-centered love of the Father, Son, and Spirit. The blessed Trinity does nothing that is not motivated by love.

Second, everything changes if we think of the relationship of the Father, Son, and Spirit as simply *a* characteristic of God, or one among many characteristics, and not the

---

17. Pope Benedict XVI, Encyclical Letter: *Spe Salvi*, 47, http://www.vatican.va/holy_father/benedict_xvi/encyclicals/documents/hf_ben-xvi_enc_20071130_spe-salvi_en.html.

fundamental truth. Take holiness again. If relationship is not the deepest truth of God's being, then the holiness of God is not a relational idea at all.[18] And if holiness is not a description of the utter uniqueness of the trinitarian life, what is it? The door is now wide open for our idea of holiness to be filled with all manner of notions. And that is what has happened in our Western conversation. The holiness of God was detached from the relationship of the Father, Son, and Spirit, and reconceived within the world of Roman law, becoming a legal idea. Instead of holiness being a name for the incomparable love of the Father, Son, and Spirit, it became a matter of law, morality, and ethical perfection (109–10).

If you start with the Father, Son, and Spirit, then the larger story of creation is about love and relationship and sharing life. "My purpose from the beginning was to live in you and you in me" (114), says Papa. If you don't start here, then creation is about something else. And what would that something else be? Law? External obedience to a distant deity? Ethical purity? Fear? Glorifying God? Promise and rewards?

In the mix and flow of Western history, a legal understanding of holiness slipped behind the fellowship of the Father, Son, and Spirit and became the fundamental truth about God—at least in our minds. This holiness is not relational, not trinitarian, not the expression of love. And without our knowing it, this legal view of holiness was carried back into God's inner sanctum, so to speak. How this happened over time is a long story, but you can see something of the point.[19]

---

18. For a treatment of holiness as relational and trinitarian, see John Webster, *Holiness* (Grand Rapids: Eerdmans, 2003).

19. For more on the legal view of holiness and how it has shaped the way we understand God and his relationship with humanity, see my book *Jesus and the Undoing of Adam*, pp. 43ff.

When legal holiness became foundational for our idea of God, the biblical story was reframed in terms of law, guilt, and punishment. God is holy (legally speaking). We have failed; there must be restitution. The story of Jesus' coming and death then followed *this* larger story, and his death was understood as God's punishment for our sins. God, on this reckoning, is too holy (legally speaking) to look upon sin, and turned his back upon his own Son when our sin was placed upon him on the cross. In our place, Jesus suffered God's punishment for our sins. You may be familiar with this version of the story.

But Young puts nail scars on *Papa's* wrists, too (97, 104, 109, 166, 224); and rightly so, for how could the One who dwells in the bosom of the Father suffer and his Father not experience his pain? What agony did Jesus bear that his *Abba* and the Holy Spirit did not also feel? How could there be a dreadful split between the Father and his Son? And how could there be a fundamental character difference between them, such that Jesus could embrace sinners, and indeed "become sin,"[20] as the apostle Paul says, and the Father be unable even to look upon us? Recall Jesus' words: "If you have seen me, you have seen the Father." "I and the Father are one." Papa puts it simply: "We were there *together*" (98); "We were all in him" (188).

As we shall see, Jesus did not come to suffer punishment inflicted by his Father, or to twist his Father's arm to accept us. We belong to the Father, Son, and Spirit; we always have, and always will. Jesus died because we are loved forever, and had gotten ourselves into such a profound and astonishing mess that it was utterly *impossible* for us to know this love and experience its freedom, joy, and life.

---

20. See 2 Corinthians 5:21.

There are two worlds of thought here, and each world ripples out of an assumption about God's fundamental character. For Young, there is nothing deeper about God than the relationship of love between the Father, Son, and Spirit. This love is good. It is right. It is incomparable. It is powerful. It is other-centered, beautiful, constant, long-suffering, full of joy and peace and free-flowing togetherness, and full of fiery opposition to our destruction. And it is this love of the Father, Son, and Spirit that frames the story of creation and history, and opens the way for us to see the astonishing dream the blessed Trinity has for the human race, and the breathtaking costs the Father, Son, and Spirit are willing to suffer together (98) to see it fulfilled.

11

THE REAL JESUS

In that day you will know that I am in My Father,
and you in Me, and I in you.

—Jesus

John's Gospel moves from the face-to-face relationship of the Father and Son to the astounding event of the Incarnation. The One who is in the bosom of the Father,[1] was loved before the foundation of the world,[2] and is himself God,[3] became flesh and dwelt among us.[4] The development of the vision of the Trinity through the first centuries of the early Church both clarified John's thought and focused the attention upon his stunning insight. Jesus was not merely an exceptional

---

1. See John 1:18.
2. See John 17:24.
3. See John 1:1.
4. See John 1:14.

man who achieved an unusually close relationship with God; he is the Father's eternal Son who shares life and all things with him in the fellowship of the Holy Spirit. And *he* became one of us, a human being. He is the *incarnate* Son.

The accent falls on the Father's eternal Son stooping to become what we are. Jesus' life on earth was the living out of his eternal relationship with his Father and with the Holy Spirit as *a human being* in our midst, in our space-time world. It was not simply God—an amorphous, monolithic abstraction—who became human, but God, the eternal Son of the Father. And he did not leave his relationship with the Father or the Holy Spirit behind when he became flesh. The Incarnation is the coming of the trinitarian life. In Jesus, Papa says, "we became fully human" (101). "Even though we have always been present in this created universe, we now became flesh and blood" (101). The triune life of God is now no longer only divine. It is divine *and* human.

Who is not stunned to silence by such an act of love and humility? The Creator became a creature. He who knows the Father became human. The One who enjoys the Holy Spirit in boundless love became a baby in Bethlehem, bringing the trinitarian life itself into our humanity. But there is more. There is another twist in the amazing tale.

The Incarnation, as Trevor Hart points out, was not "a temporary episode in the life of God."[5] The Son's becoming human was not a quick visit to a friend's house. *The Incarnation will never end.* It is an abiding reality now and forever. Stephen, the first martyr of the Church, got to see it first. Moments before he was stoned to death, Stephen gazed into

---

5. Trevor Hart, "Humankind in Christ and Christ in Humankind: Salvation as Participation in Our Substitute in the Theology of John Calvin," in the *Scottish Journal of Theology*, vol. 42, p. 72.

heaven and was given to see the most astonishing reality in the universe:

> But being full of the Holy Spirit, he gazed intently into heaven and saw the glory of God, and Jesus standing at the right hand of God; and he said, "Behold, I see the heavens opened up and the Son of Man standing at the right hand of God."[6]

It wasn't an angel or archangel that Stephen saw. It was the "Son of Man." He saw Jesus himself, the *incarnate* Son, at the Father's right hand.

After Jesus' resurrection and before he departed, he met with his disciples and spoke with them about the Holy Spirit:

> And after He had said these things, He was lifted up while they were looking on, and a cloud received Him out of their sight. And as they were gazing intently into the sky while He was going, behold, two men in white clothing stood beside them. They also said, "Men of Galilee, why do you stand looking into the sky? This Jesus, who has been taken up from you into heaven, will come in just the same way as you have watched Him go into heaven."[7]

The ascension of Jesus is to me even more shocking than the stooping of God to enter our world. Perhaps in our wildest dreams we could almost understand God becoming human for a short while to work out our salvation, but who

---

6. Acts 7:55–56.

7. Acts 1:9–11.

can understand the ascension of the *incarnate* Son?[8] For it means that the Son's becoming human is not a past event, but an ongoing reality. The humanity of Christ was not a robe that he donned for a season but has now taken off and put away in a heavenly closet. "I came forth from the Father and have come into the world; I am leaving the world again and going to the Father."[9] Jesus sits now, *as a human being*, at the Father's right hand, knowing his Father in the fellowship of the Spirit.

Like most parents, I loved my children before they were actually born. But my love for them, and their love for me, is a relationship that grows and develops through time. We are human. It takes time for our love and relationship to mature, although our love in all its fullness was present from the very beginning. It helps me to recognize that the Incarnation is not to be confused with the virgin birth of Jesus. The Incarnation stretches, as it were, from Jesus' miraculous conception through his life into his death, resurrection, and ascension. It is a movement of becoming.

At every moment Jesus is the Father's Son and the Anointed One, and he is loved and loves, yet their relationship is ever new and ever expressing itself at each stage of his human development.[10] Paul Young speaks of our freedom as "an incremental process" (97). The Incarnation, too, is a

---

8. On the ascension of Jesus, see Matthew 26:64; Luke 24:50ff.; John 6:62; 14:28; 15:5, 10, 17, 28; 20:17; Acts 1:9–11; 2:33ff.; 7:55–56; Ephesians 1:18ff.; 2:4ff.; 4:8; Philippians 3:20; 1 Timothy 3:16; 1 Peter 3:22; Hebrews 1:1–3; 4:14; 6:17–20; 8:1–16; 9:11–12; 12:2; cf. Matthew 22:41–44; Isaiah 6:1ff.; 52:13; Psalm 68:18; 110:1–5.

9. John 16:28.

10. For more on the growth and development of Jesus, see Thomas A. Smail, *The Giving Gift: The Holy Spirit in Person* (London: Hodder and Stoughton, 1988), pp. 95ff.

process in its own way. It is true at Jesus' conception. He is the Father's Son, but in our flesh he is always becoming who he is. Like the trinitarian life in eternity, the relationship of the Father and Son in the Spirit is always a life of love and oneness, yet in the Incarnation it grows and develops as we do.

If we could take a slice of any moment of Jesus' life, we would see that he is the Father's beloved Son and he is the one anointed in the Holy Spirit. But such a relationship in our space-time world takes time to express itself. At no point is it less than it always was, any more than at any point do we love our children more than we did when we first heard their heartbeats. The Father's Son becoming human involves his whole life and finds its completion in his bodily ascension to the Father's right hand.[11] "Seated with the Father" is the truth of who Jesus is, having become what he always was as the eternal Son, but now as a human being. It took time to fulfill his sonship in our human existence. It had to be lived out in our world and, as Irenaeus said, through every stage of our human existence.[12] *And it has.* In Jesus' ascension to the Father, the Incarnation reached the amazing fulfillment of what it was at conception. Now—and this is the most astonishing part—the Father's Son incarnate is *in* his Father *as a human being*, even as he was throughout his life, but now it is

---

11. See William Milligan, *The Ascension and Heavenly Priesthood of Our Lord* (Greenwood, SC: Attic Press, 1977), pp. 30ff.; and Thomas F. Torrance, *Atonement: The Person and Work of Christ*, ed. Robert T. Walker (Downers Grove, IL: InterVarsity Press Academic, 2009), pp. 264ff.

12. Irenaeus, "Against the Heresies," in *The Ante-Nicene Fathers*, vol. 1 (Grand Rapids: Eerdmans, 1987), III.17.7; IV.38.2. See also C. S. Lewis, *Miracles* (New York: Simon and Schuster, 1996), pp. 147–48.

forever.[13] Such humility and grace and love are inconceivable to us. But so it is.

And there is more! The New Testament proclaims to us that Jesus is also the Creator of all things. As we hold together the three great truths of Jesus' identity (he is the Father's Son; he is the One anointed in the Spirit; he is the Creator), we begin to see the beautiful and staggering truth of the human race. Jesus' early followers understood him to be involved in the original act of creation. This is not a side point or an obscure footnote; John, Paul, and the writer of Hebrews are emphatic:

> In the beginning was the Word, and the Word was with God, and the Word was God. He was in the beginning with God. All things came into being through Him; and apart from Him nothing came into being that has come into being. In Him was life, and the life was the Light of men.[14]
>
> For by Him all things were created, both in the heavens and on earth, visible and invisible, whether thrones or dominions or rulers or authorities—all things have been created through Him and for Him. He is before all things, and in Him all things hold together.[15]
>
> God, after He spoke long ago to the fathers in the prophets in many portions and in many ways, in

---

13. For more on the ascension of Jesus, see Gerritt Scott Dawson, *Jesus Ascended: The Meaning of Christ's Continuing Incarnation* (Phillipsburg, NJ: P&R Publishing, 2004).

14. John 1:1–4.

15. Colossians 1:16–17.

these last days has spoken to us in His Son, whom He appointed heir of all things, through whom also He made the world. And He is the radiance of His glory and the exact representation of His nature, and upholds all things by the word of His power. When He had made purification of sins, He sat down at the right hand of the Majesty on high.[16]

For these three writers, everything in creation has come into being through the Father's Son. Not a single atom or sub-atomic particle, star, animal, plant, or person has existence in and of itself; all things breathe christological air and are sustained every moment by Jesus himself. As Thomas Merton puts it, "All creatures, spiritual and material, are created in, through and by Christ... it is He Who sustains them in being. In Him they 'hold together.' Without Him they would fall apart."[17]

Commenting on John 1:4 and the phrase "in him was life," John Calvin writes, "The simple meaning is that the Word of God was not only the fount of life to all creation, so that those which had not yet existed began to be, but that His life-giving power makes them remain in their state. For did not His continued inspiration quicken the world, whatsoever flourishes would without doubt immediately decay or be reduced to nothing."[18]

---

16. Hebrews 1:1–3; see also Acts 17:28 and 1 Corinthians 8:6–7.

17. Thomas Merton, *The New Man* (New York: Farrar, Straus and Giroux, 1961), p. 137.

18. John Calvin, *The Gospel According to John*, trans. T. H. L. Parker (Grand Rapids: Eerdmans, 1988), pp. 10–11. For more on Calvin's view of Christ as mediator of Creation, see Julie Canlis, *Calvin's Ladder: A Spiritual Theology of Ascent and Ascension* (Grand Rapids: Eerdmans, 2010), pp. 55ff.

Following the apostles, both Merton and Calvin see that the entire creation was called into being through the Son, *and* that he continues to give existence and life to all things. Without him the whole of creation would instantly vanish, or "lapse back into non-existence," to borrow a great phrase from Athanasius.[19]

In creating the universe, Jesus is not like a child blowing soap bubbles through a wand. Once the bubbles are formed they detach from the wand and float away on their own. The child is involved in their creation, she is in some sense their source, but once they are formed there is a disconnect and she is no longer involved in their *continued* existence at all. The New Testament, and thinkers like Merton and Calvin, insist that, unlike the child and her soap bubbles, the Father's Son is involved in the *continued* existence of creation. Jesus is not a wand through whom we were blown into being and then disconnected, only to float away in our own lives. There is no disconnect: Jesus is the source of both our *creation* and our *continued existence*. This is a critical point, for it means that the Father's Son has a relationship with all things prior to his becoming human:

> Since he is the eternal Word of God by whom and through whom all things that are made are made, and in whom the whole universe of visible and invisible realities coheres and hangs together, and since in him divine and human natures are inseparably united, then the secret of every man, whether he believes or not, is bound up with Jesus, for it is in him that

---

19. See Athanasius, *On the Incarnation of the Word of God* (London: A. R. Mowbray, 1963), §6.

human contingent existence has been grounded and secured.[20]

Here we are a hairsbreadth from the greatest news in the universe, and from the mind-blowing glory of Jesus Christ as the center of all things.

The New Testament's witness to Jesus leads to a revolution in human understanding of God as the blessed Trinity. It also leads to a revolution in our understanding of creation and of human existence as *not separated* from the triune God, but *together with God* in relationship forever.[21] "How could it be otherwise when he who became incarnate in him is the very one through whom all worlds, all ages, were made?"[22] In becoming human, then, Jesus did not divorce his Father or leave the Holy Spirit in heaven, nor did he break his relationship with all creation. In Jesus' very existence, the shocking truth about God, creation, and humanity is being shouted to the cosmos. It would take thirty-three years, a horrible crucifixion, and a bodily resurrection and ascension to work

---

20. Thomas F. Torrance, *The Trinitarian Faith: The Evangelical Theology of the Ancient Catholic Church* (Edinburgh: T&T Clark, 1988), p. 183. Note also Colin E. Gunton's comment: "There is already and always a relationship between the Son of God and the world and it now, uniquely, takes the form of personal presence." *The Christian Faith* (Oxford: Blackwell Publishing, 2002), p. 98.

21. For more on our inclusion in Jesus, see my essay "The Truth of all Truths," available as a free download on our website, perichoresis.org. See also my books *God Is For Us* (Jackson, MS: Perichoresis Press, 1995), pp. 40ff.; *The Great Dance: The Christian Vision Revisited* (Jackson, MS: Perichoresis Press, 2000; Vancouver: Regent College Publishing, 2005), pp. 41ff.; and *Home* (Jackson, MS: Perichoresis Press, 1996), pp. 7ff.

22. Thomas F. Torrance, *The Trinitarian Faith*, p. 183.

out, but in the incarnate Son there is an astonishing coming together of the blessed Trinity and all creation—all *fallen* creation. The implications of Jesus' identity are staggering. His existence as the incarnate Son means that you are included in the life of the Trinity. So am I; we all are. "By His doing you are in Christ Jesus."[23]

To speak the name of Jesus Christ, biblically and in the tradition of the early Church, is to say, "Father's eternal Son," and it is to say, "Holy Spirit anointed," and it is to say, "Creator and Sustainer of all things"; and thus the very name of Jesus says, "The triune God, the human race, and all creation are not separated but together in relationship." Jesus is the relationship. In his own being, the Father, the Holy Spirit, and all creation are together.

This means that the mutual indwelling of the blessed Trinity now includes us! In Jesus, the human race has been gathered into the Holy Spirit's world. Adam's fallen race has been embraced by Jesus' Father and made his children forever. In Jesus, the love and joy, the fellowship and shared life, the staggering oneness of the blessed Trinity, have found us in our shacks—*us*: you, me, all of us—forever. In Jesus, "Papa has crawled inside of your world to be with you" (167).

> "Mack," said Papa with an intensity that caused him to listen very carefully, "we want to share with you the love and joy and freedom and light that we already know within ourself. We created you, the human, to be in face-to-face relationship with us, to join our circle of love." (126)

---

23. 1 Corinthians 1:30.

I fear that we in the West have been so preoccupied with guilt and sin as to have missed the astonishing fact that the Father's Son himself, the Anointed One and the Creator, has crossed all worlds to be with us and to include us in his life. Just the other day I heard a preacher on the radio holding forth about our need to receive Jesus into our lives. I could not help but be struck by how odd it sounded. When did any of us pray to receive our parents into our lives, or call our children to receive us into theirs? At its best, the preacher's call was a worthy plea for his listeners to walk with Jesus, to be his disciples, to give themselves to participate in Jesus' life. At its worst, it was a betrayal of the truth. The gospel is not the news that we can receive Jesus into our lives. The gospel is the news that Jesus has received us into his.[24]

When I was a student of Professor James B. Torrance back in the late eighties, a fellow student, Dan Price, told of seeing a little boy being hugged by his dad in the airport, and how it spoke to him of the Father-Son relationship. A week or so later the scene was replayed for me in dramatic fashion. I was reading the newspaper in the Aberdeen airport, waiting for my brother, who was coming for a visit from the States. Of the many people scurrying about, I happened to notice a dark-haired young man in his mid- to late thirties.[25] He was nervous, walking back and forth between the terminal door and the Arrivals monitor every five minutes or so. At

---

24. For more on Jesus including us in his world, see my book *Across All Worlds: Jesus Inside Our Darkness* (Jackson, MS: Perichoresis Press, 2007; Vancouver: Regent College Publishing, 2007), pp. xv, 39ff.

25. For more on this story and its meaning, see my book *Home*, pp. 12ff. This book is available as a free download on our website, perichoresis.org.

length he smiled, let out a sigh of relief, and relaxed, position-
ing himself thirty feet in front of the terminal doors in the
middle of a group of others.

As I put the paper down to watch, the doors flew open and
a few folks hustled through. Then there was a steady stream
of people, some all but running to catch a flight, some not
sure which way to go next, some smiling, obviously thrilled to
be back home in Scotland. The crowd began to disappear, and
the dad began to look anxious. *Then it happened.* A brown-
haired little boy of about eleven appeared by himself in the
doorway.

Standing perfectly still, he scanned the crowd like an
alarmed deer. I heard his dad shout something, probably his
son's name, but I couldn't tell for sure. But the boy heard his
father's voice and started running across the airport. To me it
seemed like everything in the airport went into slow motion,
and I had the perfect seat to watch it. The little boy's eyes
were full of delight as he ran. His dad just stood there with a
huge smile on his face. No parent or grandparent could have
watched without tears.

In one motion the boy dropped his bag and jumped as his
dad embraced him. They kissed each other and cried. They
laughed. But mostly they just held each other. It was a simple,
beautiful embrace. Watching through tears in my own eyes,
I heard these words whispered to me: "Baxter, Baxter, there
is the gospel. There is the resurrection and ascension of my
Son coming home from the far country. There is our embrace.
And the good news is, he is not alone, *he has you and the
whole world with him.*"

I tell this story everywhere I go, even when I return to
virtually the same group; I suppose I am forever processing the meaning of such a moment and its message. But I
knew instantly that I had seriously underestimated Jesus.

As a typical American, I was an individualist. I had always believed that Jesus was the Son of God and that he became a human being, but I thought of him as an individual who did something for us. I had not seen—even though Professor Torrance was telling us so fifty times a day, in his great phrase "the vicarious humanity of Christ"—that in Jesus something happened not only *for* us, but *to* us and *with* us.

For while Jesus Christ is a human being, he is human as the One in and through and by and for whom all things were created and are constantly sustained. He is "the Man," the one in whom we live and move and have our being.[26] What becomes of him is not of peripheral significance for his creation. If Jesus were the Lone Ranger or perhaps the Marlboro Man, he could ride into the sunset and not much more than a little dust would be disturbed. But he is the Creator. If *he* rides into the sunset, he takes the dust and the ground, the earth and the sky, the sun and the moon with him. If the human race fell in a mere man named Adam, what happened to us in the life and death of the incarnate Creator and Son of the Father?[27] If the Creator dies, the creation has no way of continuing to be. If he goes down, we go down. And that is the astonishing truth the disciples of Jesus are trying to tell us.

The apostle reaches this conclusion: "One died for all, therefore all died."[28] For Paul, Jesus is not simply one among many men. He is the Creator and Sustainer of all things. What becomes of him is not back-page, small-print news; it carries cosmic significance. There and then in Jesus, the

---

26. See Acts 17:27ff.

27. See Romans 5:12ff.

28. 2 Corinthians 5:14. "For you have died and your life is hidden with Christ in God" (Colossians 3:3). See also Romans 6:3–8, and my book *The Great Dance*, pp. 42ff.

Creator, something happened not only *for* us, but also *to* us and *with* us. When the Father's Son died, we died. In Jesus, every created person and thing—Adam, you, me, the alienated cosmos—was terminated, brought to an end.[29] "God was in Christ reconciling the world to Himself."[30] And then came Jesus' resurrection. "Blessed be the God and Father of our Lord Jesus Christ," Peter says, "who according to His great mercy has caused us to be born again to a living hope through the resurrection of Jesus Christ from the dead."[31] When Jesus rose, we rose. When he ascended to the Father's arms, we, too, were lifted up and embraced by the Father in him, and given a real place in his anointing in the Spirit.[32]

Read carefully the apostle Paul's beautiful statement:

---

29. "He has made an end of us as sinners and therefore of sin itself by going to death as the One who took our place as sinners. In His person He has delivered up us sinners and sin itself to destruction. He has removed us sinners and sin, negated us, cancelled us out: ourselves, our sin, and the accusation, condemnation and perdition which has overtaken us.... The man of sin, the first Adam, the cosmos alienated from God, the 'present evil world' (Gal 1:4), was taken and killed and buried in and with Him on the cross." Karl Barth, *Church Dogmatics*, trans. G. W. Bromiley (Edinburgh: T&T Clark, 1985), V/I, pp. 253–54. See appendix A for some beautiful quotes from a diverse group of Christian writers on our death and resurrection in Jesus.

30. 2 Corinthians 5:19.

31. 1 Peter 1:3.

32. Note Thomas F. Torrance, who says Jesus "was so one with us that when he died we died, for he did not die for himself but for us, and he did not die alone, but we died in him as those whom he had bound to himself inseparably by his incarnation. Therefore when he rose again we rose in him and with him, and when he presented himself before the face of the Father, he presented us also before God, so that we are already accepted of God in him once and for all." In *Atonement: The Person and Work of Christ*, p. 152.

But God, being rich in mercy, because of His great love with which He loved us, even when we were dead in our transgressions, made us alive together with Christ (by grace you have been saved), and raised us up with Him, and seated us with Him in the heavenly places in Christ Jesus, so that in the ages to come He might show the surpassing riches of His grace in kindness toward us in Christ Jesus.[33]

This is astonishing news. Think about it. Paul is telling us that we were made alive with Jesus, and lifted up and seated with him at the Father's right hand. F. J. Huegel sums it up by putting these words into Jesus' mouth: "The old man is crucified; I take him with me to the tomb and, as I rise, it is you who rise in me. As I ascend to the Throne it is you who ascend with me. You are a new creation. Henceforth your life shall flow from me and from my Throne."[34]

One year in Australia, I told (or retold) the story of the little boy in the airport at the end of a lecture. As I sat down I heard a young girl crying, *"Mr. Kruger, Mr. Kruger,"* as she ran down the aisle. Stephanie was her name, and as she called mine, my heart sank, for I assumed I had said something that had upset her. She sat beside me in tears. As I hugged her, I asked, "Stephanie, what's wrong?"

"Nothing is *wrong*, Mr. Kruger."

"Why are you crying?" I asked.

"When you told your story of the little boy in the airport, the Lord gave me a vision."

---

33. Ephesians 2:4–7.

34. F. J. Huegel, *The Enthroned Christian* (Fort Washington, PA: Christian Literature Crusade, 1992), p. 59.

"What did you see, Stephanie?"

"I saw God on a throne, and there were steps everywhere leading up to him. And there were heaps of people all over the steps. We were all trying to get to God, but none of us could make it; we were all bruised and cut, our knees were bloody, and we were all exhausted and sad and crying because we could not make it to God."

"That is sad," I said. "Did you see anything else?"

"Then I saw Jesus."

"And what did Jesus do?"

"Jesus walked over to us, gathered us all into his arms, and walked up the steps and sat down in his Father's lap."

We sat silent for a moment in the beauty of that vision. I gave her a kiss on the cheek and whispered, "Stephanie, that is the gospel."

Between the little boy and his father in the airport, and Stephanie's vision of Jesus taking us to his Father's lap, we have a beautiful picture of the staggering gospel of the triune God. As Lewis puts it,

> He goes down to come up again and bring the whole ruined world with Him. One has the picture of a strong man stooping lower and lower to get himself underneath some great complicated burden. He must stoop in order to lift, he must almost disappear under the load before he incredibly straightens his back and marches off with the whole mass swaying on his shoulders.[35]

---

35. C. S. Lewis, *Miracles*, p. 148. I am grateful to Roger Newell for this reference. See Roger J. Newell, *The Feeling Intellect: Reading the Bible with C. S. Lewis* (Eugene, OR: Wipf and Stock, 2010).

In Jesus himself, through his incarnate life, death, resurrection, and ascension, the human race and all creation were taken down and lifted up into union with his Father and the Holy Spirit, included in the trinitarian life itself. Jesus has prepared a place for us all in the Father's dwelling.[36]

---

36. See John 14:1–6.

PART THREE

PAPA'S DREAM

12

THE BIG PICTURE

*His unchanging plan has always been to adopt us into
his own family by bringing us to himself through Jesus Christ.
And this gave him great pleasure.*

—Saint Paul (Ephesians 1:5 NLT)

The apostle Paul begins his letter to the Ephesians with a shout of praise that doubles as a summary of the truth. "Blessed be the God and Father of our Lord Jesus Christ, who has blessed us with every spiritual blessing in the heavenly places in Christ."[1] Paul sees that something breathtaking has happened in Jesus. In him we have been blessed with every spiritual blessing. If you are like me, "every spiritual blessing in the heavenly places" seems rather vague. But notice first that Paul uses the past tense. He doesn't say that we *will be* blessed, but that we *have been*. The Father *has blessed* us. The

---

1. 1:3.

blessing has come in Jesus and it has already taken place. But what is the blessing?

The next time Paul speaks of "heavenly places" is when he is narrating Jesus' ascension to the Father's right hand,[2] and after that he uses the term again when he tells us that we were seated with Jesus.[3] While Paul did not have a worked-out vision of the Trinity, he begins all of his letters by referring to the God and Father of our Lord Jesus Christ. And he of all the disciples believed in the ascension of Jesus; it was burned into his conscience on the Damascus road. In that moment, something in what the glorified Jesus said to him imprinted his mind: "Saul, Saul, why are you persecuting *me*?" When Saul asked, "Who are you, Lord?" the answer came, "I am Jesus, whom you are persecuting." It was shocking enough for Saul that Jesus was the Lord, but Jesus' identification with the ones Saul was persecuting was even more shattering. Jesus is so close to the persecuted that he regards himself as the one attacked. Not surprisingly, then, the idea of our being "in Christ" or "in him" became the core of Paul's understanding of the truth. And it lies at the heart of the meaning of "every spiritual blessing in the heavenly places in Christ." The blessing the Father has blessed us with is Jesus himself, and all that Jesus is and has at the Father's right hand.

In the next two verses Paul fills out what he means with two beautiful images.[4] The first is the phrase "before Him." Paul says that we were chosen "to be holy and blameless before Him." Some translations take "before Him" to mean

---

2. See Ephesians 1:20.

3. See Ephesians 2:6.

4. For more on Ephesians 1:3–5, see my book *God Is For Us*, and my lecture series "You Are the Child the Father Always Wanted," both available on our website, perichoresis.org.

"in His sight," but this is too pale and distant and impersonal for what the apostle has in mind. "Before Him" moves us into the world of face-to-face fellowship, of being in his bosom. It is intimate. Here is what one commentator says:

> "BEFORE HIM" denotes the immediate presence of God to man and the closest proximity of man to God. The image suggests the position and relationship enjoyed by the cream of society at a royal court, by children to their father, by a bride to a bridegroom...[5]

Here again we come to relationship. The commentator refers to "the *immediate presence* of God to man," and "the *closest proximity* of man to God." Paul is not thinking about our being mere objects in God's sight, like my computer and desk are objects before me. He is thinking about our being the honored guests in the Father's house, about fellowship around his table in an atmosphere of warmth and intimacy. We are highly valued in the Father's presence, adored and treasured friends welcomed with open arms. And we are not alien to the Father's world; we are meant to be there, and perfectly suited for his love. I like the way Eugene Peterson translates Ephesians 1:5: "Long before he laid down earth's foundations, he had us in mind, had settled on us as the focus of his love, to be made whole and holy by his love."[6]

It is not surprising that Paul's line of thought then turns to adoption. He is desperately trying to communicate to us the breathtaking gift given to us all in Jesus. He sees that it involves our being uniquely cherished and lavishly loved by

---

5. Markus Barth, *Ephesians*, Anchor Bible (New York: Doubleday, 1974), p. 80.

6. Eugene Peterson, *The Message* (Colorado Springs: NavPress, 2002).

the Father himself, and made right for him, such that his presence is not a foreign world to us but where we belong—home. Now he adds the idea of our being included in the *family life*. The cream of society at a royal court, children in their father's arms, and a bride with her groom don't sit beside one another in a frozen stare. They share life. As Jesus says to Mack, "It's all about relationships and simply sharing life" (178).

Many years ago I met a man in Scotland named Francis Lyall who had done extensive research on the ancient idea of adoption. He pointed out that in the Roman world a natural son or daughter could be cut out of the family estate, but an adopted child could not. Once adoption had taken place, the child could never be rejected; it was a permanent position. So it is with us in Jesus: we are included forever. But Paul's focus is not only the fact that our position is eternally stable; rather, he is enamored with the nature and purpose of the gift given to us in adoption—that is, not merely legal standing, but inclusion in the life of the family. Inconceivable as it may be, in adoption we are made heirs, joint-heirs with Jesus, and what we inherit is not rights and privileges and position, but *the Father himself*.[7]

Paul is talking about being included in a family fellowship, about being given a place not just at the table, but in a shared life. Adoption is inclusion in the family itself, so that the love and joy, the interests and burdens of the family become ours, too. We are not only wanted and welcomed, but known and accepted, and so embraced as to taste and feel and experience the family life for ourselves. It's about relationship, about communion, about the sharing of souls, about knowing and being known, loving and being loved—oneness—*with the Father.*

---

7. See Romans 8:15–17.

The Father's dream is for us to be brought into his house, and not just brought into his house but honored as family members at his table, and not just at his table but at his right hand. And not just at his right hand but into conversation with him. And not just into conversation with him but into fellowship with the Father himself. Paul is talking about being ushered into a fellowship with the Father that is so close and personal, so real and intimate, that everything the Father is and has is shared with us personally through Jesus in the Spirit. Adoption means to be included in Jesus and in his shared life with his Father and the Holy Spirit. Such a dream is almost unbelievable. But there is more.

The truth is that our adoption has already happened in Jesus. Paul sees Jesus' ascension as the moment when we were included. "Every spiritual blessing in the heavenly places" is the beautiful life of the blessed Trinity itself. And the Father *has blessed* us with this life in Jesus, just as he planned it long ago. In Jesus we have been adopted into the life of the Trinity. We have been given a place in the love and laughter, the abounding life and joy, the music and creativity, the peace and freedom and unspeakable oneness of the Father, Son, and Spirit. This is the dream of the blessed Trinity, and it has now come to pass in Jesus. But, yet again, there is more.

For Paul is telling us that this was the plan from before the foundation of the world. Let me quote the three verses together so we can see his point:

> Blessed be the God and Father of our Lord Jesus Christ, who has blessed us with every spiritual blessing in the heavenly places in Christ, just as He chose us in Him before the foundation of the world, that we would be holy and blameless before Him. In love

> He predestined us to adoption as sons through Jesus
> Christ to Himself.[8]

Paul is setting before us the astonishing point that we
were chosen before the foundation of the world, and predestined to adoption. Don't let the baggage of the word *predestined* put you off. It means that you were known and loved in
the Father's heart, treasured from eternity, and that you are
not here by accident, but by his plan and purpose.[9]

Notice the two phrases "in Him" and "through Jesus
Christ." It is thrilling to think that we were so known and
loved, and destined to be included in the trinitarian life of
God. It is even more thrilling to hear that now it has come to
fruition in Jesus. Now Paul is telling us that this was the plan
before the creation of the world, and that *there and then* our
adoption was placed into the hands of Jesus Christ. "Predes-
tination means that we were eternally found in Jesus before
we were ever lost in Adam."[10]

Chosen *in Him*, predestined *through Jesus Christ*. What
could this mean but that, before Creation, the blessed Trinity
agreed upon the incarnation of the Son as the way our adoption would be accomplished?[11] Jesus was chosen first, and

---

8. Ephesians 1:3–5.

9. For a beautiful and extended treatment of election and predestina-
tion, see Karl Barth, *Church Dogmatics*, trans. G. W. Bromiley (Edinburgh: T&T Clark, 1985), vols. II.2, pp. 94ff; IV.2, pp. 31ff., and IV.1, pp.
21ff. For a simple introduction to Barth's theology, see Herbert Hartwell,
The Theology of Karl Barth: An Introduction (London: Gerald Duckworth, 1964).

10. Ken Blue's summation in a phone conversation about predestina-
tion. Used with permission.

11. See B. F. Westcott, "The Gospel of Creation," in his *Commentary on
the Epistles of St. John*, 1892.

we were chosen *in him*. It was Karl Barth in recent times who saw what this means.[12] Chosen *in* him, predestined *through* Jesus, means that Jesus Christ—and what became of us in him—was not an afterthought, but the first thought, the original and only plan of the triune God. The astonishing dream of the blessed Trinity was predestined to be accomplished in and through the incarnate Son.[13] Before the creation of the world, our adoption through Jesus was raised as the banner of all banners in heaven. In the ascension of Jesus—and of us in him—we see the "purpose and grace which was granted us in Christ Jesus from all eternity."[14]

Here in Jesus we at last find our proper bearings, the Light of the World, the true framework within which the story of Creation and human existence is understood. From the beginning it is all about the coming of the Father's Son, and *through him* the exaltation of the human race into the life shared by the blessed Trinity. For Jesus is not "Plan B," which the Father, Son, and Spirit quickly thought up and implemented after the failure of "Plan A" in Adam. Jesus is "Plan A," the first, the original, and only plan. As Papa said, "Creation and history are all about Jesus" (194). He is the Alpha and the Omega,[15] the beginning and the end. The ascension of Jesus, and ours in him, is not an afterthought, but the goal of creation. Jesus "in his Father" and "us in him" is not a half-time adjustment, but the dream of the blessed Trinity from before the foundation of the world.

---

12. Barth's treatment of "the election of Jesus Christ" is one of the greatest contributions to Christian thought. See earlier note for details.

13. See Athanasius, "Against the Arians," in *Athanasius: Select Works and Letters*, vol. 4 of *Nicene and Post-Nicene Fathers*, 2nd ser., ed. Philip Schaff and Henry Wallace (Grand Rapids: Eerdmans, 1987), 75–77.

14. 2 Timothy 1:9.

15. See Revelation 1:8; 21:6; 22:13.

13

THE WOMB OF THE INCARNATION

Have you noticed that in your pain you
assume the worst of me?

—Jesus

The fact that Jesus Christ—and our adoption in him—is not a footnote to Adam's fall but the plan from the beginning places Adam and Eve, and indeed the event of Creation itself, under the heading of "The Coming of Jesus Christ." Stop for a moment and let this sink in. Eden was never the goal, but the beginning. For the staggering gift of our adoption requires an equally staggering humility on God's part, a humility that stoops to cross all the worlds of difference between the Creator and the creature.[1] Creation was not an accident, and not

---

1. See John Calvin, *The Institutes of the Christian Religion*, ed. John T. McNeill, trans. Ford Lewis Battles (Philadelphia: Westminster Press, 1960), II.12.1.

the product of random chance, but an act of divine freedom, the first fruit of the lavish and determined love of the Father, Son, and Spirit, setting the stage for the coming of Jesus. Creation and Eden establish the personal and living context for the fulfillment of the union between the blessed Trinity and humanity in Jesus himself.

All things were created not only in and through Jesus, but also *for* him. "I am the light of the cosmos," both the *source* and the *meaning*, the *rhyme* and the *reason* of the existence of all things. It is in Jesus—and in what became of humanity and creation in him—that we see the gracious and joyful purpose of the triune God in calling forth the universe and human existence. Without seeing Jesus as the center of all things, we are doomed to live without hope in an essentially joyless and meaningless cosmos.[2] But seeing Jesus, and ourselves and all creation gathered in him, and included in his relationship with his Father and his anointing in the Holy Spirit, is seeing "the light of life."[3]

Human existence, including that of Adam and Eve, is understood in the light of Christ's coming. Creation is the first act of the triune God *preparing* for the advent of the Father's Son. It sets the stage for his story, and ours in him. There can be no Incarnation and no adoption in Jesus if there is no Creation, no people, no relationship, and no living context.

Creation establishes the place where the Trinity will become one with humanity. And this shared life will express itself in us in untold beauty and grace, and creation itself will

---

2. For a beautiful treatment of creation, see Daniel Migliore, *Faith Seeking Understanding* (Grand Rapids: Eerdmans, 1991), pp. 80ff.; and Thomas F. Torrance, *The Trinitarian Faith: The Evangelical Theology of the Ancient Catholic Church* (Edinburgh: T&T Clark, 1988), pp. 76ff.

3. John 8:12.

find in us the friendship of Jesus. The cosmos and the earth within it form the theater for the great dance of the blessed Trinity *with* the human race. Yet creation is much more than a mere theater. The created world is a cosmic sacrament, a vast, burning bush[4] baptized with the glory of the blessed Trinity. It is designed to be the "bread and wine," so to speak, in and through and by which we experience the trinitarian life for ourselves. Each and every thing, from the lowest to the highest, from the apparently insignificant to the obviously critical, has its place and value in Jesus' world. As Sarayu says in *The Shack*, "If anything matters then everything matters" (237).

"I'll never get tired of looking at this," Jesus says to Mackenzie. "The wonder of it all—the wastefulness of Creation, as one of our brothers has called it. So elegant, so full of longing and beauty even now" (115). One can only imagine what it is yet to become! As beautiful and extravagant and full of life as it is now, creation is presently more akin to a photograph than a real place,[5] but it is destined in Jesus to become real. "The created world itself can hardly wait for what's coming next. Everything in creation is being more or less held back. God reins it in until both creation and all the creatures are ready and can be released at the same moment into the glorious times ahead."[6]

---

4. See Kallistos Ware, "God of the Fathers: C. S. Lewis and Eastern Christianity," in *The Pilgrim's Guide: C. S. Lewis and the Art of Witness*, ed. David Mills (Grand Rapids: Eerdmans, 1998), pp. 62–63. "This is the Orthodox approach to the realm of nature. Creation is seen as a sacrament of the divine presence; the cosmos is a vast and all-embracing Burning Bush, permeated with the fire of God's eternal glory."

5. The analogy comes from C. S. Lewis. See *The Weight of Glory: And Other Addresses* (Grand Rapids: Eerdmans, 1965), p. 13; and *Mere Christianity* (New York: Macmillan, 1952), p. 140.

6. Romans 8:19–20, *The Message*.

I love what Jesus says after he feeds the multitude with a few loaves of bread and two fish. "Gather up the leftover fragments so that nothing will be lost."[7] This is the love of the Father, Son, and Spirit for all creation, and a beautiful expression of the trinitarian determination to bless and to include.

At the heart of the *preparation* for the coming of Jesus, of our adoption in him and the blessing of all creation, is the forming of humanity in the image of God. There could be no incarnation of the trinitarian fellowship without its counterpart on earth. Adam and Eve were not created as religious androids, but as persons in relationship. They were not extensions of God, or robots, or computers with Jesus software. While completely dependent upon the Lord for their existence, they were nonetheless distinct persons with their own minds, hearts, and wills. As the Bible makes plain on every page, and as Young makes clear throughout *The Shack*, the triune God takes *us* very seriously. We matter. We are real to God. It is above all else in the Incarnation that we see how distinct and real we are to the blessed Trinity. As Papa says, "I'm not interested in prisoners" (94). As distinct persons Adam and Eve were called to walk in relationship with the Lord, with one another, and with the whole of creation.

The pattern or blueprint of their existence was Jesus himself, in his relationship with his Father, with the Holy Spirit, and the future human race and created world. The deck was stacked. "The whole character of the creation was determined by the fact that God was to become man and dwell in the midst of his own creation."[8] Everything was designed *for* the trinitarian life, so that the life and joy, the beauty and grace,

---

7. John 6:12.

8. Thomas Merton, *The New Man* (New York: Farrar, Straus and Giroux, 1961), p. 137.

the other-centered and altruistic love and fellowship, could set up shop on earth in Jesus when the time was right.

Adam and Eve were given the central role in the plan. They were called to live in relationship with the Lord himself and to be the agents of his blessing upon creation. They were made to hear and see and know him and his love.[9] And in knowing him, in knowing his heart and love, they would experience a security and confidence not of this world—unearthly assurance. With this assurance would grow the freedom to love and be loved, to know and be known, to care and be cared for—to share life and engage in other-centered fellowship. This other-centeredness would then flow into their relationship with all creation, becoming the vehicle of blessing and shalom.

As creation has its existence, meaning, and blessing in Jesus, Adam and Eve were given a real place in his lordship. Creation was to "find itself," so to speak, or "hit its stride" through their love and leadership. Adam and Eve, first in their relationship of trust, love, and fellowship with the Lord, then in their relationship with each other, and then in their role as mediators of his blessing, formed the living context or "the womb of the Incarnation."[10] This was the earthly counterpart of Jesus and his relationships in heaven. It was the first or

---

9. For more of my thoughts on Adam and Eve, see my book *Jesus and the Undoing of Adam* (Jackson, MS: Perichoresis Press, 2002), pp. 23ff.

10. This beautiful phrase is from Thomas F. Torrance. See his essay "The Word of God and the Response of Man," in *God and Rationality* (London: Oxford University Press, 1971), p. 149. See also Thomas F. Torrance, "Salvation Is of the Jews," *Evangelical Quarterly* 22 (1950): 166; and Thomas F. Torrance, *The Mediation of Christ* (Grand Rapids: Eerdmans, 1983), p. 42; as well as my essay "On the Road to Becoming Flesh: Israel as the Womb of the Incarnation in the Theology of T. F. Torrance," available as a free download on our website, perichoresis.org.

infant form of adoption, which was destined to reach all its fullness and glory in Jesus himself.

It is here, of course, that the whole plan almost fell apart at the beginning, or so it would seem. The cunning serpent lied about the character of God. Adam and Eve believed the lie and fell to doubting the goodness of the Lord.[11] Such *doubt* as to the heart of the Lord toward them was a singular disaster, for it obliterated their unearthly assurance. Into the vacuum rose guilt and shame, fear and anxiety, and terrifying insecurity, all of which became a lethal roux within their souls, soon to poison the whole dish of their existence and that of creation. As Sarayu says to Mackenzie, "You humans, so little in your own eyes. You are truly blind to your own place in the Creation. Having chosen the ravaged path of independence, you don't even comprehend that you are dragging the entire Creation along with you" (134).

"The serpent of old who is called the devil and Satan," and "who deceives the whole world,"[12] is called by Jesus "a liar and the father of lies."[13] He is a *creature* and no equal to the triune God. He cannot create, cannot give existence or life, and has no meaning to offer; all life and meaning come from the Father, Son, and Spirit. If the evil one is to have his own world, which appears to be his dream, then he is limited to hijacking and exploiting, or "misusing," as my friend Steve Horn puts it, the trinitarian life shared with us. And he can do none of this without our permission, or against our wills. So he lies. He

---

11. For more of my thoughts on evil and the fall of Adam and Eve, see my books *The Great Dance: The Christian Vision Revisited* (Jackson, MS: Perichoresis Press, 2000; Vancouver: Regent College Publishing, 2005), pp. 67ff.; and *Home* (Jackson, MS: Perichoresis Press, 1996), pp. 27ff.

12. Revelation 12:9.

13. John 8:44.

deceives. He confuses us so that we willingly, though perhaps unwittingly, give ourselves to operate in his diabolical matrix of unbelief, confusion, and meaningless darkness. And so he finds a place for his dastardly and perverse ways in the good creation of the triune God.

His chief deception is to invite us to doubt the Lord's goodness, creating insecurity and anxiety in us, which in turn drives us into independent action. All this is then shrewdly woven into the lie that we are separated from the triune God. Adam and Eve believed the whispering doubt about the goodness of the Lord.[14] In the place of trust, love, and security rose doubt, and then fear, which inevitably turned them in upon themselves. They became self-referential and "chose independence over relationship" (125). They became self-centered, making themselves and their own judgment their point of reference and discernment rather than relationship with the Lord. The trust, love, and fellowship that had originally formed the heart of everything became mistrust, anxiety, and independence—estrangement. The divine-human fellowship, formed to be "the womb of the Incarnation," became an impossible and hopeless mess. The very relationship designed to receive the trinitarian life in Jesus became alien to the blessed Trinity.

The great disaster of Adam and Eve was not simply that they sinned or were disobedient to a divine rule.[15] The disaster was that in believing the lie of the evil one, they became blind. And by "blind" I do not mean that they could not see physically; I mean that their perception of reality became

---

14. See Genesis 3:4ff.

15. The next several paragraphs are mostly excerpts from my book *Across All Worlds: Jesus Inside Our Darkness* (Jackson, MS: Perichoresis Press, 2007; Vancouver: Regent College Publishing, 2007), pp. 23ff.

skewed, so skewed that they could no longer perceive the real truth about God or about themselves. *They hid from the Lord.*

Why? Clearly they were afraid, but afraid of what? Of course, their hiding comes on the heels of their outright disobedience, and most people would assume that they were afraid of God's punishment. But then again, how could Adam and Eve stand *in the garden*, the recipients of such astonishing blessing and love, and be afraid of *the Lord*? Had God changed? Had the Lord who created Adam and Eve out of sheer grace and love, and poured such astounding blessing upon them, suddenly made an about-face? Had he ceased to love?

Surely Adam's disobedience did not alter the being of God. *Or perhaps it did.* Perhaps God did change, abruptly and radically—not in reality, of course, but in Adam's mind. As Papa says to Mackenzie, "When all you can see is your pain, perhaps then you lose sight of me" (98). The belief in the lie about God's character swirled around with Adam's pain—the pain of his own unfaithfulness—and altered his inner vision, his perception of himself, of his world, and others. But most important, the way he saw God was altered. Adam projected his own brokenness onto God's face. He tarred the Father's face with the brush of his own angst. He took a paintbrush, dipped it into the cesspool of his own double-mindedness and guilt and shame, and painted an entirely new picture of a god with it. And it was this god, created by his own darkened imagination—not the Lord—that he feared, and from whom he hid.

The triune God did not change. How could human action of any kind change the being of God? Is the divine character so fickle, so unstable, as to be dependent upon us, or upon what we do or don't do? What changed in the relationship was not God, but Adam. He now projected his pain onto God, thereby creating an entirely mythological deity, a figment of his own baggage. But this figment was nevertheless frighteningly real *to Adam*.

Adam was scared to death. How could he not be? He believed himself to be standing guilty before a divine being who was as unstable as he. Sheer terror struck his soul. For in his fallen mind, he was staring down the gun barrel of utter rejection. In his mythology, he stood a hairsbreadth from abandonment and "the abyss of non-being."[16]

This is the problem of evil and sin. The impossible has happened: the truth about the love of the Lord is eclipsed, so eclipsed it has now become *inconceivable*. A profound blindness has taken over Adam's mind. He cannot see the Father's face. There is now a terrible incongruence between the being and character of God as Father, Son, and Spirit and the divine being Adam *perceives* and *believes* God to be. And for Adam, and indeed for all of us, the God of our imaginations is the only way God can be. Any other God is inconceivable.

From this moment, our shame will disfigure the Father's heart. The projections of our fear will rewrite the rules of his care. He will continue to bless us beyond our wildest dreams, but in our mythology we will never see it. The very presence of the Lord in love and grace will be translated through the fallen mind and perceived as the presence of "the demanding taskmaster" (198), the great critic, the Judge quick to condemn, whose judgmental, watching spirit haunts every room in the universe.

The human race is lost in the most terrible darkness, the darkness of its own fallen mind, the darkness of wrong belief

---

16. The phrase "the abyss of non-being" is from Dr. Bruce Wauchope's lecture "The Gospel and Mental Health." This lecture is available at perichoresis.org.

and unfaithfulness, of anxiety and projection and misperception. As Papa says to Mack, "It *is* the matrix; a diabolical scheme in which you are hopelessly trapped even while completely unaware of its existence" (126). Tragically, the fallen mind is consistent; it never fails. Its dark and anxious imagination creates a false deity, the proof of which it sees everywhere it looks. And this god is very, very real to us, so real it has become quite "natural"[17] to us, "*normal*" (126, 219), the most obvious thing in the world, the unquestionable truth about divinity, through which we misperceive the heart of the Father without even knowing it.

---

17. See 1 Corinthians 2:14.

14

GRACE

What was God to do in the face of this dehumanizing of mankind, this universal hiding of the knowledge of Himself by the wiles of evil spirits?

—Athanasius

The Lord's response to Adam's fall is as remarkable as it is beautiful.[1] There is no pretending that all is well, no looking the other way as if Adam's infidelity were a mere glitch in an otherwise properly functioning relationship. The Lord saw the disaster for what it was, but, to cite Athanasius again, "What then was God, being Good, to do?"[2] Pretend all is well? Lash

---

1. Most of what follows here is an excerpt from my essay "Bearing Our Scorn: Jesus and the Way of Trinitarian Love." This essay is available as a free download on our website, perichoresis.org.

2. Athanasius, *On the Incarnation of the Word of God* (London: A. R. Mowbray, 1963), §6.

out in anger? Being who he is, he accepted the Fall, without approving of it, and accepted Adam as a fallen creature. In the words of Papa, "Instead of scrapping the whole Creation we rolled up our sleeves and entered into the middle of the mess" (101). There is no divine indifference or neutrality, as if the Lord couldn't care less what happens in his creation. And there is no divine outburst of retaliatory anger. There is certainly judgment, judgment which discerns that a great wrong has happened, and judgment that insists on putting things right, on establishing peace and trust and love in the relationship. For the eternal purpose of our adoption in Jesus stands.

So as an act of sheer grace, of keen awareness of Adam's fear and identification with him in his pain, and as an act of determination to meet and relate to him in his fallen state, the Lord accepted Adam in his shame and related to him as he was. *He clothed him.*[3] Such an act was not about God or a divine need to be appeased. This was an act of love, of acceptance and real relationship, flowing out of his determination to bring the purpose of adoption to fruition.

It was the great Anselm who said to his friend Boso, "You have not yet considered the exceeding gravity of sin."[4] For Anselm, the problem of sin lay in the fact that it was committed against the great King, the eternal God himself, and therefore even the smallest sin necessarily carried the weight of an *eternal* offense.[5] But in the Garden of Eden it is difficult to find such an offended God, or to see sin being weighed over against God's eternal worth. We see the Lord, who, by *our* way of thinking, should have been highly offended, and who had every right to curse Adam and destroy him utterly—

---

3. See Genesis 3:21.

4. Anselm, *Cur Deus Homo* (Edinburgh: John Grant, 1909), XXI.

5. Ibid., XI, XX, XXIII.

but he didn't. We see the Lord putting aside all his rights to abstract justice and punishment, and we see him more concerned about his lost and terrified creatures than he is about his honor.

There are no dazzling lights, no hosts of angels, no triumphal entry of a King demanding proper recompense or vengeance for Adam's offense. The Lord comes in the cool of the day for fellowship with his beloved creature. He finds his friend hiding, ashamed and terrified. He recognizes what has happened, and without flinching moves toward Adam in tenderness and accommodating love.

The problem of the Fall, of evil and sin, is not simply that there has been disobedience to a divine command. The problem is that Adam is now so lost in his own fallen mind that he is utterly incapable of *relationship* with the Lord. How could he possibly trust the God of his broken imagination? Trapped in the tragic nightmare of his self-referential confusion, he has become the judge, and in his judgment, he believes that *the Lord* is the *enemy* to be feared and avoided. He is ashamed of himself and terrified of God. He hides.

The hiding of Adam—from the presence of the concerned and caring Lord—tells us that the Fall, at the very least, is about a terrible twisting of human perception, about an alien, ungodly confusion that so warped Adam's fundamental way of thinking that he actually *hid* from the greatest friend in the universe—*and believed he was right.*

The most penetrating commentary on the disaster of Adam's fall are the words of Jesus: "No one truly knows the Father except the Son."[6] Jesus does not say that we are doing well but need some fresh insights about his Father, or that our basic vision gets good marks but needs to be tweaked. He says

---

6. Matthew 11:27 NLT.

that *no one truly knows the Father.* What statement could be more solemn? Here is the "exceeding gravity of sin." No one— not the Jews, not the Romans, not the Greeks, no one—truly knows the Father. "For all have sinned and fall short of the glory of God," as the apostle Paul contends.[7] For Jesus, the problem of human blindness is absolute. All are so caught in the toils of Adam's confusion that there is not one who knows the Father, not one who sees him as he is, not one who is even close—except the Son.[8] "I have come as Light into the world, so that everyone who believes in Me will not *remain in darkness*."[9]

A confused mind sees only through its own confusion.[10] We cannot push the weeds of our fallen minds to the side and know the Father's heart. With Adam we are so confused, and trust is so obliterated, that adoption now seems the dream of a fool, for the rug of any possible divine-human fellow-ship has been jerked out from under our feet. And without fellowship, the "womb of the Incarnation" is simply and pro-foundly wrong for the trinitarian life. We are so trapped in our alien vision that we *will not* and indeed *cannot* let go of the way we see things, and therefore can do nothing other than impose our confusion upon the Father's face, creating a god in the image of our brokenness.[11] Jesus is dead serious: *no one knows the Father.*

---

7. Romans 3:23.

8. Note Jesus' or John's comment: "What He has seen and heard, of that He testifies; and no one receives His testimony" (John 3:32).

9. John 12:46, my italics.

10. For more on our fallen mind and inability to know the Father, see my book *Across All Worlds: Jesus Inside Our Darkness* (Jackson, MS: Peri-choresis Press, 2007; Vancouver: Regent College Publishing, 2007), pp. 7ff.

11. Ibid., pp. 21ff.

The biblical story is not about changing God, as if somehow our failure altered the Father's heart or his eternal dreams for us. The story is about how the love of the Father, Son, and Spirit finds a way to do the impossible—*reach us* in our fallen minds. As Papa says to Mack, "I understand how difficult it is for you, so lost in your perceptions of reality and yet so sure of your own judgments, to even begin to perceive, let alone imagine, *who* real love and goodness are" (192). The problem for God is: How can I restore to fellowship with me those so utterly lost in their own fallen minds that they hate me and run for cover from my sight?

How do you relate to one who does not want to relate to you? How do you get inside blindness? How do you reach one whose projecting shame so disfigures your own face that he disowns your love and hides in fear at your sight? In our pain we, like Adam, have condemned ourselves, created a god in the image of our shame and handcrafted religions to go with it, all of which we project onto the Father and defend with a vengeance.

How will the Lord get through our darkness and make himself knowable to us? Revelation seems the obvious answer, but is it? What good is revelation when our minds are so twisted that we would only misinterpret what is revealed? How can authentic communication, not to mention trust, be possible at all when our fallen imaginations paint the Lord's heart by the numbers of our own guilt and shame?

15

ADAM AND ISRAEL

You just can't get good help around here.
—Papa

Out of the twisted darkness of Adam's fall, the Lord, ever the lover of the human race, called a pagan man named Abram. He did not choose Abram because of his religious potential, but because he was as blind and fallen as everyone else on the planet. In Abram and his descendants the Lord establishes real relationship with the fallen children of Adam. But this is not going to be easy.[1] Israel, trapped in the

---

1. My discussion of the relationship between the Lord and Israel is greatly influenced by the work of Thomas F. Torrance. For a thorough treatment of Torrance's vision of Israel, see my essay "On the Road to Becoming Flesh: Israel as the Womb of the Incarnation in the Theology of T. F. Torrance." It is available as a free download at perichoresis.org. Of particular interest here is Torrance's *The Mediation of Christ* (Grand Rapids: Eerdmans, 1983), chap. 1 and 2; and his essays "The Word of God

delusions of the Adamic mind, is scared to death. The relationship between the Lord and Israel is a relationship of love and grace and promise, but it is also one of anguish.

Think of Peter in the boat with Jesus. Peter had fished all night and caught nothing. Jesus got into his boat to teach the gathering crowds, and after he had finished teaching, he told Peter to push out into the deeper water and let down his nets. Already exhausted, Peter was a little hesitant. I can imagine Peter muttering to himself, "But Jesus, we have fished all night and caught nothing." He did, however, as Jesus suggested, and they caught so many fish that two boats were filled and began to sink. Peter was surely thrilled at the prospect of having such an excellent fishing guide, but his response was surprising: he was afraid. "Go away from me, Lord, for I am a sinful man, O Lord!"[2]

At first this seems odd, but Peter's reaction is a window into Israel's world. Peter here is a picture of the history of Israel. The covenant between the Lord and Israel means that the Lord himself is in the boat, so to speak, with Israel. This is a relationship of grace, to be sure, but also one of agony and conflict, for the sheer love of the Lord, while certainly comforting and full of hope, nevertheless brings Israel's sin and brokenness to light.

When my wife, Beth, and I were first married, we got into a debate about the color of the walls in our apartment. I insisted that they were obviously white, while she smiled and said they were "off-white." To prove my point I grabbed a piece of typing paper and slapped it against the wall, and

---

and the Response of Man," in *God and Rationality* (London: Oxford University Press, 1971), pp. 137ff.; "Salvation Is of the Jews," pp. 164ff., and "Israel and the Incarnation," in *Judaica* (1957), vol. 13, pp. 1–18.

2. Luke 5:8.

to my instant horror realized that the walls were clearly off-white. This is what happens in Israel's history. The Lord's presence puts the white paper against the wall of Israel's life, instantly exposing all manner of darkness. His presence with Israel means the presence of *life*, and this life inevitably reveals that what Israel is living is not life at all but a twisted form of sadness and dying. Israel is caught between the love and grace of the Lord and the divine exposure of its broken and sinful existence. Peter's cry echoes the agonizing pain of Israel's nakedness.

The One from whom Adam hid walked into the room of Israel's conscience and closed and bolted the door. The pain of Adam's fall had nowhere to hide in Israel, for the presence of the Lord was a terrifying blessing. How could it be otherwise? For neither the Lord nor his exposing love would go away. And things got worse, much worse. For the love of the Lord "not only revealed Israel's sin but intensified it."[3]

This is about relationship, and relationship means knowing and being known. Relationship means that the Lord is not only walking in the garden, but has actually found Israel hiding in the bushes. *But Israel is fallen.* The "Go Away, Do Not Disturb" sign is blaring, and Israel is not about to allow the light of God's love to shine into the corridors of its shame and wickedness. So in tender grace and accommodating mercy,

---

3. Thomas F. Torrance, *The Mediation of Christ*, p. 38. Note the fuller quotation: "So long as the cords of the covenant were not drawn tight, and God remained, so to speak, at a distance, the conflict was not very sharp, but the closer God drew the more the human self-will of Israel asserted itself in resistance to its divine vocation. Thus the more fully God gave himself to this people, the more he forced it to be what it actually was, what we all are, in the self-willed isolation of fallen humanity from God. Thus the movement of God's reconciling love toward Israel not only revealed Israel's sin but intensified it."

the Lord established the sacrificial system for Israel's sake. But even with rivers of blood from the thousands of sacrifices, the Lord's presence in Israel was still too much for Israel to endure.

As the Lord walked into the room of Israel's conscience, his presence jabbed every raw nerve of the fallen mind, from its guilt and homemade religion to its shame and self-justification, from its fear of exposure and self-protective hiding to its pride and self-referential judgment. If relationship meant only the sharing of information, then Israel could transcribe the words, put the clay tablets on the wall, and contemplate things from a safe distance. While the Lord shows great accommodation and tenderness—he takes "baby steps"—relationship nevertheless means that God himself is in the room with fallen Israel, and therefore Israel's heresy and carnality, its heathenism and alienation, are exposed, stirring up all manner of hostility and animosity toward God. Israel's recoil, its rebellion against the love of God, was neither approved nor ignored; it was accepted as the way things are with fallen humanity. But even the Lord's acceptance of Israel's rebellion means that he is one step closer, pushing Israel's conflict with him toward fever pitch.[4]

The Lord walked with Israel and, in the genius of the Spirit, used the responses of Israel his presence provoked (both good and bad) to create a new medium for human understanding.[5] Israel's way of being and thinking were thrown into the fiery furnace of God's love, and its basic beliefs about God were melted down and remade. In the presence of the Lord, Israel's entrenched ideas were thrown onto the potter's wheel,

---

4. See Thomas F. Torrance, "The Word of God and the Response of Man," pp. 137ff.

5. Ibid., p. 147.

broken down, and refashioned. New ideas, concepts, and categories began to emerge in Adam's fallen world: the names of God, the Word and Spirit of God, the love of God, covenant, sin, atonement, grace, prophet, priest, king, mercy, and forgiveness.[6] In the glorious affliction of real relationship, the love of the Lord began to find its fruit in Israel in a restructuring of Adam's tragically confused mind, all of which would become "the essential furniture of our knowledge of God."[7]

For Israel, to walk with the Lord meant discovering a new world of understanding, and with it great hope. But it also meant feeling the pain of being stripped naked with all of its illusions exposed. Either the Lord was naive, and failed to anticipate that his life, light, and love would rattle the bones of Israel's very being and intensify Israel's conflict with him, or, inconceivable as it may sound, *the intensification was deliberate*, and the deliberate intensification of Israel's conflict with God was part of his way of establishing real relationship.[8] Far from appeasing the wrath of an offended and angry deity, or fulfilling God's honor code, or pretending there is no problem,

---

6. See Thomas F. Torrance, *The Mediation of Christ*, p. 28.

7. Ibid.

8. Note Torrance's amazing comment in *The Mediation of Christ*, p. 38: "That intensification, however, is not to be regarded simply as an accidental result of the covenant but rather as something which God deliberately took into the full design of his reconciling activity, for it was the will and the way of God's grace to effect reconciliation with man at his very worst, precisely in his state of rebellion against God. That is to say, in his marvelous wisdom and love God worked out in Israel a way of reconciliation which does not depend on the worth of men and women, but makes their very sin in rebellion against him the means by which he binds them forever to himself and through which he reconstitutes their relations with him in such a way that their true end is fully and perfectly realised in unsullied communion with himself." See also Thomas F. Torrance, "Israel and the Incarnation," pp. 6ff.

relationship is about the triune God deliberately embracing us in the twisted trauma of our fallenness and drawing so near that *we feel* the hellish anguish of our estrangement and lash out against him. Jabbing every raw nerve of Israel's fallenness is the point. For real relationship necessitates that the Lord get to the very bottom of the Fall, into the catacombs of our human hostility toward him and his love. All the poison of the Fall has to surface. Anything less leaves us lost in our delusions and the Father unknown.

The one thing that the Lord could count on from his fallen creatures was that we would not be able to cope with his presence and love, and that we would do everything within our power to escape them both, including twisting his Word into religions custom-designed by our fallen minds to keep the Lord at a distance. As the Lord in his great love drew near to Israel, the more intensely Israel wanted to run. It was too much.

The bitter enmity inherent in Israel's attempt to push the Lord out of the room and close the door is the chilling, terrifying, unnerving, yet very real and personal situation into which the Father's Son will be born. The intensifying conflict between Israel and the love of God is the womb of real divine-human relationship, the "womb of the Incarnation," and is destined to reach its boiling point as the Lord, in shocking grace, comes *in person* to meet Israel at its blind, fallen, and obstinate worst. Fallen humanity and the love of God will square off in the person of Jesus Christ.

16

THE REJECTION OF
THE ANOINTED SON

*Behold, we are going up to Jerusalem; and the Son of Man will be
delivered to the chief priests and scribes, and they will condemn
Him to death, and will hand Him over to the Gentiles to mock
and scourge and crucify Him.*

—Jesus

Conceived by the Holy Spirit, the Father's Son became a
baby in the womb of the virgin Mary. He was born a Jewish
boy in Israel, and in the midst of Israel's relationship with
God. As he grew in wisdom and stature, he became more
and more involved in the life of Israel. Entering his public
ministry around thirty, Jesus immediately began healing and
teaching. Some "beheld his glory,"[1] which means they saw

---

1. John 1:14 KJV.

Jesus for who he really is,[2] as *the* Father's own Son, *the* Creator, and *the* One anointed in the Holy Spirit. In him, the light of life was shining in the darkness—and people were drawn to him. Full of compassion for the broken and overwhelmed, he poured himself out to help others, to heal and restore, to enlighten and liberate. As his fame spread like wildfire, great crowds gathered to hear him, touch him, receive his healing, and be part of his world. For a short while it was beautiful, something like the way it should be when the Father's Son enters our world.

But things quickly changed. Conflict seemed inevitable as the religious leaders began watching Jesus with suspicious hearts.[3] They had a lot to lose—and Jesus was making staggering promises and equally staggering claims. He spoke with "revolutionary boldness,"[4] assuming superiority not only to the Jewish leaders, but also to the sacred Torah itself.[5] For Jesus, as we have seen, God was his own Father, and he was *the* unique and only Son. But Jesus made no promises that he did not keep. He delivered: he healed, he restored, he gave new sight to the blind, and he even raised the dead.

Jesus' presence—his heart, his life, his healing—forced the hand of the Jewish leadership by exposing the bankruptcy of their religion. In hush-toned, backroom meetings, they plot-

---

2. For more on "glory" as the essential nature of a person or thing, see David Kowalick's lectures on "The Hope of Glory." These lectures are available at perichoresis.org and at included.com.au.

3. This section is largely a reproduction of my essay "Bearing Our Scorn: Jesus and the Way of Trinitarian Love." This essay is available as a free download on our website, perichoresis.org.

4. See Joachim Jeremias, *New Testament Theology* (New York: Scribner's, 1975), p. 253.

5. See, for example, Matthew 5:22, 28, 32, 34, 39, 44.

ted to silence him: "If we let Him go on like this, all men will believe in Him, and the Romans will come and take away both our place and our nation."[6] So they sent out spies to find "proof," anything they could use to discredit him.[7] Even (or perhaps especially) in the face of Jesus calling Lazarus back to life from the dead, "they planned together to kill Him."[8]

It is easy for us to throw stones at the outright blindness of the Jewish leaders, but in the end Jesus had few real friends, as he died virtually alone. The great crowds dwindled and then turned against him. One of his own inner-circle disciples betrayed him into the hands of the powers that be; another denied him publicly three times. All the others, save a handful, deserted him when it mattered most. A few women and the beloved disciple gathered around him in his final hours.[9]

In the space of three or so years of biblically unparalleled ministry, the Father's Son incarnate died in apparent shame, while the scoffing of the Jewish leaders and the sneering cheers of the Gentiles filled the arena of his brutal execution.

The point here is not the way Jesus' fortunes changed or even to examine why. The point is that the almost universal response to him was one of rejection. The news that the Father's Son came to be with us and to bless us with a share in his own life is astonishing indeed—who would have ever dreamed of such divine grace and blessing?—but there is something here even more stunning. We mocked him.[10] We

---

6. John 11:48.

7. See Luke 20:20 and Matthew 26:59.

8. John 11:53; cf. Matthew 28:11–15.

9. See John 19:25–26.

10. I am using "we" here in the corporate sense of humanity as a race, and of "our" presence represented in the people responding to Jesus.

abused him. We rejected him. We plotted against him and murdered the Anointed One.

Just after John announces that it was through the Word of God that "all things" came into being, that "apart from Him nothing came into being that has come into being,"[11] he writes these terrible words: "He came to His own, and those who were His own did not receive Him."[12] In those two verses we stare into the most terrifying irony: the Creator himself stooped to become one of us, and his own creatures did not receive him.

Straightaway John prepares his readers to see that something is terribly wrong. *His own received him not.* The Son's coming was all too human, too nondivine. We did not recognize him. As the songwriter says, "No banners were unfurled as God stepped into the world, held in the arms of a little girl named Miriam."[13] The presence of the Father's Son made no sense to us. He did not meet *our* expectations of God, or of God's coming, or of God's presence and blessing, or of God's Messiah. "Is not this Jesus, the son of Joseph, whose father and mother we know? How does He now say, 'I have come down out of heaven'?"[14]

Far from being received with the honor due to the Father's eternal Son, Jesus was in fact slandered as being a bastard.[15] Think about it. The one person in biblical history who was anointed with the Holy Spirit as an abiding gift[16] was accused

---

11. John 1:3.

12. John 1:11.

13. Pierce Pettis, "Miriam," from the album *Making Light of It* (Compass Records, 1996).

14. John 6:42.

15. See John 8:41.

16. See John 1:33 and Isaiah 11:2.

of being demon-possessed.[17] The Good Shepherd,[18] appointed before the foundation of the world,[19] was thought to be leading the multitude astray.[20] But the issue of Adam's fall is far more catastrophic than a quibble over expectations or an inability to think clearly about God or God's kingdom. The fallen mind led us into serious *conflict* with the presence of the Lord. The blindness expressed in that verse, "He came unto his own and his own received him not," grew with horrifying intensity into the curse *"Away with this man! Crucify, crucify him!"*[21]

This rejection was no simple refusal to play God's game. It had a violent stinger in its tail; it was rejection with a double shot of bitterness and cruelty. The Father's Son came to share his life with us, and he was spat upon. The Anointed One was mocked, derided, scoffed at, and beaten, and then in plain view of the world he was brutally murdered while his own creatures universally approved.

Crucifixion is not simply elimination; it is rejection. It is personal rejection under a curse. What a terrible spectacle it must have been for the cosmos to watch Jesus' own creatures condemn him—the true Judge, *judged* by broken humanity, to borrow from Karl Barth.[22] Is it any wonder that the earth itself shook, and darkness fell over the whole land as the sun hid its face?[23] But then again, what reader of Scripture is really

---

17. See John 7:20; 8:48, 52; 10:20.

18. See John 10:11.

19. See Ephesians 1:4–5.

20. See John 7:12.

21. John 1:11 KJV; see Luke 23:18, 21; John 19:6.

22. See Karl Barth, *Church Dogmatics*, trans. G. W. Bromiley (Edinburgh: T&T Clark, 1985), vol. IV.1, pp. 211ff.

23. See Matthew 27:51; Luke 23:44–45; Mark 15:33.

that shocked? Didn't the prophets receive the same treatment, and didn't Jesus tell a prophetic parable about his own rejection and murder at the hands of the chief priests and elders?[24]

There is much here that will never be understood. But two things are crystal clear. First, Jesus' crucifixion—and the enmity that fueled it—shouts to us that something is hideously wrong, that humanity suffers from diabolical confusion. The Father's Son came to be with us in person, and not only did we not want him, we were hell-bent on casting him out of our world and humiliating him in the process. We could not be more wrongheaded! The fact that the presence of the Anointed One produced such a hostile reaction from us, leaving the Father's Son publicly cursed, proves the point that Adam's fall involves us in the most vile and ungodly blindness.

Second, there is serious venom in the attack upon Jesus. It is terrible enough to crucify a good and innocent man; it is even more horrific when we enjoy it. The Gospel narratives do not portray a larger crowd helplessly watching in horror as a handful of wicked men play their power politics and snuff out their greatest threat. The leadership wanted Jesus dead, gone, eliminated—but so did the crowds. And the shouts of *"Crucify, crucify him!"* say so much more than simply "We want this man out of the picture." There is deep bitterness here. *Give him vinegar. Damn him.* The astonishing blasphemy of the Jewish leaders, *"We have no king but Caesar,"*[25] betrays a feverish hostility toward Jesus that would go to any length to have him eliminated.

The inherent legalism of the Western Church[26] trains our

---

24. See Matthew 21:33–46.

25. John 19:15, my italics.

26. For more on the legalistic bent of the Western Church, see my book *Jesus and the Undoing of Adam* (Jackson, MS: Perichoresis Press, 2002), chap. 1 and 2.

eyes to see Jesus' suffering as the judgment of God upon our sin, and virtually blinds us to the more obvious point that Jesus suffered from the wickedness of humanity.[27] It was the human race, not the Father, who rejected his beloved Son and killed him.[28] The wrath poured out on Calvary's hill did not originate in the Father's heart, but in ours.[29] The humiliation that Jesus bore, the torment that he suffered, was not divine but human. *We* mocked him; *we* detested him; *we* judged him. *We* ridiculed him, tortured him, and turned our face from him. It was not the Father or the Holy Spirit who abandoned Jesus and banished him to the abyss of shame; it was the human race. *We cursed him.*

Either the Father, Son, and Spirit were caught off guard by our corporate rejection of Jesus, or there is a redemptive genius at work here that is too beautiful for words. Was the Jewish and Roman rejection of Jesus not foreseen by the triune God? Was the Father surprised when *we killed the*

---

27. "Behold, we are going up to Jerusalem; and the Son of Man will be delivered to the chief priests and scribes, and they will condemn Him to death, and will hand Him over to the Gentiles to mock and scourge and crucify Him, and on the third day He will be raised up" (Matthew 20:18–19). See also Matthew 16:21; Mark 10:33–34; Luke 24:7; and Hebrews 12:3.

28. Here, see *Stricken by God?*, ed. Bradley Jersak and Michael Hardin (Grand Rapids: Eerdmans, 2007), especially the essays by Brad Jersak, Michael Hardin, Richard Rohr, and James Alison. For my treatment of Jesus' cry "My God, my God, why have you forsaken me?" see my book *Jesus and the Undoing of Adam*, pp. 58ff.

29. On Isaiah 53:2–7, see *The New Jerusalem Bible* and Eugene Peterson, *The Message*. The key word in v. 6 is *paga*, "to meet, encounter, or fall upon": "The Lord caused the iniquity of us all to meet, encounter, fall upon (*paga*) him." On Isaiah 53:10, note *The New English Bible*, "Yet the LORD took thought for his tortured servant and healed him who had made himself a sacrifice for sin; so shall he enjoy long life and see his children's children, and in his hand the LORD's cause shall prosper."

solution? Was Jesus bewildered and the Holy Spirit shocked when things went south and the crowds turned against him? No, of course not. The animosity of the human race toward the Father's Son was anticipated, and indeed counted on, and literally incorporated[30] as the critical part in bringing about our real relationship. Here is amazing grace. In breathtaking love, the Lord's way of relationship involves the shocking acceptance of our cruelty. The Incarnation involves the inconceivable *submission* of the Trinity to our bizarre darkness and its bitter judgment.

What sin could be more heinous than rejecting—and then murdering—the Father's Son, and what grace could be more shocking and personal and real than the Lord willingly submitting himself to suffer our wrath so as to actually meet us in our terrible darkness? It is astonishing indeed that the Father's Son became what we are, and it is even more stunning that we rejected and abused and crucified him. But it is more mind-boggling still that Jesus willingly accepted and endured it all, when one word would have unleashed legions of angels to his defense.[31]

How far is the blessed Trinity prepared to go to meet us? The Father, Son, and Spirit are eternally serious about loving us and bringing us to know their love, but isn't there a line in the cosmic sand that they will not cross? Isn't there a point at which even the love of the triune God draws back?

It would seem impossible that the blessed Trinity could so enter into our miserable nightmare of projected hostility as to make contact with the *real us*. But what is relationship if it leaves the *real us* trapped in our confusion, unable to hear and see and receive the Father's love? What kind of recon-

---

30. See Acts 2:23.

31. See Matthew 26:53.

ciliation would it be that declared humanity legally clean, yet left us lost in the darkened cosmos of the fallen mind and its appalling pain?

Following Torrance's line of insight, the deliberate intensification of Israel's animosity toward God leads straight into the cruel rejection of Jesus by the Jews, and by the whole race of humanity. This is how the Lord reaches the *real us*: he comes to us in person, and submits himself to our evil, alien judgment. He does not try to win us theologically. He does not call fire down upon our brazen stupidity. He does not shame us for our self-incarcerating pride and detestable prejudice. He simply comes in person, and the conflict between fallen humanity and the Lord's presence reaches its boiling point. There is nowhere to hide. The fury of our hell breaks loose.

Unlike Adam and Israel, and all of us, the Father's Son does not run to escape the pain of real relationship. Refusing to pretend that all is well, he embraces the conflict, allowing himself to become the personal target, the *scapegoat* for all of our pain. He willfully, deliberately, humbly, and astonishingly bows to suffer our loathsome enmity. He takes a dagger to the heart—without ever approving of or agreeing with our dastardly confusion. While we are breathing christological air, he, the Creator and Sustainer of the universe, the Father's Son and the Anointed One, allows us to pour our wrath upon him.

On a human, relational level, when someone is angry with us, we have several possible avenues of response. We can pretend that there is no problem, that all is well, and go our merry way. We can invoke the "I don't care" clause and turn away in indifference. We can retaliate, matching anger with anger. But none of these responses serve the purpose of *relationship* or solve the problem. What, then, is the way forward?

Forgiveness? Yes, forgiveness clears the air for most of us, but forgiveness does not necessarily reach the other person's heart. But what if we accept the other person's way of seeing? What if we enter into their way of seeing *us*, and, without necessarily approving of their judgment, submit ourselves to their verdict? What if we were to bear their wrongheaded anger without condemning them?[32] And in doing so, in bearing the scorn of their resentment, what have we done? Have we not identified with them, embraced them, and related to them as they are? Have we not taken *them* into ourselves and established a real and personal relationship with them in their pain and estrangement? Indeed, have we not *reached them*?

Such is the way of the trinitarian love of God for us in our terrible darkness. Jesus embraced our hell as the womb of his incarnation. In person, the Son of God walked into the room of our fiery conflict with God and bore our animosity. Who would ever have imagined that the Father's Son himself would come among us, let alone allow himself to be rejected, damned, and cursed by his own creation? "Most profoundly, Jesus's death expresses the Trinitarian mystery of self-surrender at the heart of divine reality."[33] Such astounding love, such care, such determination *to be with us* and to share life, is beyond our wildest dreams. It cannot be. *But so it is.*

For the Father's Son did come. He did enter into the trauma of Adam's fall. He did not pretend that all is well; he did not abandon us and move on to other, more important things; he did not shout instructions from the sidelines of the

---

32. I am not suggesting here, of course, that anyone stay in an abusive relationship. I am only giving an analogy that helps us see how the Lord loves and endures us in our blindness in order to reach the real us.

33. Roger J. Newell, *The Feeling Intellect: Reading the Bible with C. S. Lewis* (Eugene, OR: Wipf and Stock, 2010), p. 34.

conflict; and he did not retaliate. His presence stirred up the hell of Adam's fall, and we poured out our sin upon him and cursed him. Jesus Christ, the Father's Son, the Anointed One, stepped into the arena of our hostility and deliberately submitted himself to suffer our damnation—*and we damned him.*

The sin of all sins was the irony of all ironies, and the great prophet Isaiah predicted it: "He was despised and forsaken of men, a man of sorrows, and acquainted with grief; and like one from whom men hide their face He was despised, and we did not esteem Him."[34] Twice Isaiah uses the word *despised,* emphasizing the contempt and disdain of the people toward Jesus. He heard the whispers, the snickering innuendos, the mocking shouts. While he was fully divine, to be sure, he was the Son of God *as man* and thus thoroughly human. He had no force field to protect his heart, no secret antidote to counter the gut-wrench of such personal rejection.

It is painful enough to live with the knowledge that you have disappointed a friend, but how do you bear knowing that you are a disappointment to the whole world? What Great Sadness engulfs your heart when you are sneered at by your own people as a disgrace—publicly despised and forsaken? Think of Jesus' pain as he walked into his illegal trial and allowed himself to be unjustly judged and condemned, and then endured the self-righteous grimaces and smirks of disdain, the pompous pride of those who hated him as they relished their victory.

A few years back I met a man out west. As we talked one evening he shared some stories of his own wounds. I noticed his hands quivering as he remembered the details of one particular day.

"When I was about five years old, my dad was plowing in

---

34. Isaiah 53:3.

the field behind our house," he said. "It was a hot day. Daddy whistled, and then shouted to Mama to send out some tape to cover blisters on his hands. Eager to help, I grabbed the tape and started toward Daddy. I tore off a piece of tape about seven inches long, thinking that would be good, but by the time I got there the tape was a twisted mess. I can still see the disgust on my daddy's face. And he was so mad. With disdain in his eyes he jerked the tape from my hands. Then he grabbed me on the top of my head, spun me around, and kicked me in the ass with his boot. It knocked me to the ground. I'm not proud to say it, but I peed in my pants, and cried all the way home. That was over fifty years ago, my friend. The shame still makes my insides churn."

Jesus knew the kick was coming, and he deliberately walked right into the boot. But the kick was not from his Father. "Behold, we are going up to Jerusalem; and the Son of Man will be delivered to the chief priests and scribes, and they will condemn Him to death, and will hand Him over to the Gentiles to mock and scourge and crucify Him."[35] The doom of Calvary haunted Jesus from the moment of his birth. It was always with him, the ghost of every miracle. There was no other way; this was the plan from before Creation. He was the Lamb foreknown, and the Lamb slain before the foundation of the world.[36] The "buzzing cloud of flies about the cross," as Lewis says, was foreseen from the beginning.[37]

Gethsemane is the window into Jesus' inner world. Just hours before the long agony of his execution, Jesus retreated with his closest friends to pray. "My soul is deeply grieved, to the point of death," he told them. Mark says Jesus was

---

35. Matthew 20:18.

36. See 1 Peter 1:20; Revelation 13:8.

37. C. S. Lewis, *The Four Loves* (New York: Harcourt, Brace, 1960), p. 127.

"distressed and troubled," and Luke says he was "in agony," and that his sweat "became like drops of blood."[38] Overwhelmed with the impending doom of placing himself in the crosshairs of our cruelty, Jesus fell on his face. Three times he cried out in fervent prayer, "My Father, if it is possible, let this cup pass from me; yet not as I will, but as you will." *"Abba! Father!* All things are possible for *you*: remove this cup from me—yet not what I will, but what you will."[39] Jesus is ever the faithful Son, but at this moment faithfulness leads straight into the belly of the coldhearted beast. "Behold, the hour is at hand and the Son of Man is being betrayed into the hands of sinners."[40]

What comfort Jesus found in Gethsemane was short-lived. He was soon forsaken by his own disciples, mercilessly beaten and whipped, and ridiculed at every turn. Then came the disgrace of dragging his own cross through the streets lined with murmurs of contempt, and then the nails, the crucifixion, and the belligerent derision: "He saved others; He cannot save Himself. He is the King of Israel; let Him now come down from the cross, and we will believe in Him. He trusts in God; let God rescue Him now, if He delights in Him; for He said, 'I am the Son of God.'"[41]

Jesus knew his Father would never forsake him, and not in a million millennia would the Holy Spirit abandon her post, but as he was hoisted up on the cross, as the jerking suffocation dislocated his shoulders and tormented his already-broken body, as his ears rang with the scoffing of the crowds, and as he bore the despicable treachery of the human race, he

---

38. Matthew 26:38; Mark 14:33; Luke 22:44, respectively.

39. Matthew 26:39; Mark 14:36, respectively, my translation and emphasis. See also Luke 22:42.

40. Matthew 26:45.

41. Matthew 27:42–43.

was overwhelmed. It had to be. In the lion's den of our hostility, Jesus died a humiliating death encircled by a thousand disgusted faces.

Here we must be silent in awe. "One day you folk will understand what he gave up," says Papa (193). "There are just no words."

⟐

As we poured our scorn upon Jesus, the Lord was causing the iniquity of us all to encounter or fall upon him,[42] and Jesus was becoming the scapegoat, "the Lamb of God who takes away the sin of the world."[43] Dying in the arms of our contempt, the Father's Son met us *where we are. He reached us.* Accepting us at our most wicked moment, Jesus embraced us in the terrible abyss of our gnarled and twisted pathology, thereby penetrating to the core of Adam's fall and the original sin—*and he brought his Father and the Holy Spirit with him.* "We were there *together,*" says Papa (98). Mack is shocked:

> "At the cross? Now wait, I thought you *left* him—you know—'My God, my God, why hast thou forsaken me?'"...
>
> "You misunderstand the mystery there. Regardless of what he *felt* at that moment, I never left him."
>
> "How can you say that? You abandoned him just like you abandoned me!"
>
> "Mackenzie, I never left him, and I have never left you."
>
> "That makes no sense to me," he snapped. (98)

---

42. See Isaiah 53:6, and previous note.

43. John 1:29.

On the cross Jesus bore the Great Sadness of the world; he gave himself into the trauma of our darkness. Immersed in our contempt, he lost touch with his Father's love and with the comfort of the Holy Spirit. *"My God, My God, why have You forsaken Me?"*[44]

But even this cry of despair was also a cry of solid hope; indeed, a sermon of victory.[45] For the psalm from which Jesus quotes goes on to say: "For He has not despised nor abhorred the affliction of the afflicted; nor has He hidden His face from him; but when he cried to Him for help, He heard."[46] In quoting this psalm, which ends in astonishing triumph, Jesus is interpreting his death, as if to say, "It may look to you, as Isaiah foresaw,[47] that my Father is forsaking me. But nothing could be further from the truth, as you will soon see." Breathing his last breath in the darkness, Jesus gave himself

---

44. Psalm 22:1; Matthew 27:46; Mark 15:34.

45. See John McLeod Campbell, *The Nature of the Atonement* (London: Macmillan, 1878), pp. 237ff.; and my book *Jesus and the Undoing of Adam*, pp. 58ff. Note George MacDonald's insight: "It was a cry in desolation, but it came out of Faith. It is the last voice of Truth speaking when it can but cry. The divine horror of that moment is unfathomable by the human soul. It was blackness of darkness. And yet he would believe. Yet he would hold fast. God was his God yet. My God—and in the cry came forth the Victory, and all was over soon. Of the peace that followed that cry, the peace of a perfect soul, large as the universe, pure as light, ardent as life, victorious for God and his brethren, he himself alone can ever know the breadth and length, and depth and height." "The Eloi," in *Unspoken Sermons: Series I, II, III* (Whitethorn, CA: Johannesen, 1999), p. 112.

46. Psalm 22:24.

47. Note Isaiah 53:4: "Surely our griefs He Himself bore, and our sorrows He carried; yet we ourselves esteemed Him stricken, smitten of God, and afflicted."

completely into his Father's hands in helpless trust. "Father, into Your hands I commit My spirit."[48] In the words of Papa, "Don't forget, the story didn't end in his sense of forsakenness. He found his way through it to put himself completely into my hands. Oh, what a moment that was!" (96).

This is how the Father, Son, and Spirit made their way into Adam's shack—and into Mackenzie's, and ours. And this is why Papa has nail scars on her wrists, and if Sarayu manifested physically, they would be seen on her wrists as well. For in the oneness of the blessed Trinity, the Father and the Holy Spirit suffered Jesus' hell with him. They shared fully in his trauma, feeling his abuse, tasting the salt of his tears, and (I should hasten to add) sharing his humble restraint in the teeth of such sickening injustice. They chose the way of submission, of other-centered love, of grief and shared sorrow, and in doing so drew our very hell into the bosom of the Father and into the dwelling of the Holy Spirit.

Jesus entered into the den of our iniquity, thereby establishing a real relationship between the blessed Trinity and us in our twisted prejudice. Jesus reached us in our fallen minds, personally closing the abyss between his Father's dream for our adoption and our insane blindness. The death of Jesus was an act of inclusion: he was including the real us, the fallen, helpless, broken, rebellious us in his fellowship with his Father. In dying, Jesus became the mercy seat, the place where the blessed Trinity personally suffered and endured sinners and their sin in astonishing mercy.

It deserves repeating again: the gospel is not the news that we can accept an absent Jesus into our lives. The gospel is the news that the Father's Son has received us into his. In

---

48. Luke 23:46.

Jesus the alien world of our darkness and pain, of our obstinate pride and anger, was drawn within the life of the blessed Trinity, and the trinitarian life of God set up shop inside our hell forever. Our adoption is not a mere theological doctrine. Adoption is the way things really are, now and forever.

17

THE WONDERFUL EXCHANGE

For you know the grace of our Lord Jesus Christ, that though He
was rich, yet for your sake He became poor, so that you through
His poverty might become rich.

—Saint Paul

At the heart of the universe is the shocking love of the
blessed Trinity, a love that bears all injustice and Great
Sadness to reach us, that we may taste and feel and know
the trinitarian life. Note these beautiful words from three
theologians—one from the ancient Church, one from the Ref-
ormation, and one from our own day:

> ...our Lord Jesus Christ, who did, through his
> transcendent love, become what we are, that he might
> bring us to be even what he is himself.[1]

---

1. Irenaeus, "Against the Heresies," in *The Ante-Nicene Fathers*, vol. 1
(Grand Rapids: Eerdmans, 1987), p. v.

This is the wonderful exchange which, out of his measureless benevolence, he has made with us; that, becoming Son of man with us, he has made us sons of God with him; that, by his descent to earth, he has prepared an ascent to heaven for us; that, by taking on our mortality, he has conferred his immortality upon us; that, accepting our weakness, he has strengthened us by his power; that, receiving our poverty unto himself, he has transferred his wealth to us; that, taking the weight of our iniquity upon himself (which oppressed us), he has clothed us with his righteousness.[2]

The prime purpose of the incarnation, in the love of God, is to lift us up into a life of communion, of participation in the very triune life of God.[3]

Each of these theologians set forward the meaning of the apostle Paul's famous comment: "For you know the grace of our Lord Jesus Christ, that though He was rich, yet for your sake He became poor, so that you through His poverty might become rich."[4]

Each of these quotations describes a "wonderful exchange"[5] between Jesus and the human race. For the apostle, the One who was rich before all worlds became poor in order to

2. John Calvin, *The Institutes of the Christian Religion*, ed. John T. McNeill, trans. Ford Lewis Battles (Philadelphia: Westminster Press, 1960), IV.17.2.

3. James B. Torrance, *Worship, Community and the Triune God of Grace* (Downers Grove, IL: InterVarsity Press), p. 21.

4. 2 Corinthians 8:9.

5. For more on the "wonderful exchange" in the thought of the early church, see Thomas F. Torrance, *The Trinitarian Faith: The Evangelical Theology of the Ancient Catholic Church* (Edinburgh: T&T Clark, 1988), pp. 179ff.

exchange his eternal wealth with our poverty. For Irenaeus, the Son of God became what we are to bring us to be what he is in himself. For Calvin, Jesus became one with us to make us sons and daughters with himself, and to share with us his own immortality, strength, wealth, and righteousness. For Torrance, the Father's Son became incarnate to give us a share in the very triune life of God. Here recall Young's Jesus: "I came to give you Life to the fullest. My life" (182).

In the words of the apostle Paul, Irenaeus, Calvin, and Torrance, we see that the life and death of Jesus Christ are about a wonderful exchange in which all that we are in our sin and pain and shame is taken into Jesus, and all that he is in his life with his Father and Spirit is given to us. "For he assumes the poverty of my flesh, that I may assume the richness of his Godhead."[6] Jesus is the place where the two worlds meet. At the heart of this exchange is the submission of Jesus, and indeed of the Father and the Holy Spirit, to us in our darkness. "Genuine relationships are marked by submission even when your choices are not helpful or healthy," says Jesus in *The Shack* (147). Mackenzie, like all who hear this news, was astonished:

> "Why would the God of the universe want to be submitted to me?"
>
> "Because we want you to join us in our circle of relationship. I don't want slaves to my will; I want brothers and sisters who will share life with me." (147–48)

---

6. Gregory Nazianzen, *A Select Library of Nicene and Post-Nicene Fathers of the Christian Church*, 2nd series, vol. 7 (Grand Rapids: Eerdmans, 1983), *Oration* 38.13.

Here our thoughts must move in multiple directions at once. First, in drinking the dregs of the cup of our abuse, Jesus truly entered into Adam's world and into our terrifying mythology and its pain. He saw through our eyes. He *identified* with us in our hurt and brokenness in the most profound and personal way. It is here in the bowels of our trauma, not by mere observation or extrinsic command but by personal experience of our rejection, that Jesus became our merciful and faithful High Priest,[7] able to meet us in every form of human hurt. What aspect of our personal hell has Jesus not experienced? What shame or abuse, what betrayal, rejection, or condemnation has he not suffered? What snide whisper has he not heard? Is there a single stone in our gnarled and traumatic existence that Jesus Christ left unturned?[8]

This is important. Think about it. We don't need a priest to twist the Father's arm, for the Father is for us forever. As Jesus said, his Father loves the world and judges no one.[9] We do, however, desperately need a God who knows, a God who has been there, who has suffered, bled, and died in the foxhole of human pain, a God who can identify with us in the trauma of living, who can speak to us from personal experience, and One who knows how to meet us where we are in our terrifying mythology. "Only pierced hands are gentle enough to

---

7. See Hebrews 2:17. For a beautiful song on the priesthood of Jesus, see Glen Soderholm, "Our Great High Priest," from the album *By Faint Degrees* (Moveable Feast Music), available at glensoderholm.com.

8. For more here, see my book *Across All Worlds: Jesus Inside Our Darkness* (Jackson, MS: Perichoresis Press, 2007; Vancouver: Regent College Publishing, 2007), p. 41.

9. See John 3:16; 5:22.

touch some wounds."[10] "The Bible directs man to God's powerlessness and suffering; only the suffering God can help."[11]

Jesus learned through the things he suffered, through loud crying and tears.[12] It is this Jesus, the Father's Son incarnate, crucified and resurrected, who is our Savior, our Brother, our High Priest, and our Salvation. "Therefore let us draw near with confidence to the throne of grace, so that we may receive mercy and find grace to help in time of need."[13] "For consider Him who has endured such hostility by sinners against Himself, so that you will not grow weary and lose heart."[14]

Second, in suffering our rejection Jesus became *our* representative and substitute in the depths of our unfaithfulness. As the one in and through and by and for whom all things were created and are sustained, Jesus already had a relationship with us; in submitting to our condemnation he established this relationship with us in the trenches of Adam's fall, putting himself in the place of sinners, the one for the many. And in our place, Jesus filled the covenant relationship with his own love for his Father, so that at the heart of our rebellion now stands the faith and faithfulness of Jesus himself.

The question "Where are you?"[15] asked by the Lord in Eden, echoes from Adam through Israel's history without answer. In Jesus, "Where are you?" is answered fully, person-

---

10. Elizabeth Rooney, from the poem "Hurting," in *A Widening Light: Poems of the Incarnation*, ed. Luci Shaw (Vancouver: Regent College Publishing, 1994), p. 99.

11. Dietrich Bonhoeffer, *Letters and Papers from Prison*, ed. E. Bethge, enlarged ed. (New York: Macmillan, 1971), p. 361.

12. See Hebrews 5:7–8.

13. Hebrews 4:16.

14. Hebrews 12:3.

15. Genesis 3:9.

ally, completely: "I always do the things that are pleasing to him."[16] "Father, into your hands I commit my spirit."[17]

Our contribution to the new covenant was summed up in the treachery of Caiaphas, the high priest who presided over the trial of Jesus. Jesus was causing a stir, and the priests feared that "the Romans will come and take away both our place and our nation." Addressing the council, Caiaphas said, "You know nothing at all, nor do you take into account that it is expedient for you that one man die for the people, and that the whole nation not perish."[18] As a shrewd political move, Caiaphas and the priests sacrificed Jesus to save their place. But it was an unwitting move of dramatic irony, which became the occasion of infinite grace. For in sacrificing Jesus, Caiaphas became the only high priest in Israel's long history to actually do his job: he offered up the one, true Sacrifice—though he never knew it, and did it for the wrong reason.

As Jesus humbly gave himself to the murderous intrigue of the religious and political machine, he formed a new covenant in the deepest, darkest pit of our treachery, bringing his faithfulness into our disobedience, replacing our hiding and fear and religion with his fellowship with his Father, and filling our rebellion with his love for his Father. Our hypocrisy became the place and the means whereby the new covenant relationship between the Lord, Israel, and the whole human race was cut into flesh-and-blood existence and filled with Jesus himself—and all that he is with his Father and the Holy Spirit.

Third, in dying in the terror of our hostility, Jesus made his way inside the cosmic headquarters of the domain of evil.

---

16. John 8:29.

17. Luke 23:46, my translation.

18. John 11:48–49.

"The Son of God appeared for this purpose, to destroy the works of the devil."[19] "Since the children share in flesh and blood, He Himself likewise also partook of the same, that through death He might render powerless him who had the power of death, that is, the devil, and might free those who through fear of death were subject to slavery all their lives."[20] Evil has its stronghold in our doubt as to God's goodness, and thus in our fear of separation from God. In believing the lie, we are irretrievably trapped in its confusion, pain, and projecting mythology. As Jesus bowed to be condemned by us, he suffered fully from our terrified faith in the lie of separation, and from the traumatic world of darkness that lie had engendered.

Despised, abused, and beaten to a pulp, Jesus experienced the shame and humiliation of our rejection. Therein he followed the trail of the lie through our darkness to the original sin and "the schemes of the devil"[21] behind it. In the words of one writer, "God 'defeats' evil not by ruthlessly punishing guilty parties, but by faithfully untwisting every step of false response with true submission to the Father's will."[22] At each step of Jesus' life inside our darkness, the father of lies found himself face-to-face with Jesus' undiluted trust in the love and goodness of his Father and the power of the Spirit. The victory of Jesus over the evil one was not by command, or by angelic warfare, but by willing submission to us and our evil, and to the will of his Father:

---

19. 1 John 3:8.

20. Hebrews 2:14–15.

21. Ephesians 6:11.

22. Roger J. Newell, *The Feeling Intellect: Reading the Bible with C. S. Lewis* (Eugene, OR: Wipf and Stock, 2010), p. 32.

Did not the Lord cast himself into the eternal gulf of evil yawning between the children and the Father.... Did he not foil and slay evil by letting all the waves and billows of its horrid sea break upon him, go over him, and die without rebound—spend their rage, fall defeated, and cease?[23]

In allowing himself to be banished by us into the abyss of evil's shame, Jesus pitched his tent in the stronghold of evil, faced the strong man, bound him, and plundered his house.[24] Herein lies the new exodus, for Jesus "condemned sin in the flesh," "disarmed the rulers and authorities," and "led captive a host of captives."[25]

In the genius of the blessed Trinity, our cruel rejection of Jesus became the way of our adoption; our bitter abuse became the way of the Father's embrace and the dwelling of the Holy Spirit. For how could our unfaithfulness and contempt and treachery, or the enslaving lie of the evil one, or death itself break the love and oneness and life of the blessed Trinity? In dying at our hands, Jesus brought his life into our death, his relationship with his Father into our miserable destitution, his anointing by the Holy Spirit into our despair. Out of his boundless love "he was dishonored that he might glorify us,"[26] and "he endured our insolence that we might inherit immortality."[27] Suffering our abuse to give us grace, he met our cruelty with his kindness, our rejection with his

---

23. MacDonald, *Unspoken Sermons*, p. 537.

24. See Matthew 12:29; Mark 3:27.

25. Romans 8:3; Colossians 2:15; and Ephesians 4:8, respectively.

26. Nazianzen, *Orations*, I.5.

27. Athanasius, *On the Incarnation of the Word of God* (London: A. R. Mowbray, 1963), §54.

mercy, and our dead religion with his joy; he exchanged our world with his, transforming the shack of Adam's fall into the house of his Father and the temple of the Holy Spirit.

In a variation on Saint Paul's great statement we might say, "For you know the stunning grace of the Father's Son: that though he was rich in the shared life of the blessed Trinity, yet for our sake he became poor, suffering our wrath to meet us, and that now through his suffering we who were so poor have been included in Jesus' own rich relationship with his Father in the Spirit."

18

THE SECRET

*The secret of every man, whether he believes or not,
is bound up with Jesus.*
—Thomas F. Torrance

Love Himself can work in those who know nothing of Him.
—C. S. Lewis

Understandably, the disciples were slow to grasp the full meaning of Jesus' identity and what was becoming of the cosmos and the human race in his life, death, resurrection, and ascension. The implications are simply too staggering, too revolutionary for any of us to comprehend. Even in the upper room, after several years of walking with Jesus, they struggled to understand. John 14 records part of Jesus' conversation with his disciples on the eve of his death and resurrection. It is then that Jesus summarizes the meaning of his life and work in a single statement. After promising the disciples that he and his Father will send them another soul mate, the Spirit of truth, and not leave them orphaned,[1] he says,

> In that day you shall know that I am in My Father, and you in Me, and I in you.[2]

Take a moment to read Jesus' words again. There are three critical truths: first, Jesus is *in* his Father; second, we are *in* Jesus; third, Jesus is *in* us. In astonishing grace and love he has done this for us, to us, and with us. Dying in our rejection, Jesus included us in his world with his Father and the Spirit. In the simplest of terms Jesus tells us of the world—his world, and ours in him—that awaits our discovery in the Holy Spirit. Such a world is inconceivable to us; but the Spirit of truth will bring us to know, not as theological axioms but as living experience, that Jesus is *in* his Father, and that we are not outsiders looking in but *already* insiders included in Jesus and his relationship with his Father. The deadening whisper of our separation from God, of our rejection and abandonment, is here exposed to be mere fluff. For Jesus has included us all forever.

This is the truth that sets us free.[3] We are not spectators, not mere fans watching the beautiful life of the Father, Son, and Spirit from a distance. The trinitarian life has pitched its tent inside our humanity, inside our rejection and pain. We are included in this life, so much so that the music of the great dance is already playing in our lives; it's just too close for us to see. As Thomas Merton said: "He is closer to us than

---

1. See John 14:16ff.

2. John 14:20. See also my book *Home*, pp. 7ff.

3. See John 8:31–32.

we are to ourselves and that is why we do not notice Him."[4] "I am *in* you," like "I am in my Father," and "You are in me," is not something we *make* true; it *is* the truth, part of what we will come to know as reality in the Spirit. As Mackenzie says, "That is almost unbelievable!" (115).

We are free, of course, to live our lives "on the steps" if we want, exhausting ourselves again and again with trying to get to God, or cynical and bitter because we can't, or even grossly proud because we think we actually have; but the steps are merely an illusion. The real world is Jesus *in his Father*, and *us in Jesus*, and *Jesus in us*.

One Saturday afternoon years ago, when my son was six or seven, he and one of his buddies peered around the door at me as I sat on the couch in our den, sorting through junk mail and getting ready to watch a football game. They were decked out in camouflage, face paint, plastic guns and knives, helmets—the whole nine yards. Before I knew what was happening, two camouflaged blurs were flying through the air right at me. The attack was on. For five minutes or so we went through several mock explosions and fights before the three of us ended up in a pile of laughter on the floor. It was then that a sort of ticker-tape banner scrolled past the front of my mind: "Baxter, this is important; pay attention."

I had no idea what the message meant. After all, it was Saturday, and a dad and his boy and his friend were just playing army on the floor of the den. Surely there was nothing extraordinary about that. The first clue came when I realized that I actually did not know this other little boy at all. I had never seen him, and didn't even know his name. I thought to myself: *Suppose my son was in the back room with our dog,*

---

4. Thomas Merton, *The New Man* (New York: Farrar, Straus and Giroux, 1961), p. 138.

Nessie, and this boy had appeared in the den alone. Presumably he would have known that I was Mr. Kruger, but that is about as far as things would have gone. Not in a million years would he have come flying through the air at me, not by himself.

The little boy did not know me; he did not know what I was like. But my son did—and that was my second clue. My son knows me. He knows that I love him, that he is one of the apples of my eye. He knows that I *like* him and that he is always welcome and wanted. So he did the most natural thing in the world: in the freedom of knowing my heart, he ran to me to play. The miracle was that his buddy was right in the middle of it all. Without even knowing what I was seeing, I saw my son's relationship with me, his at-homeness and freedom with me, go inside that other little boy. And the other boy got to experience our fellowship. He got to taste and feel and play in my son's freedom and joy with me.

Stop for a moment and take this in. "In that day, you shall know that I am in my Father, and you in me, and I in you." What Jesus is saying is that *we* are the other little boy. As Jesus says to Mackenzie in *The Shack*, "My purpose from the beginning was to live in you and you in me" (114). And as Papa says, "We want to share with you the love and joy and freedom and light that we already know within ourself. We created you, the human, to be in face-to-face relationship with us, to join our circle of love" (126).

Through his death Jesus has included us in his life with his Father in the Spirit. There is thus far more going on in our lives than we have ever dared to dream; in Papa's words, "There is more going on than you could imagine or understand, even if I told you" (104). Jesus Christ is already sharing himself with you, with me, with us all. The love and joy, the music and laughter, the care and sacrifice, the beauty and goodness of the blessed Trinity, are already within us. This is the mystery hidden in past ages, but now revealed in Jesus: "Christ in you, the hope of glory."[5] This is the secret behind the richness of our experience of our own motherhood and fatherhood, of our love and sacrifice, of our music and art and joy, of our lives.[6]

Let us look at this shocking truth from another angle. When Jesus transformed the water into wine, he first asked the servants to fetch water and fill the six water pots.[7] Each pot held about 30 gallons, which totals around 180 gallons of water. That is a lot of water, and a lot of work. Have you ever wondered why Jesus asked the servants to help? Think about it. If you can turn water into wine, why not just create the wine and save the servants the trouble of getting all that water? Why involve the servants at all?

Having lived forever in a fellowship of love and sharing with his Father in the Holy Spirit, Jesus is not the sort of person who does things alone. In fact, he never does. While "you and I are not necessary,"[8] the Lord "does not will to be God without us,"[9] to borrow a profound point from Karl Barth. Of course Jesus did not need the servants, but this Lord is

---

5. Colossians 1:27.

6. For more on our participation in Jesus' life with his Father in the Spirit, see my books *The Great Dance: The Christian Vision Revisited* (Jackson, MS: Perichoresis Press, 2000; Vancouver: Regent College Publishing, 2005), pp. 53ff.; and *The Secret* (Jackson, MS: Perichoresis Press, 1997).

7. See John 2:1ff.

8. Daniel Migliore, *Faith Seeking Understanding* (Grand Rapids: Eerdmans, 1991), p. 86.

9. Karl Barth, *Church Dogmatics*, trans. G. W. Bromiley (Edinburgh: T&T Clark, 1985), IV.I.7.

about sharing, about giving us a place in his life and in what he is doing. The servants got to participate in Jesus' life with his Father in the Spirit. "The prime purpose of the incarnation… is to lift us up into a life of communion, of participation in the very triune life of God."[10]

Here is another example. I was on my way to speak at a college in the Midwestern States not long ago. A young man picked me up at the airport and we started driving to the college. It was a part of our country that is extremely flat, and for mile after mile we passed farms with farmers plowing in the fields. Along the way I asked the young man what he planned to do when he graduated.

"I'm planning on going to seminary," he said.

"Do you want to be a missionary?"

"No," he answered, "I don't think so; probably a pastor."

About that time a huge tractor made a turn in the field in front of us. I pointed to the farmer and asked, "Have you ever thought about how Jesus relates to farmers and their families?"

The young man paused and said, "No, I can't say I have," and looked at me like I had a third eye.

"That farmer and his family spend sixty or seventy hours a week farming. It's what they do with most of their time. More than likely you'll have a church full of farmers and their families. So it's an important question, isn't it?"

"Well, when you put it like that, it sure is. But I don't know how to answer it."

"When you get back to your house tonight and sit down to eat, what will you do before you take your first bite?"

"I'll thank the Lord."

---

10. James B. Torrance, *Worship, Community and the Triune God of Grace* (Downers Grove, IL: InterVarsity Press, 1996), p. 21.

"Thank him for what?" I asked.

"*For the food*," he said with that same look on his face.

"Of course, but why? Why thank the Lord for something that the farmer grew? Why not thank the farmer and his family?"

"Well, I guess I should thank the farmer, but are you saying I'm not to thank the Lord?"

"No, of course not. I'm only trying to help you see that you already know how Jesus relates to the farmer's life and work. You don't have a theology that allows you to see what your prayer already knows."

"I'm not following you," he said.

"Think about it. You thank the Lord for food that the farmer grew. Now what does that tell you about the farmer?"

He paused, clearly processing his thoughts. Then a huge grin came over his face. "I think I get it. That is so cool! The farmer is part of the way the Lord provides for us."

"That's it," I said, "and so are teachers, garbage collectors, welders, workers, truck drivers, the men and women who make household cleaning products, secretaries, and scientists, to name a few. They all participate in what Jesus is doing."[11]

Jesus does not need the farmers any more than he needed the servants to get the water at the wedding in Cana. He does not need parents to make babies and care for them, or teachers to teach, or doctors and nurses to heal, or musicians to make music, or artists to create, or oilfield workers, clerks, secretaries, inventors, explorers, or theologians. He could simply command and it would all be so. But such a thought has never crossed the mind of the Father, Son, and Spirit, for

---

11. For more on how our ordinary lives are a participation in Jesus' life, see my book *The Great Dance*, pp. 47ff.

that would be to pretend that we are not wanted or included in their shared life.

Not long after my conversation with the college student, a young mother walked into my office with a stack of newsletters in her hand. She had tears in her eyes as she slammed them down on my desk, shouting, "I feel like a pile of crap!"

"What in the world has happened?" I asked.

"I've been reading these newsletters from friends and missionaries all over the world. They're all out there doing these wonderful things for God. Even their children are perfect. And it just hit me what a worthless life I have. *For Pete's sake*, I do three loads of laundry a day, and when I'm not doing laundry I'm grocery shopping, and when I'm not grocery shopping I'm unloading the groceries, or cooking the groceries, or cleaning up after cooking them. And somewhere in there I try to keep my mess of a house presentable, stay in touch with my kids, keep them clothed and on schedule, and find a little time for my husband. By the end of the day I'm too tired even to read my Bible. What do *I have* to offer God?"

"Wait!" I said. "Just wait a minute. We need to punch the Pause button and rethink all of this."

"I sure hope so."

"Do you remember what you told me the other day about your daughter's coat?"

"Which part?"

"The whole story."

"Of course, but what does that have to do with anything?"

"Well, you told me you had spent all morning shopping for a coat for your daughter to keep her warm. And not just any coat, mind you, but one that she would like, and one that would be large enough to wear next year but not look like it this year, and one that was on sale!"

"*Okay?*"

"Well, did you just decide that you were going to be a good mother and flip a switch that created this concern for your daughter? Did you take a 'good mother' pill?"

"What are you getting at?"

"I'm asking about the origin of your love for your daughter, and for your family. What is the source of your determination that they eat right every day, that they be safe and loved and nurtured and clothed?"

"*I'm their mother.* Who thinks about stuff like that?"

"*I* do, for one. These are important questions, and they might just have some serious freedom in them for you—and dignity."

"Okay, but what's your point?"

"My point is that Jesus is not up there watching you from a distance. He's not waiting for you to do something for him in his absence. *He is here, in you.*"

"I've always believed that, but what does it mean, really?"

"Well, it means that through you, the Father, Son, and Spirit have created several unique persons. Never before in the history of the cosmos have your children existed. They are one of a kind, and now that they were born through you, they will live forever in Jesus. That seems like a rather huge thing to me. It is loaded with serious dignity."

"I see that, on my good days. Somewhere inside, I know that's true, but it's hard to feel it every day."

"And it means that Jesus is sharing his love for his sheep—your family—with you. It means that he put in your heart his own concern for your daughter to have a new coat. You woke up in his love, shopped all morning in his joy. You gave yourself to participate in what he was doing, and you loved every minute of it. His joy filled your heart. It made you sing. And you found the coat. But you don't know who you are, and you can't see what is happening in your life. It is not simply *your* concern and delight, but *his*, and there is no more noble thing in all the world than cooking a meal for your family. For that is nothing short of the Father himself, through his Son and in the Spirit, sharing his royal feast with his loved ones. You are in the middle of it. There is far more going on in your life than you ever dreamed. If you don't see it, the newsletters will kill you with shame, opportunities will become exhausting burdens, life will become a long frustration, and you will not know the joy of who you are."

One more story. On my first flight out West I made sure that I had a seat by a window. At that point I had never seen the Rocky Mountains, so I was determined that I could at least see them from the air. As it turned out, the middle seats throughout the plane were empty, so everyone had plenty of room. The flight attendant closed the door and we started backing up to depart. Then the plane stopped and pulled forward, and the attendant opened the door. In a flash, a man who looked like Indiana Jones stepped onto the plane. He had the hat, the vest, and the leather satchel. Somehow I knew where he was going to sit. And he did. He walked twenty-five rows back and sat beside me.

As I greeted him, he introduced himself and sat down. He said he was a "systematic, microevolutionary microbiologist." He was returning from what seemed to me to be very much like an Indiana Jones–type expedition in the Caribbean. It was, in fact, a research trip dedicated to studying various species of plants.

We were hardly in the air before he began talking about plants, especially rare species that the average person doesn't even know exist. He knew their Latin names. With real fire in his belly he launched into this story about plants that were on the verge of extinction, how important they were, what could be done to save them, and why we must. He simply could not bear the thought that we had already lost, and were now losing, whole species of plants to extinction. He even pulled out a couple of napkins and drew diagrams and charts. I must say, I was truly fascinated.

Somewhere over Idaho he finished and looked over to me. "I suppose, being a theologian, you want to talk about evolution?"

"No, not really," I said, "but I do have a question."

"Which is?"

"Where did you get your passion for plants? I mean, it's not every day that you meet someone who has such a deep burden for the welfare of plants. I'm just curious as to its origin. Did you grow up around botanists? Were your parents botanists? Did you just decide one day that you were going to love plants?"

"I've never really thought about it much, or even at all."

"It probably just *evolved*," we both said at the same time.

"Or perhaps not," I said as I pulled out a napkin and began drawing three interrelated circles. In one circle I wrote "Father," and in the other two I wrote "Son" and "Spirit." Pointing to the circles, I said, "I know the origin of your deep passion for plants, and I know who you are. That fire in your belly is not yours; it comes first from the Father, Son, and Spirit. It is the blessed Trinity who cares so deeply about creation. They share their passion for creation with you through Jesus, and through his Spirit he humbly shares with you his delight in plants, his burden for their welfare, and his desire for their wholeness. And you are living in it! You go to sleep at night, wake up in the morning, and work all day in *his* concerns and creative ideas. You are living in Jesus' life, participating in the relationship that Jesus has with his Father in the fellowship of the Spirit, and in their zeal for the blessing of creation. You live in the circle of the triune life of God, and you're not sure that God even exists!"

"Well," he said, "if that's true, why haven't I ever been told?"

"You just were."

19

ABIDE IN ME

I am the vine, you are the branches; he who abides in Me and I in him, he bears much fruit, for apart from Me you can do nothing.
—Jesus

Perhaps if you approved of the plans of the Glad Creator, you would allow Him to make of you something divine!
—George MacDonald

Taking Jesus Christ seriously opens our eyes to the secret of our humanity, of our burdens and joys, loves and passions. It gives us eyes to see the astonishing dignity of being human in Jesus' world. There is only one circle of care and love and creativity in this universe; only one burden for right and life and blessing; one circle of harmony and other-centered sacrifice, of joy and generosity and passion for peace; one desire for all things beautiful, and it is that of the blessed Trinity. We have not been blown into existence only to drift aimlessly through life without meaning or purpose or dignity. Jesus has crossed all worlds to find us—and he *has*—and in himself he has lifted us up into the life he shares with his Father in the Holy Spirit. "I am in my Father, you are in me, and I am in you." *Nothing is ordinary.* "I am the Light of the world; the one who follows me shall never, ever walk in the darkness, but shall have *the light of life.*"[1]

Such a vision is almost too good to be true. But so it is. As Papa says to Mackenzie in *The Shack*, "Like I said, everything is about him. Creation and history are all about Jesus. He is the very center of our purpose and *in* him *we* are now fully human, so our purpose and your destiny are forever linked" (194, my italics).

There are a thousand things that must be said here, but for the moment there are three critical points that need to be noted.

First, Jesus himself is the proper content and meaning of the great themes of the New Testament: the kingdom of God, salvation, adoption, atonement, reconciliation, justification, the new covenant, heaven. The kingdom of God is the very life and love and joy of the blessed Trinity—shared with us in Jesus—coming to unique and personal expression in our lives, in our relationships with one another, and in our relationship with all creation. The very identity of Jesus Christ as the One in whom the Father, the Holy Spirit, and all creation are bound together carries profound geopolitical, racial, social, environmental, economic, and educational implications, not to mention ramifications for physics, psychology, or theology. "I am the light of the *cosmos.*" As the Creator incarnate, Jesus, in his relationship with his Father in the Spirit, is integral to every sphere and area of human life and of the life of our planet. Nothing was left behind when he ascended to

---

1. John 8:12, my translation and emphasis.

his Father's arms. Nothing is outside of his anointing in the Spirit.

In Jesus, heaven and earth are united; the life and oneness of the blessed Trinity have crossed the infinite divide and embraced us forever. All things have become new. The covenant relationship between the Lord and Israel is now filled with the relationship between the Father and the Son in the Spirit.[2] The new covenant relationship is Jesus himself, and all that he is and has and experiences in the Holy Spirit.

And what is salvation but our death in Jesus' death, and our new life in his resurrection? What could be more *at-one* than Jesus face-to-face with his Father in the Spirit, and the human race in him? Immanuel, adoption, heaven, eternal life—these are all ideas that have their fundamental meaning in the staggering grace of the triune God in Jesus whereby we were lifted up into the Father's arms, seated with Jesus at his right hand, and ushered into the world of the Holy Spirit. "This is eternal life, that they may know You, the only true God, and Jesus Christ whom You have sent."[3]

Second, the astonishing union that Jesus has established with us, and the life shared within it, does not mean that we become Jesus or that he becomes us. That would be the end of us as real persons, and the end of the dream of the blessed

---

2. Note Thomas F. Torrance's comment: "In Jesus Christ the Covenant faithfulness of God has been met and answered by a Covenant faithfulness within our humanity, so that that divine-human faithfulness forms the very content and substance of the fulfilled Covenant which is the New Covenant. Thus the Covenant relationship is now filled with the relationship or communion between the Son and the Father, and it is in that communion that we are given to share by the Spirit." From *Conflict and Agreement in the Church*, vol. 2 (London: Lutterworth Press, 1960), pp. 122–23.

3. John 17:3.

Trinity for us. In the life of the Father, Son, and Spirit there is oneness and utter union, the three Persons dwelling completely in one another, but no loss of their distinct and personal identities. They do not become one another. The Father, Son, and Spirit have found a way to give us a real place in their shared trinitarian life without losing us in the process. We are included, but not absorbed; united, but not so merged that we cease to be real. We share in the trinitarian life, but always as distinct persons with our own unique personalities. The blessed Trinity will have it no other way.

This vision walks between the extremes of pantheism, on the one side, and dualism or deism on the other.[4] In pantheism the relationship between God and the world is collapsed, so that God and the world are a single entity. Humanity is so merged with the divine that we are no more than extensions of the divine being, drops of water in the divine ocean. There is no distinct and real "us" to share in the life of God. In deism, God is a spectator watching us from an infinite distance, so that there can be no real and meaningful relationship between God and humanity; we are truly strangers forever. In pantheism the distinction between the divine and the human is lost, reducing us to nothing more than computers with divine software, while in deism the distinction is so absolute that the divine and the human are never related except perhaps by way of external instruction, and our humanity has no divine life. But the trinitarian vision holds together both the reality of our union with the triune God and the distinction between us. The union gives us a real share in the trinitarian

---

4. For more on pantheism and deism, see my book *The Great Dance: The Christian Vision Revisited* (Jackson, MS: Perichoresis Press, 2000; Vancouver: Regent College Publishing, 2005), pp. 68ff. and 94ff.

life; the distinction means that there is a real "us" to taste and feel and experience it.

Third, in Jesus we see who we are and why we are here, as well as what's wrong and the way forward. Jesus has included us in his relationship with his Father, *and* in his relationship with the Holy Spirit, *and* in his relationship with every person, *and* in his relationship with all creation. Jesus is the center of it all.[5] Life is about walking with him and participating in his relationships. We are never more alive, or free, or more ourselves, than when we are seeing with Jesus' eyes, caring with his heart, loving with his love. Death is about being alone, doing our own thing in our own way, serving ourselves and our own interests.

Think back for a moment to our discussion of the Trinity. The mutual indwelling of the Father, Son, and Spirit is both the *truth of being* and the *way of being* of the blessed Trinity at the same time. There was never a moment when the Father, Son, and Spirit did not dwell in one another, and there was never a moment when their mutual indwelling did not express itself in love and relationship. But with us, time is involved.

What Jesus has made of us in his life, death, resurrection, and ascension is the *truth* of our being, but it has not yet become our *way* of being. We are not separated from the blessed Trinity, but included in the trinitarian life. This is our identity, the *truth* of our being, and our destiny of joy. We are loved, accepted, embraced forever, and adopted. But such has not yet become our *way* of life, and herein lies our calling: our

---

5. For a beautiful song on Jesus as the center of it all, see Vanessa Kersting, "Centre of It All," from the album *For All the Times*, available at iTunes and at vanessakersting.com.

identity in Jesus calls and frees us to *become* who we *are* as those loved, accepted, and embraced forever.[6]

On the one hand, becoming who we are involves letting Jesus' Father love us, as my friend Bruce Wauchope puts it so beautifully. It's about Mackenzie "learning to live loved" (177), letting Papa's embrace have the run of the house in his soul. The truth calls us to change from believing that we are separated from God, cut off and abandoned, that we are alone and that it is up to us, to believing that in Jesus we are wanted, received, cared for, and included in the life shared by the Father, Son, and Spirit.

On the other hand, it involves giving ourselves—our minds, hearts, and wills—to participate in what Jesus is doing. Our agenda, our independence, our confused self-will must die, so that the life and concerns, the burdens and joys, the music and other-centered love of the blessed Trinity can come to undiluted and unique expression in us. As Jesus says to Mack in *The Shack*:

> Seriously, *my* life was not meant to be an example to copy. Being my follower is not trying to "be like Jesus," it means for your independence to be killed. I came to give you life, real life, my life. We will come and live our life inside of you, so that you begin to see with our eyes, and hear with our ears, and touch with our hands, and think like we do. (151, my italics)

"Abide in Me, and I in you," Jesus says in John's Gospel. "As the branch cannot bear fruit of itself unless it abides in the vine, so neither can you unless you abide in Me. I am the vine, you are the branches; he who abides in Me and I

---

6. See John 1:13.

in him, he bears much fruit, for apart from Me you can do nothing."[7] As Mackenzie learned, we cannot walk on water just by flexing our faith muscles, but only as an act of participation in what Jesus is doing. We are free to fill a thousand water pots and to invent charms and chants and recipes of our own devising, but the water will never become wine unless the Lord performs his work. It's about relationship, about the free submission of our hearts and wills to the love and life of the Father, Son, and Spirit.

Faith has no power without truth. Without reality, without Jesus, faith is simply a form of magic where we try to weave our spell over someone or wrest the cosmos to our will apart from Jesus. As we shall see, we are remarkably free to dream our own dreams of life and power and success; but how could our independent attempts at lordship and life ever work in Jesus' world? The question of Sarayu, Papa, and Jesus to Mackenzie is directed to all of us: "How is that working for you?" (199); or as *The Message* asks, "What good would it do to get everything you want and lose you, the real you?"[8]

Life in this universe is about walking with Jesus in real relationship. This will mean saving the whales, finding ways to purify water, to serve and heal the sick, to care for the poor, to be mothers and fathers, teachers, workers and farmers, cooks, musicians, and coaches. It will mean saying "No!" to racism, sexism, social injustice, denominationalism, fragmentation, and dualism of every kind, but never in our own strength and time. "'This always works better when we do it together, don't you think?' Jesus asked, smiling" (176). And later he tells Mack,

---

7. John 15:4–6.

8. Luke 9:25, *The Message*. See also Matthew 16:2.

If you try to live this without me, without the ongoing dialogue of us sharing this journey together, it will
be like trying to walk on the water by yourself. You
can't! And when you try, however well-intentioned,
you're going to sink. (182)

It is here that we can begin to understand what it means
to be sinners. Sin is not simply breaking a divine law, unless
by "law" is meant the real world in Jesus. In this sense, sin is
any thought, act, motive, or word that violates our inclusion
in Jesus and his relationship with his Father, the Holy Spirit,
and all creation. Yet at a more fundamental level, sin is not
about acts or behaviors so much as it is about the blind pride
of the great darkness. *Sin is insisting that Jesus Christ repent
and believe in us.* It is our secret demand that Jesus betray
himself and pretend that he is not in the Father, that we are
not in him nor he in us. Sin is our command that Jesus give
up his world with his Father and the Spirit, and believe in us
and ours, that he participate in our dream and agenda, and
our timing and will. And in a way he does, for Jesus meets
us in our darkness, accepts us, and loves us as we are; he
will "travel any road to find you" (184), and he has. But he
will never betray the fact that real life is living in the Father's
embrace in the Spirit. So he meets us in our darkness and sin
and confusion, and his presence means that he is our Savior, working through love to save us from our false selves so
that we may become who we truly are in him and experience
real life.

It is fascinating that the first words of Jesus in John's
Gospel are a question. John the Baptist has pointed his disciples to Jesus as the Lamb of God who takes away the sin of
the world. So John's disciples begin to follow Jesus. As they

walk behind him, Jesus turns and asks them, "What do you seek?"[9] It is a simple question, but loaded. Can you imagine Jesus himself looking straight into your soul and asking, "What *do* you want?" John's disciples, like all of us, are dazed by the question. Who wouldn't be? Simple as it was, it cut through all pretense.

John's disciples did not know how to answer. At length they managed a question of their own in response: "Rabbi, where are you staying?" At first reading, their question seems irrelevant if not inane, but then you realize that the word translated "staying" is the word usually translated "dwelling." "Rabbi, where are you *dwelling*?" Can you not see Jesus smiling in his mind's eye and thinking, *So, you want to know* where I am dwelling? The theologians among us wish that Jesus had given a careful theological answer about "dwelling" in the bosom of his Father. But to the disciples' question, "Where are you dwelling?" Jesus offered a simple command: "Come, and you will see."

It all comes down to this. On the one hand there is Jesus' question, "What do you seek? What are you after? What do you want? Is it life, real life? Do you want peace, hope, meaning, freedom to be, to live, to love, to die?" On the other is his command, "Come, and you will see." Jesus speaks to our hearts with the inviting command of love and relationship. "Walk with me. Put your agenda away and come with me. Follow me." In George MacDonald's words:

> To follow him is to be learning of him, to think his thoughts, to use his judgments, to see things as he saw them, to feel things as he felt them, to be hearted,

9. John 1:38.

souled, minded, as he was—that so also we may be of the same mind with his Father.[10]

Given who Jesus is, what he has made of us in his life, death, resurrection, and ascension, and who we are in him, his abiding question is, "Which world are you going to live in today; your own, or mine?" As Jesus says to Mackenzie in *The Shack*, "We're meant to experience this life, your life, together, in a dialogue, sharing the journey. You get to share in our wisdom and learn to love with our love, and we get...to hear you grumble and gripe and complain, and..." (177). He sets before us two choices. "I've loved you the way my Father has loved me. Make yourselves at home in my love."[11] "If you want to do your thing, have at it. Time is on *our* side" (151, my italics).

---

10. George MacDonald, *Unspoken Sermons: Series I, II, III* (Whitethorn, CA: Johannesen, 1999), p. 371.

11. John 15:9, *The Message*.

20

The Spirit of Adoption

Because you are sons, God has sent forth the Spirit of His Son into our hearts, crying, "Abba! Father!"

—Saint Paul

There is Someone dancing with you, and you are not afraid of making mistakes.

—Richard Rohr

Adoption is not the dream of a naive God; it is the simple and stunning truth in Jesus Christ. In becoming human, Jesus has crossed the impossible divide between the divine and the creaturely. And in bearing our enmity, he has established a real relationship with us not merely in our humanity, but at our broken worst. As the Father's Son incarnate, he has brought his own relationship with his Father into our fallen world, overcoming our sin and embracing us in the Father's love. *And* since Jesus is also the *Anointed One*, establishing a relationship with us at our worst means that he has brought the Holy Spirit into our world of flesh. Adoption means that in and with and through Jesus and the hostility he endured at the hands of sinners, the Holy Spirit has descended into the inner catacombs of our hell, never to leave until those catacombs become to us the bosom of Jesus' Father. Jesus is "the Lamb of God who takes away the sin of the world" *and* "the one who baptizes in the Holy Spirit."[1]

Like the Incarnation, Jesus' anointing in the Spirit took time to become what it was. At no point was he without the Spirit, but the relationship had to develop at each stage of his human growth. Conceived by the Spirit, Jesus' entire life was lived in the Spirit, yet there was growth, development, and maturity. The Father's Son became a *real* human being. He lived out his sonship and his anointing in the Spirit as a man. The Holy Spirit is not a divine liquid that could be poured into the container of Christ's humanity. She is a person to be welcomed and known and loved. Jesus' anointing was personal and relational, not mechanical or extrinsic; it was both a fact and a relationship. Jesus loved and lived in the Spirit, saying "Yes" to her at every moment of his life, and so ever becoming what he always was. Stretching from his miraculous conception into his life and death, Jesus' anointing in the Spirit reached its mature expression in his resurrection and ascension.

At the same time, Jesus was penetrating our darkness to the point of suffering death at our hands on the cross. His anointing was fulfilling itself not only in his humanity, but also through his suffering. He lived out his eternal sonship in the trenches of our broken world, under the menacing harassment of evil and inside the brutal pain of our rejection.

---

1. John 1:29, 33.

Jesus learned what it meant to be the Father's Son incarnate through the things that he suffered.[2]

It is fascinating to think of God "learning"—who could possibly know what that might mean?—but as creation itself was something *new* for God, so was the Incarnation, and so was living inside our darkness.[3] Surely the blessed Trinity anticipated what it would be like to become human, but there is a difference between anticipation and personal experience. Once the triune God called forth the cosmos and humanity within it, the trinitarian life began expressing itself within a new world of relationships. In the Incarnation, the blessed Trinity has "become" what it forever was and is, but in a *new* way—now in relationship with us as fallen creatures. And as Jesus lived out his sonship as a man, the Holy Spirit was not a bystander watching from a distance. She did far more than hand him a box of tissues as he suffered at our hands. She was in the suffering with him.

In fellowship with the Father's Son, as he endured the trauma of our blind judgment, the Holy Spirit "composed himself,"[4] as Thomas F. Torrance says, or "accustomed" himself, as the great Irenaeus puts it, "to dwell in the human race."[5] Jesus suffered, and in his pain the Holy Spirit was becoming accustomed to our humanity, and to our

---

2. See Hebrews 5:8.

3. See Thomas F. Torrance, *The Trinitarian Faith: The Evangelical Theology of the Ancient Catholic Church* (Edinburgh: T&T Clark, 1988), p. 155.

4. Thomas F. Torrance, "Come, Creator Spirit," in *Theology in Reconstruction* (Grand Rapids: Eerdmans, 1975), p. 246; see also Thomas F. Torrance, *The Trinitarian Faith*, p. 189.

5. Irenaeus, "Against the Heresies," in *The Ante-Nicene Fathers*, vol. 1 (Grand Rapids: Eerdmans, 1987), III.17.1; see also III.20.2; III.18.7; III.19.1; and IV.20.4.

alienation—from the inside. Through nurturing Jesus in the agony that he bore from us, the Holy Spirit was making our broken world part of hers.

I think the Holy Spirit "learned" how to meet us in the darkness through Jesus' affliction, through her steadfast ministry to the suffering servant of God. Just as "the Word of God was on the road to becoming flesh"[6] in the relationship between the Lord and Israel, and as that Word has in fact become flesh and dwells among *us*, so the Holy Spirit was "on the road" to dwelling with the fallen children of Adam, and in Jesus has "learned" to do so forever. To speak of the Holy Spirit "learning" is, of course, a wild speculation, but at least it helps us take the Incarnation seriously as something *new* for the Father, Son, and Spirit. Who knows? Who can say for sure? But what we do know is that the great Lover of life and freedom and wholeness has made her way inside our hell in Jesus. And here she cannot possibly sit still or be quiet; her passion for life becomes a passion for our liberation.

Pentecost is the inevitable fruit of Jesus' ascension, and of ours in him. Embracing us in our darkness, Jesus was also including us in his own anointing with the Holy Spirit. Through Jesus the Holy Spirit was poured out on *all flesh*, as prophesied by Joel.[7] The Spirit's passion is to educate every human being—to make subjectively, personally, emotionally, physically, and spiritually real *to us* in our darkness that which is already real in Jesus Christ: that we are loved, accepted, and embraced forever, included in the trinitarian life itself. She

---

6. The phrase is from Thomas F. Torrance in his essay "Our Oneness in Christ and Disunity as Churches," in *Conflict and Agreement in the Church*, vol. 1 (London: Lutterworth Press, 1960), p. 266.

7. See Joel 2:28ff. and Acts 2:17ff.

is determined that "the wonderful exchange" move from the *truth* of our being to our *way* of being.

Inside our darkness is the one, special, and unique Spirit of the Father and Son, the Holy Spirit. And she is the Spirit of truth, the Spirit of adoption, the Spirit of grace, and the Spirit of life in Christ, working with and within us that we may *become* who we *are* in Jesus. But like a briar patch, our inner world is a tangled mess of guilt and shame and anxiety, of self-centeredness, hiding, and fear, all of which coalesce to give us a profoundly wrong way of seeing. "Mack," says Jesus in *The Shack*, "there is far more going on here than you have the ability to perceive" (174). The Holy Spirit has come to do with us what we alone could never do in a million years. She walks with us relationally and in great tenderness, meeting us where we are in our hurt and confusion, gently untangling the mess to give us new sight so that we may choose life with all our hearts.

Several points emerge here that are critical for us to note. First, the Holy Spirit meets us in our *broken* inner worlds. In *The Shack*, Sarayu is present and at work in the garden that turns out to be the "mess" of Mackenzie's broken soul (140). And she is not horrified. While she does not rejoice in our sin or approve of our unrighteousness, the Holy Spirit is not a puritanical prude who cannot cope with our humanity. She is not like a sheltered young girl who knows nothing of the dark vagaries and vicissitudes of life on planet Earth. She is not shocked by our primitive crudity and devious shenanigans. More like a seasoned nurse in a mental ward than an old maid disgusted with our brokenness, the Holy Spirit has seen it all in Jesus. She knows our hell, our pain, our insane cruelty. She is not put off by the dirty job of our liberation; in fact, she loves it (140). She is the answer. As in Mackenzie's garden, the Holy Spirit is full of joy and having the time of her life in ours.

And this joy is shared by the Father. "At that moment, Papa emerged down the walkway carrying two paper sacks. She was smiling as she approached" (139). When I first read these two lines I did a double take, and then reread them to make sure they actually said what I thought they said. When I had the chance, I asked Paul about Papa *smiling* as she walked in Mackenzie's *garden*.

"Please tell me," I said, "that you wrote that on purpose."

"Well, of course," he said simply, with a huge grin on his face.

This scene of Sarayu's joy and Papa smiling in the middle of Mack's mess is worthy of a serious pause. *Do not miss this.* Both Sarayu and Papa are inside Mack's darkness and pain. Herein lies the deeply personal meaning of "the wonderful exchange." As much as I love Papa's embrace on the front porch, I think this scene in the garden is even better. Paul Young here reveals the astonishing truth of the Incarnation. The Holy Spirit and Jesus' Father are not up there somewhere watching us from a safe and unspoiled distance; they are inside our world of sin and shame. This is what Paul Young discovered in his personal despair—Jesus, his Father, and the Holy Spirit, smiling and overjoyed. "Instead of scrapping the whole Creation we rolled up our sleeves and entered into the middle of the mess—that's what we have done in Jesus," says Papa (101).

Second, the Holy Spirit comes to *liberate* us. Her presence in our inner world is not the end, but the beginning. For the dream of the blessed Trinity is not only that we would be included in the trinitarian life, but also that we would come to experience this life for ourselves. What has happened to us, with us, and for us in Jesus must become real *in* us. But such a dream can never reach fulfillment against our will, and our will is intertwined with our blind, wrong believing. So the Holy Spirit has a herculean job on her hands. She must lead us to turn against our own blindness and to believe, trust, and give ourselves to Jesus and his Father.

Never one to confuse the fruit with the root, she is not preoccupied with our sins so much as with our sin—our *unbelief.* Jesus says that the Holy Spirit "will convict the world concerning sin and righteousness and judgment," and he goes on to say, "concerning sin, because they do not believe in Me."[8]

We bring into Jesus' relationship with us a most bizarre and alien way of thinking and seeing, which, of course, makes perfect sense to us, and to which we cling with a vengeance. And as we cannot hear our own accents, neither can we see our own blindness. It is impossible for us to push aside the weeds of our fallen minds and believe in anything other than what we perceive through our blindness, but Jesus has penetrated our darkness and brought the Spirit of truth with him.

The Holy Spirit is not a spectator watching from the outside, giving abstract and external instructions that she hopes we will apply to our lives. She meets us in our gardens, in our garbage cans, in our shacks, bearing witness to the "unbelievable" world of Jesus and his Father—and our world, too. She works within us to help us see through our own blindness to know the truth in Jesus, and in this way to help us take "baby steps" (176) against our own fear and judgment, prejudice and alienation. But we are a hardheaded lot, strongwilled and obstinate. Like first graders who think they are college professors, we know it all and cannot be told a thing,

---

8. John 16:8–9.

even as we leave a trail of wreckage behind us. So the Holy Spirit gives us time to do it our own way, all the while working deep at the core of our being, bearing witness with our spirits[9] that it is true—that we are indeed sons and daughters of the Father himself—and crying the exclusive words of Jesus, "*Abba! Father!*" within us.

If you've ever written a poem or a letter, you already have an illustration of how this internal witness works. Writing, like so many other things, is a process of trial and error. Many times I write and then rewrite a chapter before I even know what I'm actually trying to say. Then there are almost endless revisions. A poet crafts a phrase or a word picture, but then scratches through it and tries again. Before long there are piles of wadded paper on the floor. But if she stays at it, and bears the gut-wrench of saying what cannot be said, the poem emerges.

But how does the poet know that this or that word is not the right one? How does she know that this turn of phrase, or image, or metaphor, is inappropriate? How does she know when they are right, and the poem is finished? The answer is simple, yet profound: she has two "knowings" at work within her.[10] One is the knowing of her mind, and the other is the knowing of her heart, what MacDonald called "the something deeper than the understanding—the power that underlies thought,"[11] and Michael Polanyi called "tacit

---

9. See Romans 8:16.

10. For more on the two knowings within us, see my book *The Great Dance: The Christian Vision Revisited* (Jackson, MS: Perichoresis Press, 2000; Vancouver: Regent College Publishing, 2005), chap. 4 and 5.

11. George MacDonald, "The Fantastic Imagination," in *The Complete Fairy Tales*, ed. U. C. Knoepflmacher (New York: Penguin, 1999), p. 9.

foreknowledge."[12] What the poet already knows in her heart, the "spirit knowing," scrutinizes her thoughts, words, and phrases, calling her to repent, to expand her thoughts "till they are worthy of the theme,"[13] until the understanding in her mind grows to express the deeper knowing of her heart.

This is what the Holy Spirit does within our hearts. "Because you are sons, God has sent forth the Spirit of His Son into our hearts, crying, 'Abba! Father!'"[14] She gives us an internal "knowing" that we belong to glory, that we are special, loved, made for life and not death, for joy and goodness and grace, not sorrow and Great Sadness. But the wounds, the trauma, the neglect, the divorce, the personal failures and disappointments, the wretched theology, all shout another message.

> Mack knew that what he was hearing, as hard as it was to understand, was something amazing and incredible. It was as if her words were wrapping themselves around him, embracing him and speaking to him in ways beyond just what he could hear. Not that he actually believed any of it. If only it were true. His experience told him otherwise. (104)

There are two knowings within us. The one is the knowing of the Spirit, the other is the knowing formed in the crucible of our own experience and the whisper of the father of

---

12. See Michael Polanyi, *The Tacit Dimension* (New York: Doubleday, 1966), p. 23. I am grateful to Lance Muir for this reference.

13. Saint Hilary of Poitiers, "On the Trinity," in *A Select Library of Nicene and Post-Nicene Fathers*, vol. 9 (Grand Rapids: Eerdmans, 1983), I.18.

14. Galatians 4:6, my italics.

lies. The witness of the Spirit gives us a divine basis, within our own darkness, for repentance and new faith, which leads into liberation and life. Repentance is a radical recasting of our minds, a deep and wide and fundamental change in the way we think and see and understand. It is nothing short of a revolution in the way we see God, ourselves, others, and life itself. The Spirit's witness forms a new knowing within us, creating a suspicion that we may be blind as bats and dead wrong about God, and giving us permission within our own souls to believe in the goodness of Jesus' Father against our own entrenched prejudices and mythology. "Do not be conformed to this world, but be transformed by the renewal of your mind."[15] "Now may the God of hope fill you with all joy and peace in believing, so that you will abound in hope by the power of the Holy Spirit."[16]

Third, the Holy Spirit treats us with profound respect. We are real to the blessed Trinity, and we matter deeply. Overriding our hearts and wills is simply not part of the trinitarian way of life; that would be to destroy us as distinct persons. We are highly treasured and precious to the Father, Son, and Spirit. They relate to us as we *are* in our hurt, darkness, and confusion. "Without the violation of one human will" (127), and "without brutalizing anyone" (183), the Holy Spirit works with a purpose in our hearts, always enlisting our participation in the process. As Sarayu says to Mack, "I would like your help clearing this entire plot of ground. There is something very special that I want to plant here tomorrow, and we need to get it ready" (133). "Together, you and I, we have been working with a purpose in your heart" (140).

Freedom and respect, honor and patience are themes

---

15. Romans 12:2.

16. Romans 15:13.

throughout the biblical story as they are in *The Shack*. Only moments after the front porch embrace, Papa realizes that although she has made her way into Mack's darkness and embraced him, he is hesitant to open up. She sees that he is not ready. "That's okay," she says, "we'll do things on your terms and time" (85). This is the heart of the biblical story. The blessed Trinity takes us seriously. The Father, Son, and Spirit want relationship and shared life with us.

A few moments later Mack asks Jesus what he is supposed to do:

> "You're not *supposed* to do anything. You're free to do whatever you like." Jesus paused and then continued, trying to help by giving Mack a few suggestions. "I am working on a wood project in the shed; Sarayu is in the garden; or you could go fishing, canoeing, or go in and talk to Papa."
>
> "Well, I sort of feel obligated to go in and talk to him, uh, her."
>
> "Oh," now Jesus was serious. "Don't go because you feel obligated. That won't get you any points around here. Go because it's what you *want* to do." (91)

Our freedom is not an illusion. We are free to be exactly what we are. For the Father, Son, and Spirit want the *real* us, not the Sunday church version, to experience their shared life and love.

This respect for us as real persons with our own hearts, minds, and wills, broken as they are, shines in the conversation about Mack's children. "When he spoke of his concerns for Kate, the three only nodded with concerned expressions, but offered him no counsel or wisdom" (108). They do not rescue Mackenzie. Jesus, Papa, and Sarayu *listen*. They want to know, to hear, to understand what is going on in Mackenzie's heart. They are more interested in knowing him as he is than offering quick suggestions. Sarayu explains a moment later: "We have limited ourselves out of respect for you. We are not bringing to mind, as it were, our knowledge of your children. As we are listening to you, it is as if this is the first time we have known about them, and we take great delight in seeing them through your eyes" (108).

Seeing through the eyes of others is the hallmark of intimacy and real relationship. The Holy Spirit cares deeply about where we actually are in our understanding and believing (and lack of same), and cares about what we want. She gives us plenty of time and space to make a mess of ourselves. We are shockingly free to do our own thing, to chase one scheme after another, to try to be sorcerers and wizards imposing our own will upon others and creation. She lets us live with ourselves and the consequences of our vaunted ideas, our appalling self-righteousness, and our sin. In the words of Mr. Raven in MacDonald's *Lilith*, "Indeed the business of the universe is to make such a fool of you that you will know yourself one, and become wise."[17] The Holy Spirit does not forsake us in our folly, but is quick to utilize every opportunity in her determination that *we* come to *know* the truth, and experience its freedom and life. For the dream of the blessed Trinity must become ours, too.

I, for one, would prefer a quick fix, but zapping our blind eyes with light cannot make them see. And even if it could, *we* would never believe what we saw. This is about relationship, and it's about the education of our fallen minds, and the liberation of our wills. It takes time. It is about our com-

17. George MacDonald, *Lilith* (Grand Rapids: Eerdmans, 2000), p. 26.

ing to *know* Jesus, and *knowing* in the Bible is a long way from just reciting information, quoting Scripture, or going to church. Knowing involves repentance, the radical conversion of our minds; and it involves personal experience, trust, and self-giving, communion, and oneness. The Spirit of adoption wants *us*—the people we are—to *believe*, to trust, to walk with, and give ourselves to participate in Jesus' life with his Father. It has never crossed her mind to force her will upon us. In Jesus she has come to relate to us in our darkness and hurt, and gently bring *us* to see.

Fourth, the Holy Spirit never sleeps, but works around the clock to bring life out of our misery, good out of our wrong, and healing out of our personal disasters. I love this the most about the Father, Son, and Spirit. They don't have a hair trigger. They are patient and brilliant strategists in their love.

Young captures this beautifully in three places. The first is in the garden with Sarayu; Mack and Sarayu have been preparing the garden, and he realizes that he has made a mess. "But it really is beautiful, and full of you, Sarayu. Even though it seems like lots of work still needs to be done, I feel strangely at home and comfortable here" (140). Papa and Sarayu cannot help but look at each other and wink, as Mack has no clue. Sarayu enlightens him:

> And well you should, Mackenzie, because this garden is your soul. This mess is *you*!... And it is wild and beautiful and perfectly in process. To you it seems like a mess, but to me, I see a perfect pattern emerging and growing and alive—a living fractal! (140)

The second illustration comes when Jesus and Mack are talking after Mack's "visit" with Sophia about judgment, and after he has "seen" Missy alive and playing. Mack asks Jesus why he has not told him before about Missy, and Jesus answers:

> I've been talking to you for a long time, but today was the first time you could hear it, and all those other times weren't a waste, either. Like little cracks in the wall, one at a time, but woven together they prepared you for today. You have to take the time to prepare the soil if you want it to embrace the seed. (178)

The third comes when Papa and Mackenzie are enjoying scones on the front porch. It is a meeting of hearts, as Mack is apologizing for having judged Papa and thought such ill of her. Then Papa opens her heart and lets Mackenzie in on a simple, but rather life-changing secret about how she works:

> "Let's say, for example, I am trying to teach you how not to hide inside of lies, hypothetically of course," she said with a wink. "And let's say that I know it will take you forty-seven situations and events before you will actually hear me—that is, before you will hear clearly enough to agree with me and change. So when you don't hear me the first time, I'm not frustrated or disappointed, I'm thrilled. Only forty-six more times to go. And that first time will be a building block to construct a bridge of healing that one day—that today—you will walk across." (189)

This is beautiful—and absolutely true—and Paul Young did not learn it in a book. This insight, this hope-begetting, joy-inspiring revelation, comes only when we get real with ourselves and honest with the Father, Son, and Spirit.

The recovery world teaches us that it is essential to take the time to write out a personal inventory of our lives. Such an inventory, "fearless and searching" as they call it in Alcoholics Anonymous, is to be brutally honest and as exhaustive as possible, a veritable catalog of all our sins, lies, character defects, and personal failures. Facing yourself honestly is the scariest thing in the world, but as you do, you see not only your own brokenness; you meet the grace of the Lord Jesus, and the compassion—indeed, the humor—of his Father, and the comfort of the Holy Spirit. "Blessed are the poor in spirit, for theirs is the kingdom of heaven. Blessed are those who mourn, for they shall be comforted."[18]

I was shocked when I understood this. The fingerprints of the blessed Trinity were all over my life; not for a second had I ever been abandoned. And the best part was seeing how the Holy Spirit used my mistakes, my character defects, and outright folly to help me see that I was loved and included. She transforms our shame into sacraments of our Father's love.

Just as the Holy Spirit accustomed herself to dwell in our flesh, she is, step-by-step, helping us grow accustomed to Jesus' world and Papa's fondness. Just as she "learned" in Jesus to meet us in our darkness, she is helping us learn to live loved, because we *are* loved—and she uses our own blunders to do so. Perhaps the robe of Stephen, the first martyr reported in the book of Acts, became a sacrament of grace and love to the apostle Paul, who had watched approvingly as he was killed. Who knows, the ladybug pin left as a calling card by Missy's murderer in *The Shack* may become a sacrament to him and to Mack, a visible sign of the unsearchable love of the blessed Trinity.

Fifth, in the Spirit the sheer love of the blessed Trinity

18. Matthew 5:3–4.

becomes a fiery *judgment* within us. Jesus died in our loathing and rose in our hell, and we cannot kill him again or separate ourselves from his presence. As Karl Barth says, "We cannot break free from this Neighbor."[19] And his presence is one of love and grace and acceptance, and therefore of *judgment*. "For love loves unto purity," as MacDonald put it.[20] "God will never let a man off with any fault. He must have him clean."[21] The love of the blessed Trinity would never have us alien to the trinitarian life. "Therefore all that is not beautiful in the beloved, all that comes between and is not of love's kind, must be destroyed."[22]

Missy's murderer is not going to skip through the pearly gates playing with ladybugs. To begin with, heaven is where the blessed Trinity dwells, and the evil that has hijacked and so horribly twists and misuses this man avoids the light at all costs. While this murderer is forgiven, loved, and accepted, while he is embraced and included, he does not *know* it by any stretch of the imagination, and such unknowing leaves him writhing in pain and trapped in the clutches of darkness. He belongs to the Father, Son, and Spirit—always has, always will—but he has given himself to participate in darkness. He acts out of the lie of the evil one and its grotesque meaninglessness, wreaking havoc in the lives of all around. He has become a terrible monster, living an alien form of existence in violation of his true self in Christ, and this alien existence must be transformed in the fire of Jesus' love.

This man, like each of us, must be *judged* by the living

---

19. Karl Barth, *Church Dogmatics*, trans. G. W. Bromiley (Edinburgh: T&T Clark, 1985), III.2.133.

20. MacDonald, *Unspoken Sermons*, p. 19.

21. Ibid., 529.

22. Ibid., pp. 18–19.

Word of God.[23] That is to say, he must be divided; the evil must be discerned, and separated from his true self in Jesus. "Much in us will appear to us ourselves, and especially to the Judge, as worthy of damnation; it belongs in the fire,"[24] writes one theologian. All that is alien in us to the trinitarian life and way of being must die. The poison of the darkness must be removed from us so we can become who we truly are in Jesus. We must repent and believe, *not* in order to be accepted and loved and included, but to *live in that reality*.

The Holy Spirit is the Spirit of adoption, and therefore in our darkness she is a refining fire.[25] "All that comes between and is not of love's kind, must be destroyed." Otherwise, we are doomed to be included in a life we can never live. Thus the Spirit works to free us so that we may choose to forsake our sin and flee all that is not truth, all that is foreign to the other-centered, self-giving love and grace and life of the Father, Son, and Spirit. Her transforming and freeing fire is her witness, *"Abba!* Father!" She uses the truth—our adoption, our salvation in Jesus Christ—to bring us into judgment, creating the crisis of our personal liberation.[26]

"Abba! Father!" is a cry full of hope for us, the new life already alive within us yearning and pressing for expression, and at the same time it is inevitably the white paper against the walls of our twisted inner worlds, exposing our darkness as darkness. Such exposure or judgment is painful, even

---

23. See Hebrews 4:12.

24. Hans Urs von Balthasar, *Credo* (New York: Crossroad Publishing, 1990), p. 71.

25. See Luke 3:16.

26. For more on the crisis of Jesus in our lives, see my book *Across All Worlds: Jesus Inside Our Darkness* (Jackson, MS: Perichoresis Press, 2007; Vancouver: Regent College Publishing, 2007), pp. 51ff.

withering.[27] But as the songwriter says, "Burning ember, let me never curse the pain you bring."[28] For the pain of exposure is the fruit of our salvation; indeed, it is our salvation saving us, our adoption finding us out in our insanity and fear and alien way of being, the love of the triune God loving us into freedom to let go of that which is destroying us. Hence, the songwriter continues, "Somehow I know I will be whole in your burning."

The Holy Spirit draws our minds and hearts and wills away from ourselves to focus on what became of Jesus, and on what became *of us* in him: "I am in my Father, you in me, and I in you." The Spirit works within us to reveal this truth, this fact, this reality, this Person. *"Abba!* Father!" is not simply a Bible phrase; it is the voice of Jesus himself *in us*. The Holy Spirit reveals Jesus not simply *to* us as a distant object, but *in* us,[29] leading to a personal encounter with Jesus himself. We gaze upon him whom we have pierced,[30] and find ourselves undone by his unaccountable and unsearchable love. We begin to know Jesus and ourselves. We begin to understand that there is more to us than we ever dared dream, that we belong to glory, that we are known and loved and a delight to Jesus and his Father. We begin to see our motherhood and fatherhood, our relationships, our farming and work, our botany and burdens and music, even our theology in a glori-

---

27. For a wise and beautiful discussion of the pain of Jesus' liberating judgment, see Pope Benedict XVI, Encyclical Letter: *Spe Salvi*, 47.

28. Steve Bell, "Burning Ember," from the album *Burning Ember* (Peg Music, 1998), available at stevebell.com.

29. See Galatians 1:16.

30. See Zechariah 12:10 and John 19:37. See also Richard Rohr's essay "The Franciscan Opinion," in *Stricken by God?*, ed. Bradley Jersak and Michael Hardin (Grand Rapids: Eerdmans, 2007), pp. 206ff.

ous new light. And at the same time, this encounter reveals the life we are living as an unholy labyrinth of freedom and bondage, joy and sadness, hope and desperation, participation and perversion, riddled with insecurity and self-centeredness, pride, fear, hiding, lust, greed, and envy.

The revelation of Jesus Christ in the Spirit is at once grace and judgment, painful hope and burning light, for it reveals both the stunning truth of who we are in Jesus and how shockingly far we are from being ourselves. In revealing Jesus, the Spirit of adoption brings us into the crosshairs of divine judgment, where "there is no creature hidden from His sight, but all things are open and laid bare to the eyes of Him with whom we have to do."[31] As with Mackenzie in the cave with Sophia, so it is with us: before Jesus there is nowhere to hide. He sees right through us. He is not moved by the lip-quiver, dazzled by marketing hype, or confused by religious dress or political rhetoric. In his presence there are no calls to make, no strings to pull, no deals to cut. "Before his gaze all falsehood melts away."[32] We know that he knows that we know that he knows. We are naked. And such judgment is inescapable grace—the exposing, discerning, enlightening, withering, healing, and liberating love of the blessed Trinity.

Here in our own shacks, naked, vulnerable, and helpless, we meet not shame or disappointment or condemnation, not the angry gods of our fallen imaginations, but the one true God, the blessed Trinity—Jesus, his Father, and the Holy Spirit—and that love which never seeks its own, but suffers all things, endures all things, hopes all things, and never fails.[33]

Here, inside our own souls and our great darkness—inside

---

31. Hebrews 4:13.

32. Pope Benedict XVI, Encyclical Letter: *Spe Salvi*, 47.

33. See 1 Corinthians 13.

our garbage cans, where we have hidden our heartache, our gut-wrenching wounds, our guilt and shame, where the whisper of evil has enslaved us and the lie "I am not" was born, at the fountainhead of our fear of abandonment and our terrifying insecurity—we encounter the real Jesus. His pierced hands free us to allow ourselves to be known and loved in his Father's embrace, to be (in the words of C. S. Lewis, quoted earlier) "united with the beauty we see, to pass into it, to receive it into ourselves, to bathe in it, to become part of it." Our traumatized souls hear Papa shout our names, and Jesus' own unearthly assurance baptizes us in the power of the Spirit of adoption. We are free to rest, to let go, to weep in love's embrace. Peace and hope and joy are born in our pain and Great Sadness. We are called to a radical change of heart and mind, to rethink everything we thought we knew, to forsake the lie and believe in Jesus, the Father's Son and the Anointed One, our crucified Lord and Savior and our salvation and life. In the corridors of our shame, the *truth* of our being becomes our *way* of being.

From creation to the birth of Jesus, the womb of the Incarnation was being prepared. In Jesus, the dream of the blessed Trinity for our adoption was fulfilled inside our darkness. And from Pentecost on, human history is about the Holy Spirit's work within us, corporately and individually, bringing us to encounter Jesus within our own brokenness so that we can begin to discern good from evil, light from darkness, life from death, and heaven from hell.

Hint by hint, line upon line, insight following insight, the Spirit is leading us into a radically new mind. We are beginning to smell the rat and see through the powerlessness of our religions. We long for home, for glory, for life, for truth and freedom and justice, for shalom. A baby step of hope in Jesus releases a baby step of the Spirit's freedom and power—and all her gifts—in us. One little "amen" of faith in Jesus is an "amen" of accepting our acceptance; it is opening our hearts and letting the Father love us, so that Jesus' own *parrhesia*— his unearthly assurance, confidence, freedom, boldness, and life—is free to thrive within us. His anointing with the Holy Spirit begins to flourish in our broken humanity, in our relationships, our music, our gardening, our work and play. Our self-centeredness and detestable pride, our fear and prejudice and judgment, our greed, envy, and lust, our terrible anxiety, all begin to die. We become free to love Jesus for his sake, and others and creation for their own benefit.

The hope of the human race is that we belong to the Father, Son, and Holy Spirit; we always have, and always will. And the Spirit of adoption will not give up on our coming to *know* that truth personally and corporately. The Spirit's passion is to bring her anointing of humanity in Jesus to full and personal and abiding expression in us, and not only in us personally, but in our relationship with the Father through the Son, and in our relationships with one another, and indeed with the earth and all creation.

The Spirit of truth, the Spirit of adoption, the Spirit of grace will not rest until we are all judged to the roots of our souls, and until our reconciliation, adoption, and anointing— made real in Jesus himself—have taken shape on earth and throughout the cosmos. As the apostle Paul says, "Until we all attain to the unity of the faith, and of the knowledge of the Son of God, to a mature man, to the measure of the stature which belongs to the fullness of Christ."[34] In the meantime, humanity lives under the judgment of the love of the blessed Trinity,

---

34. Ephesians 4:13.

in the unnerving and liberating crisis of Jesus' real presence and the Holy Spirit's revealing ministry, between the revelation of the beauty of the trinitarian life of grace and freedom and its exposure of the mess we are making of our own.

Some, perhaps, are won with the Spirit's first "Hello," but most of us run and hide, burying the dream and living in compromise—for now. We are Israel desperately trying to run from the Lord, Peter in the boat with Jesus, Saul of Tarsus on the Damascus road—and perhaps Mackenzie shaking his fist at God. But even when we run, or shake our fist, the Holy Spirit does not forsake us. Having met us in our cruel rejection of Jesus, she is able to find us in our sin, and even in our wildest heresies. She meets us in our running, and in time turns our mistakes, our character defects, our blunders and shenanigans into a way of revealing the truth to us again—leaving a trail of sacraments behind her. Only three hundred more to go, or perhaps it's three million; who knows? "The whole thing is a process, not an event" (183). It does not happen overnight, but through a lifetime, and perhaps beyond.[35] Is this not what history is about? Our prayer, like Mackenzie's, is simple: "So please, help me live in the truth" (201).

Life in the world of the Holy Spirit is always personal and relational. She is determined and faithful, kind, mostly gentle, and always true. She is most competent to meet us where we are in our darkness; and without overwhelming us or violating our will, she leads us to begin to use Jesus' right mind, to risk leaving our own darkness and its strange comfort (172) in order to embrace the shocking new world of the Father and

---

35. For a careful and honest treatment of hope, hell, and judgment, see Bradley Jersak, *Her Gates Will Never Be Shut* (Eugene, OR: Wipf and Stock, 2009).

his incarnate Son. In the words of Papa to Mackenzie in *The Shack*,

> The Truth shall set you free and the Truth has a name; he's over in the woodshop right now covered in sawdust. Everything is about *him*. And freedom is a process that happens inside a relationship with him. Then all that stuff you feel churnin' around *inside* will start to work its way *out*. (97)

As my friend Ken Blue likes to say, "Thank you, Holy Spirit; we will have more, please."

> "Jesus?" he whispered as his voice choked. "I feel so lost."
> A hand reached out and squeezed his, and didn't let go. "I know, Mack. But it's not true. I am with you and I'm not lost. I'm sorry it feels that way, but hear me clearly. *You are not lost.*" (116, my italics)

Holy Spirit, have your way with us, that we may feel the squeeze of Jesus' hand, and hear his Father shout our name. Do what you must, that we may repent and believe and so taste and feel and experience the life and freedom of our adoption in Jesus.

ACKNOWLEDGMENTS

All thoughts, even God's, arise in relationship. This book has my name on it, but it is the fruit of a lot of conversations. I am grateful to many people around the world. To Paul Young, thank you for your courage and freedom to write *The Shack*, for your priceless friendship, and for your encouragement at every step in the incremental process of writing this book. My brother from another mother, it is a great joy to walk with you.

To the Perichoresis family at home and abroad: You have saved me again and again with your questions, your longing, your relentless desire. To my Australian family: I come to you each year to be born again, and you always deliver. Thank you for your hunger for truth, and for your zero-tolerance for blarney in things that matter. There is more going on here than we would dare to dream.

I am deeply grateful to David Jennings, Christy Jones, Ken Courtney, Julian Fagan, Louis d'Alpuget, and John and Lorraine Baker. Without you this book would not have been. Thank you from the bottom of my heart. You have inspired me. And thanks to my mom and dad, who years ago taught me to walk, and gave me the freedom to run. You have always stood behind me, the most blessed gift of all.

To Steve Horn, Larry Bain, Ken Blue, Bruce Wauchope, David Kowalick, David Upshaw, and David Peck: Thank you for the years of real friendship and serious conversation, and for your care for me and my family. *You are my brothers.* I am eternally indebted to you. If I am remotely sane, it is your fault. Hang with me, I will teach you how to fish.

To John MacMurray, Wayne and Wendy Marchant, Bill Winn, Timothy Brassell, Tony Murphy, Betty and Doug (Tom Bodett) Johannson, Chris and Sarah Failia, Ernie and Carol Tolive, Jim and Jon Sawyer, Lance Muir of Ontario Christian Books, Jeff and Janice McFall, Dirk Vanderleest, my brother Stuart, Harry and Robbie Phillips, and Paul Fitzgerald: Your friendship makes me grateful to be alive. Thank you for your hearts and prayers, for taking the time to read this book, and for your suggestions. May the Lord grant the day when Carol will cook her famous meatballs for thousands, and Lance will be honored as the captain of all things trinitarian, and Fitzgerald will lead countless souls through one breakthrough after another. Meanwhile, Doug will "leave the light on for us."

To Beth, my wife of thirty years: You deserve the best. Thank you for enduring. We are not alone. Life is ours. To my "boy," J. E. Baxter Kruger: No dad could be prouder of his son. You are the crown of your old man's name. You belong to the glory of the blessed Trinity.

I am blessed with a great son and three wonderful daughters, Laura, Kathryn, and Caroline. Not a day goes by that we don't grieve Caroline's passing to glory. Caroline, we did not get to know you, but the Lord will restore the years that the locusts have eaten. That will be a large time! Thank you for the courage that you somehow share with me. Kathryn, our child of joy and color, you are a blessing beyond words. Your smile and wit light every room. Your heart is beautiful. The next is yours, I promise. And finally, to Laura, O beautiful daughter of mine, you have made me smile every day of your life. What a privilege it is to be your dad. To you this book is dedicated, with all joy and gratitude.

APPENDIX:
A FEW QUOTATIONS ON OUR
INCLUSION IN JESUS' DEATH

In the context of this statement [2 Corinthians 5:17] Paul located this transition from the old to the new at a single point: the death of all men in Christ's death for all, and the living of all men for him who was raised for all. To the apostle, what had happened in Christ simultaneously transformed not only the status of creation but also the vantage point from which this creation must be viewed.

Paul S. Minear, *Images of
the Church in the New Testament*

In all that, Christ was on the one hand so one with God that what he did, God did, for he was none other than God himself acting thus in our humanity. And therefore there is no other God for us than this God, and no other action of God toward us than this action in which he stood in our place and acted on our behalf. On the other hand, he was so one with us that when he died we died, for he did not die for himself but for us, and he did not die alone, but we died in him as those whom he had bound to himself inseparably by his incarnation. Therefore when he rose again, we rose in him and with him, and when he presented himself before the face of the Father, he presented us also before God, so that we are already accepted of God in him once and for all.

Thomas F. Torrance, *Atonement: The Person and Work of Christ*, ed. Robert T. Walker

With the birth and resurrection of Jesus, with Jesus himself, the relation of the world to God has been drastically altered, for everything has been placed on an entirely new basis, the unconditional grace of God.

Thomas F. Torrance, *Space, Time and Resurrection*

Our resurrection has already taken place and is fully tied with the resurrection of Christ, and therefore proceeds from it more by way of manifestation of what has already taken place than as new effect resulting from it.

Thomas F. Torrance, *Space, Time and Resurrection*

He has made an end of us as sinners and therefore of sin itself by going to death as the One who took our place as sinners. In His person He has delivered up us sinners and sin itself to destruction. He has removed us sinners and sin, negated us, cancelled us out: ourselves, our sin, and the accusation, condemnation and perdition which has overtaken us.... The man of sin, the first Adam, the cosmos alienated from God, the "present evil world" (Gal 1:4), was taken and killed and buried in and with Him on the cross.

Karl Barth, *Church Dogmatics*,
trans. G. W. Bromiley

He has ceased to be. The wrath of God which is the fire of His love has taken him away and all his transgressions and offences and errors and follies and lies and faults and crimes against God and his fellow men and himself, just as a whole burnt offering is consumed on the altar with the flesh and skin and bones and hoofs and horns, rising up as fire to heaven and disappearing. That is how God has dealt with the man who broke covenant with Himself.

Karl Barth, *Church Dogmatics*

When God comes to humanity in the history of Jesus Christ, humanity at the same time is brought to God in that history objectively. It is not faith which incorporates humanity into Jesus Christ. Faith is rather the acknowledgement of a mysterious incorporation already objectively accomplished on humanity's behalf. "One had died for all; therefore all have died" (2 Cor. 5:14). That all have died in Christ (and been raised with him) is the hidden truth of humanity as revealed to faith. Our true humanity is to be found not in ourselves but objectively in him. God's real presence to humanity in Jesus Christ (revelational objectivism) is paralleled by humanity's real presence in Jesus Christ to God (soteriological objectivism).

George Hunsinger, *How to Read Karl Barth*

We must not think of our salvation as less than a complete exchange, for there is nothing good in fallen Adam, he is totally and incurably corrupt in all his parts and passions. There is therefore no hope for him; death is the only "cure," for it is by death only that Adam can be saved from his fallen self and become a new creation. This is what Christ has done for Adam. He took his place, not only as his Substitute to take way his sins, but as his Representative to crucify his fallen nature, that in his sinless body he might slay and remove the old, and by his resurrection replace it with the new.

The ground of this truth is in Romans 6:3-8. There, Paul repeats the truth verse after verse in varying forms of words: we are "baptised into his death"; "we are buried with him by baptism into death"; we are "planted together within the likeness of his death"; "our old man was crucified with him"; "he that is dead has been justified from sin"; we are "dead with Christ." Could anything be more plain? Paul says that when Jesus died, we died with him.

William Still, *Towards Spiritual Maturity*

He was crucified: then what about us? Must we ask God to crucify us? Never! When Christ was crucified we were crucified; and his crucifixion is past, therefore ours cannot be future. I challenge you to find one text in the New Testament telling us that our crucifixion is in the future. All the references to it are in the Greek aorist, which is the "once-for-all" tense, the "eternally past" tense. (See Rom 6:6; Gal 2:20; 5:24; 6:14.)

Watchman Nee, *The Normal Christian Life*

When therefore the Lord Jesus was crucified on the cross, he was crucified as the last Adam. All that was in the first Adam was gathered up and done away in him. We were included there. As the last Adam he wiped out the old race; as the second Man he brings in the new race.

Watchman Nee, *The Normal Christian Life*

It does not depend on your feelings. If you feel that Christ has died, he has died; and if you do not feel that he has died, he has died. If you feel that you have died, you have died; and if you do not feel that you have died, you have nevertheless surely died. These are divine facts. That Christ has died is a fact, that the two thieves have died is a fact, and that you have died is a fact also. Let me tell you, *You have died!* You are done with! You are ruled out! The self you loathe is on the Cross in Christ.

Watchman Nee, *The Normal Christian Life*

Frequently the old man is taken in an individual sense and the crucifying and putting off the old man as the personal breaking with and fighting against the power of sin....But we shall have to understand "old" and "new man," not in the first place in the sense of the *ordo salutis*, but in that of the history of redemption; that is to say, it is a matter here not of a change that comes about in the way of faith and conversion in the life of the individual Christian, but of that which once took place in Christ and in which his people had a part in him in the corporate sense described above.

Herman Ridderbos, *Paul: An Outline of His Theology*

The unmistakable fact is passed over that in Paul
dying, being buried, etc., with Christ does not have
its ultimate ground in the ceremony of incorporation into the Christian church, but rather in already
having been included in the historical death and
resurrection of Christ himself. Of particular significance is the pronouncement of 2 Corinthians 5:14ff.,
where a clear transition becomes perceptible from
the "Christ for us" to the "we with [or in] Christ."…
From this it is to be concluded that "having died,"
"being in Christ," "being new creation," the fact that
his own are no longer judged and "known according the flesh" (namely, according to the world mode
of existence), has been given and effected with the
death of Christ himself.

Herman Ridderbos, *Paul: An Outline of His Theology*

Lutherans generally treat the doctrine of the mystical union *anthropologically*, and therefore conceive
of it as established by faith. Hence they naturally
take it up at a later point in their soteriology. But
this method fails to do full justice to the idea of our
union with Christ, since it loses sight of the eternal
basis of the union and of its objective realization
in Christ, and deals exclusively with the subjective
realization of it in our lives, and even so only with
our personal conscious entrance into this union.
Reformed theology, on the other hand, deals with the
union of believers with Christ *theologically*, and as
such does far greater justice to this important subject. In doing so it employs the term "mystical union"
in a broad sense as a designation not only of the

subjective union of Christ and believers, but also of the union that lies back of it, that is basic to it, and of which it is only the culminating expression, namely, the federal union of Christ and those who are His in the counsel of redemption, the mystical union ideally established in that eternal counsel, and the union as it is objectively effected in the Incarnation and the redemptive work of Christ.

Louis Berkhof, *Systematic Theology*

The old man is crucified; I take him with me to the tomb and, as I rise, it is you who rise in me. As I ascend to the Throne it is you who ascend with me. You are a new creation. Henceforth your life shall flow *from me and from my Throne.*

F. J. Huegel, *The Enthroned Christian*

SUGGESTIONS FOR FURTHER STUDY

Anatolios, Khaled. *Athanasius: The Coherence of His Thought.* London: Routledge, 1998.

Athanasius. "Against the Arians." In *Athanasius: Select Works and Letters.* vol. 4 of *Nicene and Post-Nicene Fathers,* 2nd ser., edited by Philip Schaff and Henry Wallace. Grand Rapids: Eerdmans, 1987.

_____. *On the Incarnation of the Word of God.* London: A. R. Mowbray, 1963.

Aulen, Gustaf. *Christus Victor.* London: SPCK, 1950.

Bailey, Kenneth. *Jesus Through Middle Eastern Eyes.* Downers Grove, IL: InterVarsity Press Academic, 2008.

Barth, Karl. *Church Dogmatics.* Translated by G. W. Bromiley. 13 vols. Edinburgh: T&T Clark, 1985.

_____. "The Covenant as the Presupposition of Reconciliation." In *Church Dogmatics* IV/1, pp. 22–54.

_____. "Creation as Benefit." In *Church Dogmatics* III/1, pp. 330–44.

_____. "Faith in God the Creator." In *Church Dogmatics* III/1, pp. 3–41.

_____. "God with Us." In *Church Dogmatics* IV/1, pp. 3–21.

_____. "The Homecoming of the Son of Man." In *Church Dogmatics* IV/2, pp. 36–116.

_____. "The Judge Judged in Our Place." In *Church Dogmatics* IV/1, pp. 211–83.

_____. "The Miracle of Christmas." In *Church Dogmatics* I/2, pp. 172–202.

_____. "The Problem of a Correct Doctrine of the Election of Grace." In *Church Dogmatics* II/2, pp. 3–93.

_____. "The Sloth and Misery of Man." In *Church. Dogmatics* IV/2, pp. 378–83.

_____. "The Way of the Son of God into the Far Country." In *Church Dogmatics* IV/1, pp. 157–211.

Berry, Wendell. *What Are People For?* New York: North Point Press, 1990.

Blue, Ken. *Authority to Heal.* Downers Grove, IL: InterVarsity Press, 1987.

_____. *Healing Spiritual Abuse.* Downers Grove, IL: InterVarsity Press, 1993.

Bonhoeffer, Dietrich. *Letters and Papers from Prison.* Edited by E. Bethge, enlarged ed. New York: Macmillan, 1971.

Boyd, Gregory A. *Repenting of Religion.* Grand Rapids: Baker, 2004.

Buckley, Michael J. *At the Origins of Modern Atheism.* New Haven, CT: Yale University Press, 1987.

Buechner, Frederick. *Telling Secrets.* San Francisco: Harper, 1991.

Calvin, John. *The Institutes of the Christian Religion.* Edited by John T. McNeill and translated by Ford Lewis Battles. Philadelphia: Westminster Press, 1960.

Campbell, Douglas A. *The Deliverance of God.* Grand Rapids: Eerdmans, 2009.

Campbell, John McLeod. *The Nature of the Atonement.* Grand Rapids: Eerdmans, 1996.

Canlis, Julie. *Calvin's Ladder: A Spiritual Theology of Ascent and Ascension.* Grand Rapids: Eerdmans, 2010.

Capon, Robert Farrar. *The Mystery of Christ and Why We Don't Get It.* Grand Rapids: Eerdmans, 1993.

————. *The Parables of Grace.* Grand Rapids: Eerdmans, 1988.

————. *The Parables of Judgment.* Grand Rapids: Eerdmans, 1989.

————. *The Parables of the Kingdom.* Grand Rapids: Eerdmans, 1985.

Chesterton, G. K. *The Everlasting Man.* San Francisco: Ignatius Press, 1993.

Dawson, Gerritt Scott. *Jesus Ascended: The Meaning of Christ's Continuing Incarnation.* Phillipsburg, NJ: P&R Publishing, 2004.

Erskine, Thomas. *The Unconditional Freeness of the Gospel.* Edinburgh: Waugh and Innes, 1829.

Farrow, Douglas B. "The Doctrine of the Ascension in Irenaeus and Origen." *Journal of the Faculty of Religious Studies, McGill University* 26 (1998).

Fee, Gordon D. *God's Empowering Presence.* Peabody, MA: Hendrickson, 1994.

Forsyth, P. T. *The Person and Place of Jesus Christ.* London: Hodder and Stoughton, 1909.

————. *The Work of Christ.* London: Hodder and Stoughton, 1946.

Gary, Bert. *Jesus Unplugged.* Grand Haven, MI: FaithWalk Publishing, 2005.

Giles, Kevin. *The Trinity and Subordinationism.* Downers Grove, IL: InterVarsity Press, 2002.

Gregory, John. *The Platonists.* New York: Routledge, 1999.

Gunton, Colin E. *Christ and Creation.* Grand Rapids: Eerdmans, 1992.

————. *Father, Son and Holy Spirit: Toward a Fully Trinitarian Theology.* London: T&T Clark, 2003.

————. *The Promise of Trinitarian Theology.* London: T&T Clark, 1991.

————. *The Triune Creator.* Grand Rapids: Eerdmans, 1998.

Hart, Trevor. "Humankind in Christ and Christ in Humankind: Salvation as Participation in Our Substitute in the Theology of John Calvin." *Scottish Journal of Theology*, vol. 42.

————. *Regarding Karl Barth*. Carlisle, England: Paternoster Press, 1999.

————. *The Teaching Father: An Introduction to the Theology of Thomas Erskine of Linlathen*. Edinburgh: St. Andrews Press, Devotional Library, 1993.

Hartwell, Herbert. *The Theology of Karl Barth: An Introduction*. London: Gerald Duckworth, 1964.

Hawthorne, Gerald. *The Presence and the Power*. Dallas: Word, 1991.

Hollis, James. *The Eden Project: In Search of the Magical Other*. Toronto: Inner City Books, 1998.

————. *The Middle Passage: From Misery to Meaning in Midlife*. Toronto: Inner City Books, 1993.

Huegel, F. J. *The Enthroned Christian*. Fort Washington, PA: Christian Literature Crusade, 1992.

Hunsinger, George. *How to Read Karl Barth*. New York: Oxford University Press, 1991.

Irenaeus. "Against the Heresies." In *The Ante-Nicene Fathers*, vol. 1. Grand Rapids: Eerdmans, 1987.

Jeremias, Joachim. *The Central Message of the New Testament*. New York: Scribner's, 1965.

————. *New Testament Theology*. New York: Scribner's, 1975.

————. *The Prayers of Jesus*. Naperville, IL: Alec R. Allenson, 1967.

Jersak, Bradley. *Her Gates Will Never Be Shut*. Eugene, OR: Wipf and Stock, 2009.

Jersak, Bradley, and Michael Hardin, eds. *Stricken by God?* Grand Rapids: Eerdmans, 2007.

Jinkins, Michael. *Invitation to Theology*. Downers Grove, IL: InterVarsity Press, 2001.

Konig, Andrio. *The Eclipse of Christ in Eschatology.* Blackwood, South Australia: New Creation, 2003.

Kruger, C. Baxter. *Across All Worlds: Jesus Inside Our Darkness.* Jackson, MS: Perichoresis Press, 2007; Vancouver: Regent College Publishing, 2007.

————. "The Big Picture: From the Trinity to Our Adoption in Christ." Lecture series, 2000. perichoresis.org.

————. *God Is For Us.* Jackson, MS: Perichoresis Press, 1995; Carlisle, England: Paternoster Press, 1995.

————. *The Great Dance: The Christian Vision Revisited.* Jackson, MS: Perichoresis Press, 2000; Vancouver: Regent College Publishing, 2005.

————. *Home.* Jackson, MS: Perichoresis Press, 1996.

————. "Inside the Soul: An Anatomy of Darkness." Lecture series. perichoresis.org.

————. *Jesus and the Undoing of Adam.* Jackson, MS: Perichoresis Press, 2002.

————. "On the Road to Becoming Flesh: Israel as the Womb of the Incarnation in the Theology of Thomas F. Torrance." 2007. perichoresis.org.

————. *Parable of the Dancing God.* Jackson, MS: Perichoresis Press, 1995; Downers Grove, IL: InterVarsity Press, 2001.

————. *The Secret.* Jackson, MS: Perichoresis Press, 1997.

————. "The Trinity and the Christian Life." Lecture series, 1999. perichoresis.org.

————. "You are the Child the Father Always Wanted." Lecture series, 2002. perichoresis.org.

Lewis, C. S. "Beyond Personality: Or First Steps in the Doctrine of the Trinity." In Lewis, *Mere Christianity*, pp. 135–90.

————. *The Chronicles of Narnia.* New York: Collier Books, Macmillan, 1946.

————. *The Four Loves.* New York: Harcourt, Brace, 1960.

_____. *The Grand Miracle and Other Selected Essays on Theology and Ethics from "God in the Dock."* Edited by Walter Hooper. New York: Ballantine Books, 1970.

_____. *The Great Divorce.* New York: Collier Books, Macmillan, 1946.

_____. *A Grief Observed.* New York: Bantam, 1976.

_____. *Mere Christianity.* New York: Macmillan, 1952.

_____. *Miracles.* New York: Simon and Schuster, 1996.

_____. *Surprised by Joy: The Shape of My Early Life.* London and New York: Harcourt, Brace, 1956.

_____. *Till We Have Faces.* New York: Harcourt, Brace and Jovanovich, 1980.

_____. "The Weight of Glory." In *The Weight of Glory: And Other Addresses*, by C. S. Lewis, pp. 1–15. Grand Rapids: Eerdmans, 1965.

Lossky, Vladimir. *The Mystical Theology of the Eastern Church.* New York: St. Vladimir's University Press, 1998.

MacDonald, George. *The Complete Fairy Tales.* Edited by U. C. Knoepflmacher. New York: Penguin, 1999.

_____. *The Fisherman's Lady.* Edited by Michael R. Phillips. Minneapolis: Bethany House, 1982.

_____. *The Golden Key.* Grand Rapids: Eerdmans, 1982.

_____. *Lilith.* Grand Rapids: Eerdmans, 2000.

_____. *The Marquis' Secret.* Edited by Michael R. Phillips. Minneapolis: Bethany House, 1982.

_____. *Unspoken Sermons: Series I, II, III.* Whitethorn, CA: Johannesen, 1999.

Manning, Brennan. *Abba's Child.* Colorado Springs: NavPress, 2002.

_____. *The Ragamuffin Gospel.* Sisters, OR: Multnomah, 2000.

_____. *Ruthless Trust.* San Francisco: Harper, 2000.

McVey, Steve. *Grace Amazing.* Eugene, OR: Harvest House, 2001.

Merton, Thomas. *The New Man.* New York: Farrar, Straus and Giroux, 1961.

Meyendorff, John. *Byzantine Theology.* New York: Fordham University Press, 1974.

Migliore, Daniel. "The Triune God" and "The Good Creation." In *Faith Seeking Understanding.* Grand Rapids: Eerdmans, 1991.

Mills, David, ed. *The Pilgrim's Guide: C. S. Lewis and the Art of Witness.* Grand Rapids: Eerdmans, 1998.

Molnar, Paul D. *Incarnation and Resurrection: Toward a Contemporary Understanding.* Grand Rapids: Eerdmans, 2007.

Moltmann, Jürgen. *The Spirit of Life.* Minneapolis: Fortress, 1992.

––––––. *The Trinity and the Kingdom: The Doctrine of God.* London: SCM Press, 1981.

Nazianzen, Gregory. *A Select Library of Nicene and Post-Nicene Fathers of the Christian Church.* 2nd ser., vol. 7. Grand Rapids: Eerdmans, 1983.

Newell, Roger J. *The Feeling Intellect: Reading the Bible with C. S. Lewis.* Eugene, OR: Wipf and Stock, 2010.

Pascal, Blaise. *Pensees: Thoughts on Religion and Other Subjects.* New York: Washington Square Press, 1965.

Payne, Leanne. *The Healing Presence.* Grand Rapids: Baker, 1989.

––––––. *Restoring the Christian Soul.* Grand Rapids: Baker, 1996.

Placher, William C. *The Domestication of Transcendence.* Louisville: Westminster John Knox Press, 1996.

––––––. *A History of Christian Theology.* Louisville: Westminster John Knox Press, 1983.

––––––. *Narratives of a Vulnerable God: Christ, Theology, and Scripture.* Louisville: Westminster John Knox Press, 1994.

Polanyi, Michael. *The Tacit Dimension.* New York: Doubleday, 1966.

Pope Benedict XVI. Encyclical Letter: *Spe Salvi.* http://www.vatican.va/holy_father/benedict_xvi/encyclicals/documents/hf_ben-xvi_enc_20071130_spe-salvi_en.html.

Purves, Andrew. *The Crucifixion of Ministry.* Downers Grove, IL: InterVarsity Press Books, 2007.

———. *Reconstructing Pastoral Theology.* Louisville: Westminster John Knox Press, 2004.

Richard of St. Victor. "Book Three of the Trinity." In *Richard of St. Victor.* New York: Paulist Press, 1979.

Rohr, Richard. *The Naked Now: Learning to See as the Mystics See.* New York: Crossroad Publishing, 2009.

Smail, Thomas A. *The Forgotten Father.* London: Hodder and Stoughton, 1980.

———. *The Giving Gift: The Holy Spirit in Person.* London: Hodder and Stoughton, 1988.

———. *Once and For All: A Confession of the Cross.* Eugene, OR: Wipf and Stock, 1998.

Smith, Malcolm. *The Power of the Blood Covenant.* Tulsa, OK: Harrison House, 2002.

Tarnas, Richard, *The Passion of the Western Mind.* New York: Ballantine Books, 1993.

Taylor, John V. *The Go-Between God.* London: SCM Press, 1972.

Torrance, Alan J. *Persons in Communion.* London: T&T Clark, 1996.

Torrance, James B. "Covenant or Contract." *Scottish Journal of Theology* 23, no. 1 (February 1970).

———. "The Vicarious Humanity of Christ." In *The Incarnation: Ecumenical Studies in the Nicene-Constantinopolitan Creed.* Edited by Thomas F. Torrance, pp. 127–47. Edinburgh: Handsel Press, 1981.

———. *Worship, Community and the Triune God of Grace.* Downers Grove, IL: InterVarsity Press, 1996.

Torrance, Thomas F. *Atonement: The Person and Work of Christ.* Edited by Robert T. Walker. Downers Grove, IL: InterVarsity Press Academic, 2009.

————. "The Atoning Obedience of Christ." *Moravian Theological Seminary Bulletin* (1959): 65–81.

————. *The Christian Doctrine of God*. Edinburgh: T&T Clark, 1996.

————. "The Eclipse of God" and "Cheap and Costly Grace." In *God and Rationality*. London: Oxford University Press, 1971, pp. 29–85.

————. *Incarnation: The Person and Life of Christ*. Edited by Robert T. Walker. Downers Grove, IL: InterVarsity Press Academic, 2008.

————. "Karl Barth and the Latin Heresy." In *Karl Barth: Biblical and Evangelical Theologian*. Edinburgh: T&T Clark, 1990, pp. 213–40.

————. *The Mediation of Christ*. Grand Rapids: Eerdmans, 1983.

————. *Preaching Christ Today*. Grand Rapids: Eerdmans, 1994.

————. *Space, Time and Resurrection*. Edinburgh: Handsel Press, 1976.

————. *Theology in Reconstruction*. Grand Rapids: Eerdmans, 1975.

————. *The Trinitarian Faith: The Evangelical Theology of the Ancient Catholic Church*. Edinburgh: T&T Clark, 1988.

von Balthasar, Hans Urs. *Credo*. New York: Crossroad Publishing, 1990.

————. "Our Capacity for Contemplation." In *Prayer*. New York: Sheed and Ward, pp. 27–67.

Ware, Kallistos, "The Human Person as an Icon of the Trinity." *Sobernost* 8, no. 2 (1986): 6–23.

————. *The Orthodox Way*. London: A. R. Mowbray, 1979.

Wauchope, Bruce. "The Gospel and Mental Health." Lecture series. perichoresis.org.

Webster, John. *Barth's Ethics of Reconciliation*. Cambridge: Cambridge University Press, 1995.

Weinandy, Thomas G. *In the Likeness of Sinful Flesh*. Edinburgh: T&T Clark, 1993.

Wright, N. T. *Paul*. Minneapolis: Fortress, 2005.

————. *Surprised by Hope*. New York: HarperCollins, 2008.

Yoder, Wes. *Bond of Brothers*. Grand Rapids: Zondervan, 2010.

Zizioulas, John. *Being as Communion*. London: Darton, Longman and Todd, 1985.

For more information about Dr. Kruger and the ministry of Perichoresis, visit these websites:

thegreatdance.org
perichoresis.org
included.com.au

It's the powerful story that stole the hearts of millions of readers worldwide, making it a phenomenon in publishing history.

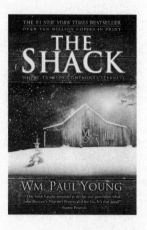

Mackenzie Allen Phillips's youngest daughter, Missy, has been abducted during a family vacation, and evidence that she may have been brutally murdered is found in an abandoned shack deep in the Oregon wilderness. Four years later, in the midst of his great sadness, Mack receives a suspicious note, apparently from God, inviting him back to that shack for a weekend.

Against his better judgment he arrives at the shack on a wintry afternoon and walks back into his darkest nightmare. What he finds there will change his life forever.

In an age where religion seems to grow increasingly irrelevant, THE SHACK wrestles with the timeless question: Where is God in a world so filled with unspeakable pain? The answers that astounded and transformed Mack will do the same for readers.

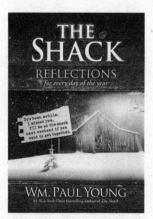

THE SHACK: REFLECTIONS FOR EVERY DAY OF THE YEAR provides an opportunity for you to journey with Mack and his remarkable friends, Papa, Sarayu, and Jesus, in a fresh and unique way.

This 365-day devotional contains meaningful quotes from *The Shack*, along with insightful and thought-provoking prayers written by the author of *The Shack*, Wm. Paul Young. It is designed to inspire, encourage, and uplift you every day of the year.